Open Road's
Paris Kids
with

by Valerie Gwinner

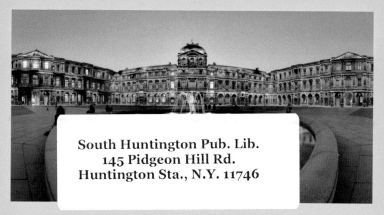

Open Road Travel Guides
The only travel guide your family really needs!

"Our family is similar to the authors: Franco-American, two kids (also boys) and a love of Paris. We thought we knew everything there was to know about Paris with kids, but this book taught us a wealth of new material, revealing an entire "new" city. If it could teach these old Paris hands a thing or two, just think what families new to Paris will learn. This book has a great mix of facts, fun, frivolity and fascination scattered throughout its pages, and is all you really need for a well-rounded trip to the City of Light. Buy it, pack it, and go!" – *Amazon.com*

944.36

Open Road Publishing

Open Road's new travel guides cut to the chase.
You don't need a huge travel encyclopedia – you need a
selective guide to steer you right. If you're going on vacation for
a few weeks or less, get a guide that brings you the *best* of any
destination for the amount of time you *really* have for your trip!

Open Road – the guide you need for the trip you want.

The New Open Road *Best Of* Travel Guides.
Right to the point.
Uncluttered.
Easy.

Open Road Publishing
P.O. Box 284, Cold Spring Harbor, NY 11724
www.openroadguides.com

Text Copyright©2010 by Valerie Gwinner
- All Rights Reserved -
ISBN 13: 978-1-59360-121-8
ISBN 10: 1-59360-121-2
Library of Congress Control No. 2008940466
Maps by Andy Herbach.

The author has made every effort to be as accurate as possible, but neither she nor the publisher assumes responsibility for the services provided by any business listed in this guide; for any errors or omissions; or any loss, damage, or disruptions in your travels for any reason.

About the Author
Valerie Gwinner is also the author of *Open Road's London with Kids.*

Acknowledgments
For their tips and moral support. my sincere thanks go to Kevin Reese and Mary Hall Surface, Brian and Deborah Howes, Mark Haskell and Elise Stork, Susan Campbell and Mark Pugliese, Charlie and Sue Calhoun, Victoria and Dale Pedrick, Karen Kuhlke and Suman Beros, Pam Roos, Zack Sorensen, Pernette Lezine, Camille and Fernand Beaucour – and to my mother, Anta Montet White.

For photo credits turn to page 222.

CONTENTS

Maps

Open Road's
PARIS WITH KIDS

1. INTRODUCTION

You're going to **Paris**? And taking the kids!!?

We heard this over and over when we first took our kids to Paris. For many people, a trip to Paris conjures images of beauty and romance, not strollers and diaper bags. It is a place for misty sunsets over the Seine, couples kissing under the chestnut trees, and lazy hours on café terraces.

Yes, Paris is all those things. However, what many people don't realize is that Paris is also the capital of one of the most kid-friendly nations in the world. France has prenatal care, parental leave, and child care policies that are the envy of most other industrialized countries. The country's national education budget surpasses its budget for national defense. Very simply, **children are a priority in France** – and it shows. It shows in the quality and creativity of the local playgrounds. It shows in the fact that every major museum and monument in Paris caters to children with special activities and workshops. It shows in the care that goes into products that are designed for children, whether it's books, clothing, or toys.

Even French food, a source of great national pride, caters to kids. Children in France are not just small people – they are gourmets-in-training. Thus you have cooking classes for kids at the Ritz Hotel, special children's menus in major restaurants, and jars of

Major Sights

1. Arc de Triomphe
2. Centre Pompidou
3. Champs-Élysées
4. Eiffel, Tour
5. Hôtel des Invalides
6. Jardin des Tuileries
7. Jardin du Luxembourg
8. Louvre
9. Musée de l'Orangerie
10. Musée d'Orsay
11. Musée Picasso
12. Musée Rodin
13. Notre-Dame
14. Palais de Chaillot
15. Palais Royal
16. place des Vosges
17. Sacré-Coeur
18. Ste-Chapelle

M Métro Stop

baby food at your local grocery store that feature choices such as sole meunière and canard à l'orange.

Paris offers a seemingly unlimited supply of activities and wonders for visitors of all ages – and many opportunities for reconciling the interests of adults and children. Admire **Nôtre Dame Cathedral** and have your kids hunt for their favorite gargoyles. Search for the **Secret of the Sorcerer's Stone** together through the historic Marais neighborhood. Enjoy the serene beauty of the Luxembourg gardens as your children play with **miniature sailboats** in the central fountain. Take the stairs down the **Eiffel Tower** and check out the view from the inside of the structure. Run a rat through a maze at the **Palais de la Découverte science museum**. Look for the Phantom's traces on a tour of the Paris **Opera house**. Go to the **horse races** in the Bois de Boulogne. Admire Monet's *Water Lilies* like the storybook character Linnea. View some of Paris' greatest buildings, bridges, and monuments from a *bâteau mouche* **tour boat**. Enjoy scoops of **Berthillon ice cream** on the Ile Saint Louis. Go on a candlelit tour of the **Vaux le Vicomte Palace**. Have lunch in a café under the chestnut trees of the **Tuileries Park** while your children go on a pony ride (*see photo below*). See a **magic show** at the *Musée de la Magie*. Take a family bike ride along the canals of the **Versailles Palace** gardens. Discover the underground labyrinth of Paris' **Catacombs**.

These are just some of the adventures that await you. Many more are described in the pages of this book. You'll also find kid-friendly strategies for visiting museums and monuments. There are recommendations for family-friendly hotels and restaurants, as well as tips on where to enjoy a light meal or snack, as well as historical facts, legends, and anecdotes to bring the stories of Paris to life for kids and adults.

So what are you waiting for? Isn't it time you discovered Paris – with kids?

2. OVERVIEW

See It As a Great Adventure

Discovering a new place and culture with your children can be highly rewarding and supply family memories that last a lifetime. It's a chance to connect with each other without the distractions of home. It's also an opportunity to try new things that you might be embarrassed to do at home. For example, my first and only archery experience took place during a Medieval Festival in a French Château. The boys talked me into it, and they were more than pleased when I managed to hit the bull's eye in front of a cheering crowd. If that's not reason enough to pack up the family bags, here are a few more:

- **Children bring new perspectives to your travels**. They see the world from a different angle. Kids point out details we might miss, such as how the Coca Cola tastes different, the sidewalks are wider, or that there are more mopeds and motorcycles than at home.
- **Kids take you places you might otherwise skip**, but secretly enjoy: for example, to the top floor of the Eiffel Tower, onto that old-fashioned carrousel, or into the Museum of Magic.

- **Traveling with kids helps break down cultural barriers**. It gives you something in common with other parents and brings out the kid-lovers in people who don't have children of their own.
- **Traveling with children reminds us that it's okay to slow down.** Enjoy the city at a human pace.

Take an afternoon nap. Have a leisurely café au lait while the kids quietly play in the hotel room. Spend some time watching the world go by from a park bench or café terrace. After all, you're on vacation.

Involve Your Kids

Children will be much more enthusiastic about traveling to Paris if you give them a role in the planning process – remember it's their trip, too. Even small kids can feel like they are part of the action if you include them in some background research. One of the best methods with young children is to introduce them to Paris ahead of time with books and videos that feature the city. It gives them a taste of what is ahead and things to look forward to. With small children, you can bring along the Madeleine books by Ludwig Bemelmans or *Eloise in Paris* by Kay Thompson and see how many places they recognize from the illustrations. In this guidebook we also highlight visits based on the story *Linnea in Monet's Garden* by Christina Bjork and Lena Anderson, the book/film of *The Red Balloon* by Albert Lamorisse, and the character Nicolas Flamel from the first Harry Potter volume.

If your children are older, encourage them to help plan your itinerary. You don't have to build your entire trip around their ideas, but you can give them a chance to pick their top choices. Cater to their interests. For example:

• **Is your daughter a fashion slave?** Take her to a (free) fashion show at the Galeries Lafayette Department Store. Follow up with lunch on the rooftop café where there is a magnificent view of the city.

• **Is your child a budding scientist?** Spend a morning in the *Cité des Sciences* at La Villette. Take a break in the park's wonderful playgrounds, then embark on a canal boat tour for a unique ride through the locks.

• **Does someone in your group love horses?** Plan a day trip to Chantilly with its magnificent live horse demonstrations and museum. Have an afternoon snack in the gardens of the Chantilly Palace. Give everyone a treat by ordering desserts smothered in Crème Chantilly (whipped cream).

• **Do your kids play soccer?** Tour the Paris team's Stade de France sports stadium in the nearby suburb of Saint Denis. While there, drop in to see the magnificent Saint Denis Cathedral with its tombs of all the French kings.

Balance Everyone's Desires

The secret to a successful family trip is to find ways to have something for everyone. If you build your whole trip around your children's desires, you will come home exhausted and frustrated. Similarly you can't expect a child to love Paris if he or she is made to sit through too many two-hour meals, wait for you to try on clothes in one store after another, or visit endless museums at a crawling pace. Paris is dotted with wonderful parks and playgrounds; pastry shops; and fun boutiques that spark kids' imaginations. It's easy to intersperse these with visits to museums, monuments, or other sights. Kids also love riding on a double-decker bus, taking a boat tour, or enjoying views from high places, so build these into your sightseeing plans.

Make Museums Fun

Few of us, kids or adults, can bear dragging ourselves through every room of a museum at a snail's pace. However, that doesn't mean museums can't be fun. Here are a few ideas:

- **Go on a treasure hunt**. You can let your kids choose some favorite post cards at the gift shop before your tour, and have them search for the objects they represent during the visit. You can also pick favorite themes, such as animals, dancers, or depictions of children, and hunt for these as you explore the museum.
- **Pick up the free kids' booklets offered in most Parisian museums**. They feature games and explanations. Although they are in French, kids can still enjoy the pictures, mazes, and other activities.
- Give your kids a lesson in navigation by **handing them a copy of the museum's map** (distributed for free at the entrance) and following their lead.
- **Rent audioguides** (available in English versions in many museums for a small fee) for your kids. They appeal to kids' natural love of gadgets and let them enjoy a private tour at their own pace.
- **Cater to kids' interests**. Paris has wonderful museums specializing in dolls, magic, science, fashion, ships, models, weapons and armor, animals, history, giant crystals, and more.
- **Play "pick your favorite."** Encourage your kids to choose which paintings, pieces of furniture, or objects they would put in their room if they could. Which armor would they wear if they were a knight? Which Greek god would they want to be? Which room would they want to sleep in if this was their mansion?
- **Go for gore**. Really! Kids are fascinated by tales of guillotines, monsters, martyrs, stranded sailors, and the like. You will find plenty of examples of these in paintings and historical objects in many Paris museums.

- **Play a pretend round of Clue or another imaginary game.** When visiting a museum that is housed in a mansion or palace (as many are), have your kids imagine in which room a crime would be committed, against whom, and with what weapon. Or have kids invent their own game based on favorite TV characters, video games, or collectors' cards.
- **Surf online before you go.** The major Parisian museums have websites that your kids can browse to pick out what they'd like to see.
- **Take a break during your visit.** Most Parisian museums have lovely cafés where you can refuel and rest weary feet.
- **Divide and conquer.** Split up. Let one adult have a few hours of culture while the rest of the group goes on a boat tour, plays in a park, or does some shopping.

The Demography & Geography of Paris

More than 2 million people live in the city of Paris, more densely populated than any other city in the developed world. For example, there are about twice as many people per square mile in Paris than in Tokyo, three times more than in London, and 2.5 times more than in New York.

Paris Arrondissements

Paris is divided into 20 city districts known as *arrondissements*. The first arrondissement is located in the center of the city, near Les Halles, and the numbers radiate out following the pattern of a snail shell. The 1st, 2nd, 3rd, and 4th arrondissements are on the Right Bank of the Seine River. The 5th, 6th, and 7th are on the Left Bank. The 8th, 9th, 10th, 11th, and 12th form a second tier of districts on the Right Bank. The 13th, 14th, and 15th make up a second tier on the Left Bank. Finally, the 16th, 17th, 18th, 19th, and 20th, constitute a third tier of arrondissements on the Right Bank. Mailing addresses for Paris will start with the number 75 for Paris. The last two digits of the postal code indicate the arrondissement. Thus 75005 indicates an address in the 5th arrondissement and 75016 is in the 16th arrondissement.

Here are some of the sights you'll find in each arrondissement:

1st: Les Halles, Louvre, Place Vendome, Tuileries

2nd: Opéra Garnier, Place des Victoires, Galerie Vivienne, Passage des Panoramas

3rd: Marais, including Pompidou Center, Musée Carnavalet, Musée Picasso, Musée des Arts et Metiers, Nicholas Flamel's House

4th: Nôtre Dame and Ile de la Cité, Ile Saint Louis, Marais, including Jewish neighborhood and Place des Vôsges

5th: Latin Quarter, including Boulevard Saint Michel, Sorbonne, Cluny Museum, Rue Mouffetard, Jardin des Plantes, Natural History Museums, Paris Mosque, Arènes de Lutèce (Roman Arena)

6th: Saint Germain neighborhood, Luxembourg Gardens, Saint Sulpice

7th: Invalides, Musée Rodin, Musée d'Orsay, Eiffel Tower

8th: Arc de Triomphe, Champs Elysées, Grand Palais, Palais de la Découverte, Parc Monceau, Place de la Concorde, Gare Saint Lazare, Rue du Faubourg Saint Honoré Luxury Shops.

9th: Grands Magazins (Haussman Department Stores), Passage Jouffroy, Passage Véro Dôdat

10th: Gard du Nord, Gare de l'Est, Canal Saint Martin

11th: Bastille neighborhood

12th: Saint Antoine neighborhood, Viaduct des Arts, Promenade Plantée, Gare de Lyon, Bercy neighborhood and gardens, Bois de Vincennes

13th: Les Gobelins, Butte aux Cailles, Chinatown, Gare d'Austerlitz

14th: Montparnasse neighborhood, Gare Montparnasse, Catacombs, Parc Montsouris, Rue d'Alésia discount clothing stores

15th: Parc André Citroën, Parc Georges Brassens, Aquaboulevard (Water Park)

16th: Trocadéro, Maritime Museum, Musée de l'Homme; Musée des Plans Reliefs; Musée d'Art Moderne, Balzac's House, Passy Cemetary, Musée de la Mode et du Costume, Musée Marmottan, Bois de Boulogne, Jardin d'Acclimatation

17th: Residential

18th: Montmartre neighborhood, Porte de Clingancourt Flea Market

19th: Parc de La Villette, Cité des Sciences (Science Museum), Parc des Buttes Chaumont

20th: Belleville neighborhood, Père Lachaise Cemetery

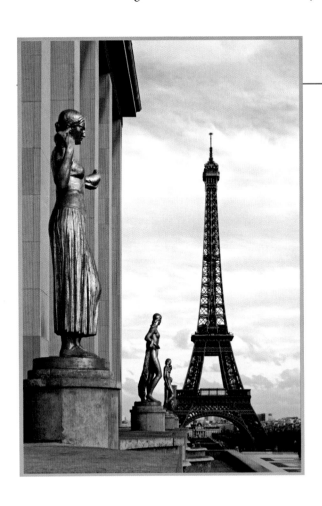

3. THE ISLANDS

Ile de la Cité

The **Point Zéro**, from which all distances to Paris are measured, is located on the Ile de la Cité. This is only fitting since this City Island (originally a cluster of smaller islands) is where the first inhabitants of Paris settled in about 250 BC. When the Romans took over in 50 BC, they expanded the city (then known as Lutetia) across the Seine River to the south, in the section now known as the Latin Quarter. But Ile de la Cité remained the political, judicial, and religious center of the city. It housed both the Temple of Jupiter, in honor of the most important of the Roman gods, and the Roman Governor's Palace.

During the medieval period, the Temple of Jupiter was replaced with a small Christian church and later with the great Nôtre Dame Cathedral. The Roman Governor's Palace was rebuilt as a Royal Palace. One wing, known as the Concièrgerie, was later turned into a prison. This is where Queen Marie Antoinette was held before she was guillotined.

NÔTRE DAME CATHEDRAL, *Place du Parvis de Nôtre Dame, on Ile de la Cité (Metro: Cité or Saint Michel-Nôtre Dame). Open daily, 8 am-6 pm. Entrance to the cathedral is free. The Tower visit is open daily 9 am to 6:30 pm (Apr-Sep) and 10 am to 5:30 pm (Oct-Mar). Entrance on the left as you face the cathedral. Adults: €7.50; Kids: free. To avoid long lines, plan on climbing up the towers when they first open or later in the afternoon, when crowds are thinner.*

Nôtre Dame Cathedral is truly the city's great lady, where some of Paris' most joyful or solemn moments have been celebrated. It was here that Napoleon crowned himself Emperor and that funeral services were held for Victor Hugo and Charles de Gaulle. Nôtre Dame was also the sight of joyous masses to celebrate the ends of both world wars.

Work on Nôtre Dame began in 1163 and took nearly 200 years to complete. The cathedral was built in the Gothic style, recognizable for its high walls, peaked arches, flamboyant decorations, and stained glass windows that seem to reach to the sky. Another telltale sign of a Gothic cathedral is the presence of flying buttresses, those elegant arcs that help carry the weight of the stone roof and walls.

Kids will enjoy yet another classic feature of Gothic architecture – the gargoyles. But here's something you should know. Real gargoyles have to be able to gurgle. True gargoyles are actually part of the roof's drainage system. When it rains, they collect water from the gutters and spew it out away from the building to protect the walls and windows from water damage. Those other monstrous sculptures, often depicted as gargoyles in movies and comics, are just decorative statues known as grotesques. See if your kids can spot the difference. Both serve a common purpose: to warn passers-by of the scary fate that awaits them if they lead a sinful life.

If you want to see the gargoyles and grotesques up close, you should climb the 386 steps to the top of the **north tower**. You'll get to seem them up close, and you'll enjoy one of the best views of Paris around. The visit takes you up the north tower, across the balconies and rooftops and down through the south tower. Before you descend, check out the enormous bell that hangs in the south tower. It is called Emmanuel (yes, big bells have names) and weighs 13 tons. It takes 8 people to ring the bell by hand. The Emmanuel bell rings a perfect F sharp. It was the first bell in the city to

Islands
1. Ancien Cloître Quartier
2. Cathédrale Notre-Dame
3. Hôtel Dieu
4. Ile St-Louis
5. Mémorial des Martyrs Français de la Déportation
6. Musée de la Conciergerie
7. Ste-Chapelle

announce the end of World War I as well as the Liberation of Paris in World War II. Today it is only rung to celebrate big events or holidays.

The façade of Nôtre Dame has three entrances. The left doorway is dedicated to Mary, the mother of Jesus. The middle one represents the last judgment. The doorway on the right is dedicated to Saint Anne, the mother of Mary. Notice all the statues and sculptures. Did you know that, originally, they were all painted in bright colors (even the gargoyles)? Besides being decorations, these works served a practical function. In medieval times, most people were illiterate, but they did know the stories of the bible. They could thus "read" the illustrations and moral lessons depicted in the church's statues, carvings, and stained glass windows.

Ile de la Cité Highlights

• Find the Point Zero
• Hunt for gargoyles at Nôtre Dame Cathedral
• Go underground into the Crypte Archeologique
• Visit Marie Antoinette's prison cell and others at the Concièrgerie
• See the spectacular stained windows at the Sainte Chapelle
• Visit the Sunday Bird Market on the Place Louis Lepine
• Take a boat ride on a Bâteau Mouche
• See the Pont Neuf and Place Dauphine
• Spend a moment of contemplation at the Deportation Memorial

Inside Nôtre Dame there are spectacular stained glass windows, particularly the three round rose windows. The largest of these, above the front entrance, depicts Mary and the Infant Jesus flanked by two angels. The north rose window in the transept dates from the 13th century. It depicts the Virgin Mary surrounded by figures from the Old Testament. The south window, dating from the 14th century, depicts Christ surrounded by angels and saints. If you walk around the choir (the U-shaped area behind the altar), you can see 14th century wooden sculptures representing stories from the life of Jesus. Notice the organ. Built in 1730, it has nearly 8,000 pipes and 5 keyboards. There are free organ concerts on Sunday afternoons.

The cathedral can seat 6,000 people. It fills up for major holidays, funerals, or big events. On Christmas Eve, entrance is restricted to members of the parish and special guests.

Before we leave this magnificent cathedral, here's one more item of interest: More than 12 million people visit Nôtre Dame each year, but some of its most regular visitors are not people. They are birds, known as kestrels or sparrow hawks. Pairs of these birds nest in high perches above the gargoyles each year. Bird watchers gather behind the cathedral every June to watch the birds feed their newly-hatched chicks.

PARVIS DE NÔTRE DAME. The large esplanade in front of Nôtre Dame is known as the **Parvis**. If you look carefully on the pavement in front of the main entrance, you will find the brass marker that indicates the **Point Zero.** Here you can really say that you are in the center of Paris. It is the point from which all distances to the city are measured. You'll also notice lines on the pavement that delineate old streets and buildings. In medieval days, the Parvis was much smaller than it is today, and it was crowded with street vendors, musicians, jugglers, even dancing bears.

Notice the statue of a man on a horse on the Parvis (toward the right as you face the cathedral)? It depicts Charlemagne, a great French king, who ultimately became Holy Roman Emperor in the year 800 and ruled over an area that stretched across France, Germany, Switzerland, Holland, Belgium, and most of Italy. Charlemagne had five wives, and encouraged trade, literature, and education even though he himself never learned to read or write.

The Parvis pavement also covers a wealth of Paris history that you can discover in the CRYPTE ARCHEOLOGIQUE. *Place du Parvis de Nôtre Dame (Metro: Cité) Open daily, 9:30am-6pm (Apr-Sep), 10am-4:30pm (Oct-Mar). Adults: €3.30; Youth: €1.60; Kids under 13: free.*

This is an interesting tour for any budding archeologist or explorer. The visit takes place underground, past ruins spanning 16 centuries.

SQUARE JEAN XXIII. This small park is located behind Nôtre Dame Cathedral. Here you can find plenty of shade, benches, and room for children to run. There are also water fountains to quench your thirst or clean off sticky fingers. It's a great place to stop for a snack. You can pick up food at one of the shops lining the cathedral (north side) or cross the pedestrian bridge to Ile Saint Louis where you can get some of the city's best ice cream cones.

MEMORIAL TO THE DEPORTATION. *Located across the small street from the Square Jean XXIII. Open daily 10am-12pm, 2pm-7pm (closes at 5 pm Oct-Mar). Adults and Kids: Free.*

Touching in its simplicity, this memorial begins with a narrow staircase that takes you to a triangular courtyard. From there you enter a small chamber lit with hundreds of thousands of lights. These represent the men, women, and children of France deported to Nazi prison and concentration camps during World War II. Their names are inscribed on the walls. An eternal flame lights a tomb to the unknown deportee.

SAINTE CHAPELLE. *4, Boulevard du Palais. Metro: Cité. Open daily, 9:30am-6pm (Mar-Oct), 9:30am-5pm (Nov-Feb). Ticket sales stop 1/ 2 hour before closing time. Adults: €7.50; Kids under 18: free if accompanied by an adult. You can purchase a combined ticket for both the Sainte Chapelle and Concièrgerie. Adults: €9.50; Kids under 18: free. A free description of the stained glass windows is available in English.*

Parent Tip: If you think that you will only be able to drag your child inside one church in Paris, the Sainte Chapelle is the one to see. The first view of the stained glass windows will surprise even the most reluctant visitor, especially on a sunny day. ❖

The Sainte Chapelle (Holy Chapel) was built in the 13th century by France's most zealously religious king, Louis IX (also known as Saint Louis). Saint Louis hired the same architect who had designed the plans for Nôtre Dame Cathedral. However, while it took 200 years to finish Notre Dame, the Sainte Chapelle was built in only seven years.

The Sainte Chapelle actually contains two parts: an upper chapel and a lower one. The lower chapel is more somber, but has a beautiful painted ceiling of golden fleur-de-lys against a royal blue background. It looks like a star filled sky. The walls are also painted, as were those in most churches. Look on the floor. There are large engraved slabs of stone that cover tombs from the 14th and 15th centuries. Some children will enjoy their almost comic-book quality.

A small, spiral staircase leads to the upper chapel. This was the part reserved for the royal family and high officers. Unlike the lower chapel, the ceiling of this one seems to reach to the sky. The stained glass windows are spectacular. They are 15 meters (nearly 50 feet) high, and most contain their original 13th century glass. They are the oldest stained glass windows in Paris. The windows depict stories from the old testament and from the life of Jesus. The chronology progresses from left to right, and from bottom to top in each window.

CONCIÈRGERIE. *1, Quai de l'Horloge. Metro: Cité. Open daily, 9:30am-6pm (Mar-Oct), 9am-5pm (Nov-Feb). Adults: €7.50; Kids under*

18: free if accompanied by an adult. You can purchase a combined ticket for both the Sainte Chapelle and Concièrgerie. Adults: €9.50; Kids under 18: free. Ticket sales stop hour before closing.

This was originally part of a royal palace, but it was turned into a prison in the 14th century. Poor prisoners were put in cells called **paillasses** that were dirty, crowded, and lined with hay. Those who could afford it payed rent for better prison cells with furniture and more privacy.

The Concièrgerie is especially famous for the many prisoners who were held here following the French Revolution. During the Reign of Terror from 1794 to 1795, the revolutionary tribunal condemned nearly 3,000 people to their deaths. Most of them spent at least some time in the Concièrgerie.

You can visit the Concièrgerie and tour the guard room, kitchen, and prison cells. Some of the cells have been rebuilt as they would have looked during the Revolution, complete with wax figures depicting guards and prisoners.

The visit begins with the guard room with its four large fireplaces. The pillars are decorated with sculptures of animals and people. Notice the giant slab of dark marble on one wall of the guard room. This used to be a table top used for royal feasts. When the palace became a prison, this was the room where trials were held and prisoners condemned.

The kitchen is up a small stairway. It has several huge fireplaces for cooking food for as many as 3,000 people. The windows were originally just above the level of the river, so that supplies could be easily delivered by boat.

The next part of the visit takes you to the prisoners' galleries. There were separate sections reserved for men and women. You can see the courtyard with its fountain where the female prisoners washed their laundry. There was a gate through which the women could speak to the male prisoners. You can also see the special cell reserved for Queen Marie-Antoinette (note that this is a re-creation of her original cell, which was later turned into a chapel). Upstairs you can visit other prison cells, including those reserved for the poor and the more upscale ones for people who had access to money or political influence.

Famous Concièrgerie prisoners include:

- **Ravaillac**, a Catholic monk and religious extremist who murdered King Henri IV. He was executed.
- **Damiens**, who struck and lightly injured king Louis XV in 1757. He was tortured and executed.
- **Marquise de Brinvilliers**, who poisoned her father, brothers, and sister. She escaped but was ultimately caught, condemned, and beheaded.
- **Cartouche**, a popular, Robin Hood-like leader of a band of thieves. He died on the rack.
- **Jeanne de Valois**, a noblewoman who wrote false letters to persuade the Cardinal of Rohan to buy a diamond necklace for Queen Marie-Antoinette, which she kept for herself. She escaped from prison but later died in poverty in London.
- **Charlotte Corday**, who assassinated Jean-Paul Marat in his bathtub for being one of the leaders of the Terror. His death is depicted in a famous painting by David. She was guillotined.
- **Marie Antoinette**, married to King Louis XVI, born in Austria, and hated by her subjects. Her hair is said to have turned white overnight after her arrest by the revolutionaries. She was spared while they tried to negotiate a peace deal with warring Austria. It failed, and she was condemned to death. A faithful servant tried to help her escape. She was betrayed and transferred to a more secure cell. She was guillotined in 1793.
- **Danton and Robespierre**, revolutionary leaders who sent many others to the guillotine, only to be later executed themselves for their excesses.

During the day, prisoners who had already been condemned to death by guillotine were allowed to wander around in the prison. Each evening, there would be an announcement declaring who would die the next day. Then a bell would ring and all the prisoners would return to their cells. Those who were condemned to die were sent to the Salle de la Toilette where they were searched and their valuables removed. Their collars were cut off, their hair was cut, and their neck was shaven to leave a clear target for the guillotine's blade

A small museum on the upper floor features artifacts from the history of the prison and some of its more well-known residents.

As you leave the Concièrgerie, notice the beautiful **clocktower** on the corner of the Quai de l'Horloge and Boulevard du Palais. It was completed in 1371 and has never stopped working.

PLACE LOUIS LEPINE MARKET. *Metro: Cité.*

There is a lovely flower market here Monday through Saturday. Then on Sundays, it is transformed into a lively pet market that features all sorts of colorful birds, as well as Guinea pigs, rabbits, and other small animals that will delight kids.

The imposing building you see on the east side of the Place Lepine is the Hôtel Dieu, Paris' oldest hospital. To the west of the Palais de Justice complex is a pretty triangular-shaped square called the **Place Dauphine.** It was built during the reign of King Henri IV in honor of his son (the Dauphin is the title of the king's heir).

PONT NEUF. *On the western edge of the Ile de la Cité. Metro: Pont Neuf.*

Although its name means New Bridge, this is actually the oldest bridge in Paris. It was built from 1578 to 1604 and was the first bridge in Paris to be made of stone. If you look at the Pont Neuf from below, you can see that it is decorated with hundreds of grimacing faces. According to legend, the artist designed these faces as caricatures of famous men of the day.

BATEAUX VEDETTES DU PONT NEUF (TOUR BOATS) *Square du Vert Galant. Down the steps on the Pont Neuf, behind the equestrian statue of King Henri IV. Boats leave every 30-45 minutes, 10am-10pm. Adults: €11. Kids age 4-12: €6. Kids under age 4: free. Note: Lower rates area available if you book your tickets via Internet in advance.*

If you are jet-lagged, foot-sore, or just want a change of pace, this one-hour boat tour is a great way to see some of Paris' major sights and monuments. Kids enjoy the ride, and you'll see Nôtre Dame, the Eiffel Tower, and other attractions from a unique perspective. Tour guide explanations are in both English and French.

Ile Saint Louis

This small island in the middle of the Seine River is **one of the fanciest neighborhoods in Paris.** However, it wasn't always such a splendid spot. In the 17th century, the area was swampy and uninhabited. There were actually two separate islands. One was called the Ile Nôtre Dame, named for the cathedral. The other was called the Ile aux Vaches (Cow Island) – hardly a romantic beginning. In the 1660s, a building developer named Jean Christophe Marie got permission from King Louis XIII to drain and connect the islands. He then built elegant mansions that were bought up by wealthy financiers and magistrates. The island was named for King Louis IX, also known as Saint Louis.

The main street of this small island is filled with fun shops and lively restaurants. Sunbathers flock to the "shores" of the island on warm, summer days. Those in the know head to Ile Saint Louis for the ice cream. (See below.)

GLACES BERTHILLON. *#31, Rue Saint Louis en l'Ile. Metro: Pont Marie.*

The official vendor for Berthillon ice cream and sorbet is located at this address, though you can find stalls selling it all over the island. It is a treat not to be missed (*see photo below*)! They use only natural ingredients. The scoops are small, but loaded with flavor – ranging from dark chocolate to green apple, wild strawberry, and many wonderful choices in between.

4. LATIN QUARTER

The history of this neighborhood is seeped in its Latin roots. These roots stretch back through medieval days when great scholars and students walked its narrow streets speaking Latin. They reach back even further to the 1st century BC, when the Romans occupied Paris and built a great city in this area south of the Ile de la Cité. Today, the Quartier Latin still bustles with students and scholars. However, its rich assortment of museums, parks, markets, and shops also make it an ideal spot from which to discover some of the kid-friendly sides of Paris.

Roman Occupation of Paris

In the year 52 BC, Julius Caesar's Roman army defeated the Gauls (inhabitants of France) and captured their main city, **Lutetia** (today's Paris). When the Gauls saw that they were losing the battle, they set their city on fire so as to leave nothing for their enemies. The Romans rebuilt Lutetia, transforming it into a great Roman city, which served as a base for conquests further north. They constructed a forum, numerous aqueducts and public bath houses, an amphitheater, and an arena. They created a grid of paved roads. They built a Governor's Palace and judicial buildings. The Romans also erected many temples to their gods, including ones to Jupiter, Juno, Minerva, Mercury, Apollo, Bacchus, Hercules, Mars, Venus, Vulcan, and Ceres.

Several of the Latin Quarter's main avenues still follow the trace of old Roman roads, including the Boulevard Saint Michel, Rue des Ecoles, and Rue Monge. Many Roman vestiges were either reused subsequently to build defensive walls and buildings, or they remain buried under modern

Paris. However, you can still travel back in time to a gladiator battle in the Roman Arena or imagine a steam room in the old Roman bath house.

ARENES DE LUTECE. *Entrances from the Rue des Arènes, Rue de Navarre, and through a passageway in the Rue Monge (Metro: Place Monge or Jussieu). Open daily, 8am-sunset. Entrance is free.*

The Arènes de Lutèce were built by the Romans in the 1st century BC. They featured entertainment such as gladiator matches, chariot races, Christians thrown to the lions, and even naval battles. There were also mime and dance performances. Dramatic plays were performed at the Roman Theater, now gone, that was located near the Cluny Roman Baths (*see later in this chapter*).

The arena was built right into the side of a hill. There were 35 rows of seats that could hold as many as 17,000 spectators. It was used until the 3rd century A.D., at which time Paris was repeatedly invaded by Vikings, Goths, and Huns, and the Roman Empire began to crumble. The arena was abandoned, and many of the stones were used to build defensive walls and towers to protect the city.

For hundreds of years the Arènes de Lutèce were forgotten under rubble and new constructions. Then in 1869, workers widening the Rue Monge came upon some of the ruins of the old arena. At the time, the city was more interested in modernization than historical preservation, so a bus depot was built on top of them. In 1883, more of the ruins were discovered on the southern side of the arena. This time there was a great public outcry to save the site, including a letter to the President of the City Council from Victor Hugo (author of *Les Misérables* and *The Hunchback of Notre Dame*). The ruins of the arena were preserved and restored, although some parts remain buried under the Rue Monge and Rue de Navarre.

Today, people play much

Latin Quarter Highlights

- Have a mock gladiator battle in the Roman Arena (Arènes de Lutèce)
- Find the unicorns in the Cluny Museum
- Look for plaques to fallen heroes by the Place Saint Michel
- Play like princes and princesses in the Luxembourg Gardens
- Try some mint tea at the Paris Mosque
- Hunt for extinct and endangered animals at the Jardin des Plantes
- Shop for wild strawberries at the Rue Mouffetard market
- Buy a book at Shakespeare and Company
- Find a 400-year-old tree that's still alive!

5th/6th
(Left Bank)
1. Arènes de Lutèce
2. Eglise St-Germain-des-Prés
3. Eglise St-Sulpice
4. Institut du Monde Arabe
5. Jardin des Plantes
6. Jardin du Luxembourg
7. Mosquée de Paris
8. Musée de Cluny
9. Musée National d'Histoire Naturelle
10. Panthéon

tamer games in the Arènes de Lutèce. It is a favorite spot for a round of boules, friendly soccer match, and children's games. There is a pretty little playground, just down the hill from the arena in the park.

THERMES DE CLUNY. *Located in the same building as the Musée National du Moyen Age (described below), 6, Place Paul Painlevé, just off the Boulevard Saint Michel. Metro: Cluny-La Sorbonne or Saint Michel. Open 9:15am-5:45pm (last entry tickets sold at 5:15). Closed Tues. Adults: €7.50 (includes audioguide); Kids: free. Free to everyone on the first Sunday of each month.*

These Roman Baths were built in the 2nd and 3rd centuries AD. They included at least a dozen different rooms on two floors, including steam rooms, warm baths, and cool pools. There were also gymnasiums and rooms reserved for conversation. They were richly decorated with marble and bronze statues, painted murals, and elaborate mosaic floor tiles. There was a sophisticated water system that provided steam and filled the pools.

The Roman baths were free to the public. However, people didn't just go to the baths to get clean. They also went to socialize, conduct business, exercise, and visit the library. Special pools were reserved for women. Men often took part in wrestling matches or calisthenics before going into the bathing rooms. Businessmen would meet in the baths or in the surrounding gardens. There were masseuses and hairdressers. There were food and drink vendors and other boutiques. All in all, it was a very lively place.

As you visit the museum, you can still see the large **Frigidarium** (cold room) that had a pool with cool water, much like a modern swimming pool. The room has a high ceiling supported by beams and arches. At the base of the arches you can make out decorations representing the hulls of ships. They were originally decorated with mermaids and tritons (male mermaids) and filled with goods and weapons. Archeologists disagree about what the ship hulls stand for, but they may be a tribute to the importance of shipping in early Lutetia. The Tepidarium (warm room) and Caldarium (hot steam room) were to the west of the Frigidarium. They are now part of the outside gardens along the Boulevard St. Michel.

With the barbarian invasions of Paris in the middle of the 3rd century AD, the inhabitants of Paris fled to the fortified part of the city on the island of Ile de la Cité. The Thermes de Cluny were abandoned and fell into ruin. Some of the stones from the building were reused to build fortification walls.

MONTAGNE SAINTE GENEVIEVE. *Hill leading from Cluny and the Sorbonne up to the Pantheon.*

This hill is named for the patron saint of Paris, **Sainte Geneviève**, to whom people pray when the city is in trouble. Geneviève was young shepherdess, born in 422 in a village west of Paris. She was extremely pious, had religious visions, and is said to have started performing miracles at age 9 when she cured a blind girl by sprinkling water in her eyes. She saved villagers from illness and Parisians from starving. However, Geneviève's most famous moment came in the year 451 when Paris was threatened by Attila the Hun, who led his invaders from Germany through eastern France, killing and pillaging all the way. Word came that Attila was approaching Paris. The Parisians panicked and began to flee, but Geneviève gave them the courage to stay, convinced by a dream that their city would be spared. In the end, the Huns never reached Paris. They were defeated, and Geneviève was credited with having saved the city.

Geneviève could not save Paris from the Franks, however, who took over the city in 464. She ultimately befriended their king, Clovis and his wife, Clothilde, and persuaded them to become Christians. When Geneviève died in 512 at the age of 90, she was buried next to Clovis. Today her remains are in the Eglise Saint Etienne du Mont, which sits atop the Montagne Sainte Geneviève.

There is a statue of Sainte Geneviève on the Pont de la Tournelle (a bridge behind Notre Dame Cathedral).

EGLISE SAINT ETIENNE DU MONT. *Place Sainte Geneviève. Metro: Cardinal Lemoine. Open 10am-12pm, 4pm-7pm. Closed Mon.*

This church was built during the 1500s and 1600s and is named for Saint Stephen, who was stoned to death by an angry mob in 34 AD for preaching the teachings of Christ. He is the first Christian martyr, and you can see a statue of him, with a pile of rocks, by the church's entrance. The other statue depicts Sainte Geneviève. Inside there is a feature called a rood screen, a set of finely carved stone balconies and double spiral stairs, designed to separate the area reserved for the clergy from the more public part of the church. Though they used to be common, this is the only rood screen left in Paris. On the right, beyond the rood screen is a shrine with Geneviève's relics. Pilgrims still come and ask her for favors, or leave plaques of thanks for her miracles.

The Medieval Latin Quarter

In the 1100s, Paris became one of Europe's most important centers of learning. Many important scholars and students congregated in the neighborhood around the **Montagne Sainte Geneviève.**

Students came from all over Europe. There were so many of them that there was a serious student housing crunch. In the 1200s, many "colleges" began to form. These started out as places for students to live and study together, often under the direction of resident "masters." One of these was founded in 1253, by Robert Sorbon, a priest at Nôtre Dame Cathedral and confessor to King Saint Louis. It was built to house students, professors, and a library. It would soon become one of the most famous and powerful universities in the world, the **Sorbonne**.

CLUNY -MUSÉE NATIONAL DU MOYEN AGE, *in the same building as the Thermes de Cluny at 6, Place Paul Painleve, off Boulevard Saint Michel. Metro: Cluny-La Sorbonne or Saint Michel. Open 9:15am-5:45pm. Closed Tues. Closed Tues. Adults: €7.50 (includes audioguide); Kids under 18: free, but pay €1 for an audioguide. Free to everyone on the first Sunday of each month. Access to the Medieval Garden along the Boulevard Saint Germain is free.*

The Cluny museum is a charming place to visit, and parents are surprised at how much their children enjoy it. The museum is not terribly big, but offers interesting glimpses at both Roman and medieval life. The visit takes you through beautiful examples of stained glass, gold work, jewelry, fabric, ivory carvings, and illuminated books. It takes you into the old Frigidarium of the Roman Baths building (see above). There are the 21 stone heads that were knocked off the statues of the biblical kings of Notre Dame Cathedral during the French Revolution. There is the tombstone from the grave of **Nicholas Flamel**. You may remember him from the first Harry Potter book as the discoverer of the Sorcerer's Stone. (Yes, he was a real person.) But the part that will most delight children is near the end of

the museum visit. It features the famous **Woman with a Unicorn** tapestries. There are six of these tapestries, and they are magnificent. The first five depict the five senses: taste, touch, smell, hearing, and sight. The sixth one is called "My Only Desire" and its meaning is not entirely clear. Children delight in looking at the magical unicorn, and searching out all the different animals in each scene. One more note to Harry Potter fans. If they've seen the film version of the books, they may recognize these tapestries; their design decorates the Gryffindor Common Room.

The courtyard in front of the Cluny museum features a 15th century well, and a facade decorated with gargoyles and other Gothic decorations.

Downhill from the museum is a nice medieval Garden that features medicinal and decorative plants of the period. **BOULEVARD SAINT MICHEL NEIGHBORHOOD.** *Metro: Saint Michel.* The Boulevard Saint Michel is one of the major thoroughfares of the Latin Quarter, and has been since Roman times when it was lined with Roman Baths, a Theater, and a Forum. Today, the boulevard bustles with college students and tourists. It is lined with lively cafés, fast-food places, clothing stores, shoe stores, pedestrian streets, and the big Gibert bookstores that have been around for over 100 years.

PLACE SAINT MICHEL AND QUARTIER DE LA HUCHETTE *Side streets to the east of the Place Saint Michel.*

This neighborhood of cobbled pedestrian streets is filled with tourist shops and restaurants. The streets date back to Roman times, including the tiny Rue du Chat Qui Pêche (Street of the Fishing Cat), which is the smallest street in the city. If your party includes a high schooler who is studying French, he or she may enjoy seeing Ionesco's The Bald Soprano, which has been playing at the little Théâtre de la Huchette since the play was written in the 1950s.

If you cross the Rue Saint Jacques, you can admire the old medieval houses in the rue Galande.

SQUARE VIVIANI. *Between Eglise Saint Julien le Pauvre and the Seine. Metro: Maubert Mutualité or Saint Michel*

If you've ever read the book, *Linnea in Monet's Garden*, you might recognize this lovely little park. It is just across the Seine River from Notre Dame Cathedral and across the street from the Hôtel Esmeralda, featured in Linnea's story. It was once the garden for the Eglise Saint Julien le Pauvre.

It also holds Paris' second oldest tree. Planted in 1681, the tree is a False Acacia, so old and gnarled that it leans on a stone crutch for support. The square offers a great view of Nôtre Dame Cathedral. This is a good place to take a break or enjoy a snack. Right around the corner to your left as you face the river is the famous English-language bookshop, Shakespeare and Company.

SHAKESPEARE AND COMPANY. *37, Rue de la Bûcherie, across the river from Nôtre Dame Cathedral (Metro: Saint Michel). Open daily. Note: This store does not accept any credit cards.*

Filled with expatriate Brits and Americans, this is one of the English-language bookshops of Paris where you can stock up on new and used books, for kids or adults. It has an interesting history that actually involves two bookshops:

The original Shakespeare and Company was located at 12, Rue de l'Odéon and run by a woman named Sylvia Beach. It was here that writers such as Ernest Hemingway, F. Scott Fitzgerald, James Joyce, and Gertrude Stein crossed paths. It was both an English-language bookshop and a lending library. During the German occupation of Paris in World War II, Beach refused to sell her last copy of James Joyce's *Finnegan's Wake* to a German officer. He threatened to confiscate all her books. She was forced to close the shop, and it never re-opened. During the Liberation of Paris, Ernest Hemingway, a war correspondent who was among the first Allied troops to enter the city, made a point of dropping by Sylvia Beach's place to officially liberate it.

In 1951, George Whitman opened up his English bookshop, called Le Mistral, in a little street across the Seine from Nôtre Dame Cathedral. He also had a lending library on the second floor, and his shop became a meeting place for a new generation of English-language poets and writers. These included Americans, such as Alan Ginsberg, William Burroughs, Henry Miller, and James Baldwin. Whitman installed cots in the library where struggling young writers could spend the night for free provided they read a book a day, worked an hour in the shop, and left a short autobiography and photo. They still do. When Sylvia Beach died in 1962, Whitman renamed his shop Shakespeare and Company to honor her. The shop extends a warm welcome to all book lovers, whether they are starving writers or not.

LUXEMBOURG GARDENS. *Located between the Boulevard Saint Michel, Rue de Vaugirard, and Rue d'Assas. Metro: Luxembourg or Nôtre Dame des Champs. Open sunrise to sunset. Entrance is free.*

The Luxembourg Palace and Gardens were built in the 17th century by Queen Marie de Médicis after the assassination of her husband King Henri IV. She bought the property from a Duke of Luxembourg, which is where it gets its name. The queen had the palace built to look like one in

Florence, Italy where she had spent her childhood. However, Marie de Médicis did not get to enjoy her new palace for long. Her son, Louis XIII, banished her from France, and she was forced to live the rest of her life in Germany.

The palace served as a royal residence until the French Revolution when it was used as a prison. During the German Occupation of Paris in World War II, the palace was taken over as central headquarters for the German Luftwäffe (Air Force). Today it houses the French Senate.

In front of the palace is the **central fountain** of the Luxembourg Gardens (*see photo on page 44*). On weekends and holiday afternoons it is dotted with miniature sailboats that you can rent by the hour from a little stand. This is one of our boys' all-time favorite activities in Paris. It also provides great photo opportunities. Keep an eye on small children, however. The edges of the fountain slope downward, and I've seen more than one child slide into the water head first.

The central fountain is a favorite hangout for students and other Parisians relaxing in the green metal chairs that fill the park. It is a lovely spot to rest your feet and soak in the sun on a nice day. As you sit there, notice the statues of the queens of France looking benevolently down at you from the surrounding terraces. Up the steps on the eastern side of the park there is a bandstand that offers free concerts in the summer, when the nearby outdoor café is also open.

Just east of the palace is the pretty, shady Médicis Fountain. Filled with goldfish, it presents an interesting optical illusion. Since the edges of the pool are on an incline, it looks like the water is slanted even though it is flat. The statue that adorns the fountain depicts a scene from the Greek myth of Acis and Galathea. Here is their story: Galatea was a water nymph. Acis was a fawn. They fell in love and became engaged. But the giant, one-eyed Cyclops, Polyphemus, wanted Galatea for himself. When he found the two lovers kissing in a cave, he threw a huge stone at Acis and crushed him. Galatea escaped into the water. Acis was turned into a river god. Polyphemus later had his eye poked out by Odysseus. The western side of the park has public tennis courts, a place reserved for playing *boules*, chess tables, a puppet theater, a wooden merry-go-round, and old-fashioned two-person swings. This is also where you will find the Luxembourg's amazing **playground**. Although there is a small fee to enter, it is well worth it. (It's the only place I know in Paris where kids pay more than adults.) If you have small children you will want to go in with them. If they are a little older and more independent, you can do what many Parisian parents and nannies do: watch them from the metal chairs around the perimeter of the playground. The small building in the playground has a restroom and snack bar.

In the summer months there are also pony rides and little race cars for rent on the western side of the park. There is a beekeeping school (near the rue d'Assas entrance) with classes twice a week. You can buy the honey each October in the garden's **Orangerie**, which doubles as a small museum featuring temporary art exhibits. If you wander through the shady paths on the western side of the park, you may come across a small replica of the Statue of Liberty. It was one of the models for the big one in New York harbor.

On the southeastern side of the park are the garden's greenhouses (not open to the public). There is also an orchard that is nearly 200 years old. The apples and pears from these trees are reserved for members of the Senate.

On the north side of the Luxembourg Gardens at #36 Rue de Vaugirard under the arcades, there is an inscription in the wall designating the official length of one meter. It is on a building that used to be the Agency for Weights and Measures and harkens back to the time (1795) when France adopted its first standardized system of measures: the metric system. The length of the meter, which was the baseline of the system, was calculated to be the equivalent of one-ten-millionth of the distance of the arc of the earth from the North Pole to the Equator. To help people get used to using meters, meter-stick measures such as this one were inscribed on the walls of buildings throughout the city.

PANTHEON, *Place du Panthéon. Metro: Luxembourg or Cardinal Lemoine. Open 9:30am-6:30pm (summer); 10am-6pm (winter). Adults: €7; Kids under 18: free.*

Initially designed as a church, the Pantheon is now a burial place for illustrious men and women; for example, Victor Hugo (author of *Les Miserables* and *The Hunchback of Notre Dame*), Louis Braille (who invented Braille writing for the blind), and Pierre and Marie Curie (who studied radioactivity). Paintings inside the Pantheon depict the life of Sainte Geneviève, death of Saint Denis, story of Joan of Arc, and crowning of Charlemagne.

Behind the Pantheon, you can take the Rue Clovis to the Rue Descartes. Notice half a block further down the Rue Clovis is a remnant of the **12th century defensive wall** that used to protect Paris from invaders, such as the English King Richard the Lionheart. If you take the Rue Descartes to the Place de la Contrescarpe, you will enter the Mouffetard neighborhood, famous for its ancient market street, shops, and restaurants.

RUE MOUFFETARD, *between Place de la Contrescarpe and Avenue des Gobelins. Metro: Place Monge or Censier Daubenton.*

This charming street has been paved with stones ever since Roman times when it led all the way to Italy. The road used to go along the Bièvre River, which now runs underground as part of the Paris sewer system. For centuries, the Mouffetard area was dotted with farms and vineyards. In the 12th century, wealthy Parisians built their country villas around here. Over time the Rue Mouffetard was lined with narrow houses (many of which are still there), shops, tanneries, cloth dyers, and an open-air market.

The Mouffetard neighborhood (familiarly known as **La Mouf**) has been home to many famous residents. Medieval author, Rabelais, used to get drunk in a tavern called the Pomme de Pin (Pine Cone) on the Place de la Contrescarpe. Age of Enlightenment thinker Denis Diderot lived at #3, Rue de l'Estrapade, and René Descartes lived at #14, Rue Rollin. Sculptor Auguste Rodin was born at #3, Rue de l'Arbalète. Ernest Hemingway lived around the corner at #74 Rue du Cardinal-Lemoine and at #39, Rue Descartes. He described the neighborhood in his books, *The Snows of Kilimanjaro* and *A Moveable Feast.*

At #60, Rue Mouffetard, there is a small fountain called the Fontaine du Pot de Fer that dates back to Roman times. It was later connected to an aqueduct used by Queen Marie de Médicis to bring water to her Luxembourg Gardens and Palace.

The house at # 53, Rue Mouffetard is famous for its hidden treasure. On May 24, 1938, workers tearing down an old house found gold coins in the walls, stamped with the likeness of King Louis XV. There were 3,351 coins in all. They had been left there by a man named Louis Nivelle, who had been Louis XV's secretary. Nivelle disappeared mysteriously in 1757, but left a will that was found with the coins. In the will, Nivelle bequeathed the treasure to his daughter, who died in 1810. The discovery of the coins led to a 15-year legal battle between Nivelle's heirs and the people who uncovered the treasure. In the end, the gold was split between Nivelle's 84 descendants. However, they had to pay fees to the genealogists and the construction crew, as well as a big inheritance tax to the City of Paris.

RUE MOUFFETARD STREET MARKET. *Metro: Censier Daubenton or Place Monge. Open Tuesday-Saturday, 8am-1pm, 4pm-7pm and Sunday 8am-1pm. Closed Sunday afternoon and Monday.* This market has been here for hundreds of years. Notice some of the old shop signs on the buildings. It is famous for its wide variety of fresh produce, meats, cheeses, and ethnic boutiques. Check out the wonderful bakeries and delicatessens with their specialties from France, Greece, Italy, and Asia. On weekends, French shoppers come in from the suburbs to enjoy the colors and tastes this market offers.

Parent Tip: Now that you've loaded up with food from the Rue Mouffetard, it's time to feed the budding scientist in every child with a visit to the nearby **Jardin des Plantes**. Here, children can run, have a picnic, ride a merry-go-round of extinct and endangered animals, get lost in a labyrinth, visit the zoo, and enjoy the wonderful **Natural History Museums**. ❖

JARDIN DES PLANTES *(Botanical Gardens), Located between the Rue Cuvier, Rue Geoffroy Saint Hilaire, Rue Buffon, and Seine River. Metro: Jussieu or Gare d'Austerlitz. Open sunrise to sunset. Museums open daily except Tues, 10am-6pm (Thurs. until 10pm). Greenhouses open daily 1pm-5pm. Menagerie (zoo) open daily 9am-5pm (summers until 6pm). Entrance to the park is free, though you do have to pay to enter the zoo, greenhouses, and museums.*

This park is a kid's haven. It contains a zoo, playground, labyrinth, and merry-go-round featuring extinct or endangered animals. There are huge greenhouses and botanical gardens. There is a paleontology museum, featuring skeletons of current and extinct animals; a gallery of evolution filled with real (stuffed) animals; a mineralogy museum with giant crystals; and a botanical museum.

The Jardin des Plantes began as a place where the royal botanists grew medicinal plants for the family of King Louis XIII. It was expanded during the reign of Louis XIV to accommodate plants brought back from expeditions to the New World and other foreign parts. The king's chief doctor headed the gardens. He oversaw the building of two greenhouses, including the Grande Serre (Large Greenhouse) that was designed to house France's first coffee tree. A 600-seat lecture hall was also added to promote the teaching of natural sciences and pharmacy.

Over time, many rare trees and plants were added to the park's collection. Some are still there today, including the oldest tree in Paris, planted in 1635. It is a False Acacia tree, and a twin to the one in the Square Viviani featured in *Linnea in Monet's Garden*. It is located in the Allée des Becquerels, near the Minerology Museum. The gardens also house a 150-year-old Ginkgo tree and a 250-year-old Chinese Sophora.

The park's **Labyrinth**, near the Rue Geoffroy Saint Hilaire side of the park, was built in 1640 on an artificial hill that had served as a trash pile. In the middle of the Labyrinth is a Cedar of Lebanon. This tree was secretly carried to Paris from London by botanist, Bernard de Jussieu in 1734. Along the route, the flower pot that held the small sapling broke. Legend has it that Jussieu carried the plant in his hat for most of the trip, catching a head cold as a result. The more reliable version of the story says that the pot broke only a few blocks from the park. Either way, the tree was safely delivered thanks to the botanist's hat.

MENAGERIE (ZOO). *Northwest corner of the Jardin des Plantes. Open daily except Tues. 9am-6pm (summer); 9am-5pm (winter). Closed Tues. Adults: €7; Kids ages 5-16: €5; Kids under 5: free. You can get a map at the entrance indicating where to find different animals.*

The Menagerie was created in 1793. It is the oldest public zoo in the world. Its first residents were animals that had been part of the royal menagerie at Versailles and were brought here after the French Revolution. They were joined by other animals that were confiscated from carnivals and street performers. More animals were added in 1795, including France's first live elephants, stolen from a Dutch zoo after a successful French military campaign. The first giraffe arrived in 1826. It was a gift from the King of Egypt. The giraffe went by boat to Marseilles, then traveled slowly up to Paris to give people a chance to see it. It was such a hit that giraffe decorations on combs, umbrellas, and other items became all the rage.

In 1870, the Prussians laid siege to the city of Paris, ultimately forcing ruler Napoleon III to surrender. During the siege, the people of Paris were cut off from their food supplies and had to eat anything they could find. Even the zoo animals were killed, and their meat was sold to local restaurants.

Today, the zoo is home to some 800 animals. There are many large mammals, reptiles, and birds. There is also a "microzoo," where you can look at tiny creatures through a microscope.

GALERIE DE PALEONTOLOGIE. *Northeastern edge of the park (near the Seine entrance). Open daily except Tues, 10am-5pm (weekdays); 10am-6pm (weekends). Closed Tues. Adults: €6; Kids ages 5-18: €4. Kids under 5: free.*

Note: This museum is slated to be renovated, so catch it while you can.

This museum holds an impressive array of animal skeletons, including a mammoth and an entire blue whale. The upper floor features magnificent dinosaur skeletons and fossils. The building was first opened in 1898 and with its intricate ironwork decorations is itself well worth the visit.

GRANDE GALERIE DE L'EVOLUTION. *Southeastern side of the park, by Rue Geoffroy Saint Hilaire and Paris Mosque. Open daily except Tues, 10am-6pm (until 10pm Thurs). Adults: €8; Kids 4-18: €6; Kids under 4: free.*

This is a wonderful place to visit with kids. The building was renovated after being closed for decades and now offers exhibits of animals of all types. The great hall is quite spectacular, featuring a long caravan of mammals ranging from very large (elephants and giraffes) to smaller ones. The lower level has marine animals on exhibit. Birds are represented in flight along the upper floors, and there are monkeys climbing up the levels near the elevators. There is a fascinating room upstairs (level 2) featuring animals that are extinct or endangered. The top level has a rhinoceros that belonged to the royal menagerie of Louis XIV. It is the oldest animal in the museum.

GALERIE DE MINEROLOGIE. *Southern side of the park, near the Grande Galerie. Open daily except Tues, 10am-5pm. Adults: €6; Kids: €4.*

This is an interesting visit for anyone who really digs rocks and crystals. It features the world's greatest collection of giant crystals. There are jewels from the reigns of Louis XIII and Louis XIV. There are also meteorites from outer space. Unfortunately, this museum is in dire need of updating and is arranged like a dusty, private collection. It is not air conditioned, which can make it hard to tolerate if the weather is hot.

JARDIN ALPIN. *Near the Menagerie. Entrance is free.*

This small garden-within-a-garden features plants that would normally be found in mountains such as the Alps, Pyrenees, or Himalayas. They survive here thanks to careful placement and attention. It is a quiet place, rarely crowded, where kids can run happily through the alley ways and adults can get the impression of being in the fresh mountain air.

PARIS MOSQUE. *1, Place du Puits de l'Ermite. The restaurant, tearoom, and Turkish bath entrances are located at 39, Rue Geoffroy Saint Hilaire. Metro: Place Monge. The Mosque is open for visits daily except Fridays, from 9am-12pm, and 2pm-6pm. The restaurant is open daily, 10am-9pm.*

The Paris Mosque was built from 1922 to 1926 as a gesture of thanks to the North African troops who fought alongside the French during World War I. It was designed to look like the mosque in the Moroccan city of Fez. Four hundred fifty artisans and technicians from Morocco, Algeria, and Tunisia worked on the building. It is beautifully decorated with mosaics, intricate wood carvings, fine rugs, and shady gardens. The minaret tower is 33 meters (109 feet) high.

Across from the entrance to the Jardin des Plantes is the entrance to the Mosque's **restaurant and tearoom**. You can enjoy tea and snacks inside or in the outdoor gardens, which are decorated with beautiful tiles, shady trees, and a fountain. The restaurant offers couscous and other North African culinary specialties eaten on huge brass tray tables. It's a taste of the exotic in the middle of Paris.

OPEN-AIR SCULPTURE GARDEN. *On the Seine, along the Quai Saint Bernard. Metro: Jussieu or Gare d'Austerlitz. Open daily, sunrise to sunset. Entrance is free.*

This spot combines a park, art, and nice views of the Seine River. The sculpture garden runs along the river from the Jardin des Plantes to the Institut du Monde Arabe. It is filled with works by modern artists such as Joan Arp, Constantine Brancusi, and Cesar – who sometimes appeal more to children than to adults. There are also paths for roller blading, ping-pong tables, and a playground. Sometimes after a particularly wet winter, the park becomes flooded by the rising waters of the Seine. Then some of the sculptures end up partially submerged.

INSTITUT DU MONDE ARABE. *1, Rue des Fossés-Saint-Bernard. Metro: Jussieu, or Cardinal Lemoine. Access to the building is free. The museum is open, 10am-6pm, Closed Mon. Adults and Children 12 and up: €4. Children under 12: free. There are often special exhibits with separate entrances and entrance fees.*

This Institute celebrates Arab culture and heritage with a museum, films, concerts, dance performances, and food. The museum has a permanent collection but is especially interesting for its temporary exhibits – like a recent one on the Egyptian pharaohs. There is a nice café and gift shop on the ground level. Even if all you do is walk by, take a look at the windows on the south side of the building. They are designed to look like Arab mosaics. But they also serve a practical purpose. Like the lens of a camera or the pupil of your eye, the openings are designed to widen or narrow automatically depending on how bright the light is outdoors.

CLAUDE NATURE SHOP. *32, Boulevard Saint Germain. Metro: Maubert Mutualité.*

This little shop appeals to bug lovers of all ages. It sells collectors' quality butterflies and other exotic bugs.

MAGIC SHOW - METAMORPHOSIS. *On a houseboat across from 55, Quai de la Tournelle (Apr-Sep), Metro: Maubert Mutualité. Sunday Brunch at 12:30pm and plus magic show at 3 pm. Adults: €38 for brunch and show, €16 for show and snack. Kids: €32 for brunch and show, €6 for show and snack. Note: from Oct to Mar this boat moves upstream to by 7, Quai*

Malaquais across from the Pont des Arts, Metro: Pont Neuf or Saint Germain des Près.

This houseboat offers floating magic shows. Special family-friendly shows are presented on Sunday afternoons. Other performances are presented Tuesday-Saturday at 9:30 pm.

PIRATE SHIP. *11, Quai Francois Mauriac, Metro: Quai de la Gare. Shows daily at 3pm during summer holidays. During the school year, there are shows every Wed, Sat, and Sun afternoon at 3. Price: €3.50 (includes snack).*

This surprising ship, moored on the Seine near the Bibliothèque Nationale Francois Mitterand, is actually a real Chinese Jonque. Built in China during the 1980s, it has sailed around the world several times. Now, it is permanently stationed in Paris, where it offers live, kid-friendly shows. It's also a family-friendly restaurant.

GARE D'AUSTERLITZ. *Along the Boulevard de l'Hôpital by the Quai d'Austerlitz.*

This train station is named for one of Napoleon Bonaparte's successful battles against the Austrians and Russians. It is where you come to catch trains coming and going from southwestern France, Spain, or Portugal. You can catch up on some of your correspondences at the station restaurant. The menu is printed on a postcard.

5. SAINT GERMAIN

Saint Germain des Près is home to Paris' first official café, established in 1686. It is famous for attracting the intellectual crowd and fancy fashion designers. There are also plenty of treats for children, too, in the side streets of Saint Germain. These range from the magnificently restored **Musée d'Orsay** (formerly a train station) to the mysteries of a summer solstice at the **Place Saint Sulpice**.

ÉGLISE SAINT GERMAIN DES PRÈS, *Place Saint Germain des Près. Metro: Saint Germain des Près. Entrance is free.*

This is the oldest church in Paris. It was first built in 543 AD, by the Merovingian king, Childebert, who was feeling guilty for having murdered so many relatives and rivals to get to the throne. The church has had to withstand many attacks from invading Vikings and others. It was originally fortified, complete with watchtowers and a moat. The bell tower (still standing) was built in the year 1,000 AD. It was part of the defensive walls and is the oldest bell tower in Paris. Much of the church you see today dates from the 11th and 12th centuries and is a good example of the Romanesque architectural style. In the late 1600s, the Église Saint Germain des Près was turned into a prison. With the Revolution of 1789, it was changed into a saltpeter factory (used to make gunpowder). After the Revolution, the church resumed its religious role.

Next to the church, along the Boulevard Saint Germain, there is a little park with a small playground called the **Square Boucicault**. It is named for Aristide Boucicaut, the man who invented the first department store, the nearby Bon Marché.

Saint Germain Highlights

- Check out the 1000 year old church tower
- Find the portrait of Benjamin Franklin in the Cour du Commerce Saint André
- Look for the brass Paris Meridian line in the Eglise Saint Sulpice
- Find the polar bear sculpture and bedroom furniture by Macintosh at the Musée d'Orsay
- Check out the animals at Deyrolles, Paris' finest taxidermist shop
- Go for a Canal Boat Ride

RUE DE BUCI. *Just east of the Eglise Saint Germain des Près.* This street is lined with wonderful bakeries, food shops, and cafés. It is a good spot to take a break and watch the fashionable Saint Germain crowd go by.

RUE SAINT ANDRE DES ARTS. *Just east of the Rue de Buci, Metro: Odéon.*

This bustling street is lined with shops, small restaurants, and an artsy movie theatre. It is a fun way to get from the Rue de Buci to the Place Saint Michel. You can also take an interesting detour into the **Cour du Commerce Saint André** (heading east, on the right, shortly after you enter the street). This cobbled lane has welcomed pedestrians to its shops and restaurants for hundreds of years. It leads to the Carrefour de l'Odéon. On the right, you will see the Paris' oldest café, the Café Procope. Notice the portraits in the window. There's one you should recognize from American history books: Benjamin Franklin.

ÉGLISE SAINT SULPICE, *Place Saint Sulpice. Metro: Mabillon or Saint Sulpice. Open daily, 8am-7:30pm. Entrance is free.*

The outside of this church is odd and slightly out of proportion. That's because it was built and rebuilt over the centuries and combines a mishmash of different architectural styles. The tower on the right was never completed.

The inside of Saint Sulpice is more interesting, especially if you are traveling with any fans of Dan Brown's *The DaVinci Code*. One of the scenes in that story takes place here in Saint Sulpice and has to do with a clue connected to the brass line, which you can see on the floor of the church leading to a white marble obelisk. The line and obelisk are part of a **gnomon**, a sort of sundial that indicates days of the year, instead of hours of the day. Here's how it works: If you look up at the stained glass windows above the meridian line, you can make out a circular hole in one of the windowpanes. On the stroke of noon, the light from the sun (provided it isn't cloudy) goes through the round hole in the window and lands on a point along the brass line. That point indicates the day's date. There is a special marble plaque indicating the spot where the light hits on the day of the Summer Solstice (June 21). Small brass plaques mark the Spring and Fall Equinoxes. On the day of the Winter Solstice (December 21) the sunlight hits a spot on the obelisk decorated with the Zodiac symbol, Capricorn. A Sagittarius symbol marks the date for November 21, and Aquarius marks the spot for January 21.

A small chapel (called Chapelle des Anges) on the right as you enter the Eglise Saint Sulpice features three famous paintings by Eugène Delacroix. One depicts Saint Michael fighting the Devil. Another depicts the story of Heliodorus, ordered by the king of Syria to steal the treasure from a Temple, but chased away by three angels (one on a horse). The third painting shows Jacob wrestling with an angel as he is being tested by God.

In another side chapel, there is also a small organ that once belonged to Queen Marie-Antoinette, and on which a young Mozart performed.

MARCHÉ DE SAINT GERMAIN DES PRÈS. *12, Rue Lobineau. Metro: Mabillon.*

This covered market once housed the Saint Germain Fair. Today it has food stalls and shops on the main level. There is a public swimming pool in the basement.

MUSÉE D'ORSAY. *1, Rue de la Légion d'Honneur (formerly Rue de Bellechasse). Metro: Solférino or Musée d'Orsay. Open 10 am-6 pm (winter), 9 am-6 pm (summer). Open until 9:45 pm on Thurs. Closed Mon. Adults: €9.50 (Sundays: €7). Kids under 18: free. Free to teachers, artists, museum employees, and journalists with presentation of professional card. Free to all on the first Sunday of each month. Combined Adult ticket for Musée d'Orsay and Musée Rodin: €12. Audioguide rental: €5. Free children's guides, Carnet-Parcours-Jeunes, and family guide, Carnet-Parcours-Famille, are available at the entrance. Wheelchairs and strollers available free of charge.*

This magnificent museum has something for (almost) everyone – Impressionist paintings and sculptures, cool furniture, models of buildings, and more – and it is in the very impressive setting of a former train station, known as the Gare d'Orsay.

The Gare d'Orsay was one of the first train stations in Paris built for electric trains. It was very modern for its time, with electric elevators and more metal than was used in the construction of the Eiffel Tower. However, as trains became longer, the station became to be too short to accommodate them. By 1939, the Gare d'Orsay no longer serviced passenger trains. During World War II, the station was used as a center for sending care packages to war prisoners. When the war was over, it became a triage center for returning prisoners. It remained empty and out of use for decades, until it was refurbished and reopened as a museum in 1986.

Today the museum features a magnificent collection of art and architecture dating from 1850 to 1915. You still get a feel for the beauty of the original train station as you walk in the central exhibition hall with its soaring ceiling. This area contains grand statues from the 19th century. Smaller exhibit halls on each side feature works by Ingres, Delacroix, Millet, Daumier, and Courbet. Toward the back of the main floor is an interesting wooden model of the Paris Opera and small scenes from famous operas. The upper levels feature exhibit rooms that take you through late 19th and early 20th century painting. These range from a large white statue of a polar bear (generally a big a hit with young children) to works by Dégas, Cézanne, Renoir, Manet, Monet, Van Gogh, and Toulouse Lautrec.

The exhibit spaces in the back of the museum feature beautiful examples of Art Nouveau and Arts and Crafts style furniture and decorative arts. Keep going up the steps, they cover several floors. Believe it or not, many children really enjoy this section. It doesn't take much for them to imagine what it would be like to live with such cool furniture.

If you need a break during your visit, you can enjoy the Café des Hauteurs on the top level, which offers snacks and light meals with an impressive view of the back side of the building's giant clock – a remnant of its days as a train station. If your kids are up for a fancier setting, they might enjoy the museum restaurant, which offers a kids menu for lunch and teas and cakes for afternoon snack.

Near the Musée d'Orsay, at 56, Rue Jacob is the former **Hotel York** mansion. This is the spot where Benjamin Franklin, John Jay, John Adams, and representatives from Britain and France signed the Paris Peace Treaty of September 3, 1783. It was this treaty that officially recognized American Independence from Britain.

DEYROLLE, *46, Rue du Bac. Metro: Bac. Open 10am-6:45pm, Mon-Sat. Closed Sun.*

This surprising store is Paris' last taxidermy shop. It has animals ranging in size from insects to grizzly bears. There are also drawers filled with fossils and minerals. You will feel like you've walked into a natural history museum, except that you can actually purchase the displays. The shop adheres to strict rules regarding endangered species. The large animals come from zoos and farms where they died of natural causes.

AU BON MARCHÉ DEPARTMENT STORE. *24, Rue de Sèvres (Metro: Sèvres-Babylone), Open Mon-Sat 9:30 am-7 pm.*

This is the world's first department store. When it was launched in 1876 by Aristide Boucicaut it was an instant success. The original building was designed by Gustave Eiffel (of Eiffel Tower fame). The kids' toys section, called **3 Hiboux** is in the basement. **La Grande Épicerie**, on the ground floor, offers gourmet foods from France and around the world.

PARIS CANAL BOAT RIDES. *By the Musée d'Orsay, on the Quai Anatole France. Metro: Solférino. Departs at 9:30am, daily, from late March to early November. Arrives at La Villette at 12:30pm. Adults: €14; Kids 4-11: €8.*

This is a 3-hour canal boat ride that takes you along the Seine, to the Paris Marina, up through the Saint Martin Canal, and to the Parc de La Villette. You get wonderful views of major Paris sights, pass through numerous locks, under lovely foot bridges, and through a long tunnel under the Place de la Bastille. It's a unique way to experience Paris. For children who enjoy boats, it's a delightful tour, though it may be too long for small tikes. Don't forget to bring snacks or a full picnic. When you get to the Parc de la Villette, you can enjoy its wonderful science museum, museum of music, and playgrounds.

6. MONTPARNASSE

The **Montparnasse** neighborhood gets its name from Greek mythology, where Mount Parnassus is home of the god Apollo and his muses. In the early 20th century it was a hangout for many artists, such as Picasso, Chagall, and Man Ray; writers such as Jean-Paul Sartre and Simone de Beauvoir, and composers such as Erik Satie and Igor Stravinsky. After World War I, the so-called "lost generation" of American writers also settled around Montparnasse. These included Ernest Hemingway, Gertrude Stein, Alice B. Toklas, F. Scott Fitzgerald, Henri Miller, Anais Nin, and Ezra Pound.

Much of the area's Bohemian charm has been erased either through urban renewal projects in the 1970s or because of rising property prices in the city. But the old streets and sights have not all disappeared. And the kid-friendly attractions of this neighborhood give you a chance to appreciate both the old and new aspects of this Mont-Parnassus, home of the Muses.

TOUR MONTPARNASSE. *Rue de l'Arrivée. Metro: Montparnasse-Bienvenue. Viewing galleries open 9:30am-10:30pm, Mon-Thur; 9:30am-11:00pm, Fri-Sun. Adults: €8.50, Kids: €5.80.*

Unlike many American cities, Paris does not have a skyline dotted with skyscrapers. But it does have the Tour Montparnasse. Completed in 1973, this is the tallest building in Europe. It has 59 stories. Many Parisians

will tell you that the top of the Tour Montparnasse offers the best view in the city. Why? Because you can see everything but the tower itself, which they consider to be terrible eyesore.

The view from the tower is spectacular. A 38-second elevator ride takes you up to an observation space on the 56th floor with a 360 degree view of the city. There is also a small museum, a movie that offers a bird's-eye view of Paris, and a snack bar.

Most of the Tour Montparnasse is filled with offices. There is a shopping mall on the ground floor with several nice department and chain stores. There is a large, public, indoor swimming center on the lower level with pools for water lovers of all ages.

Montparnasse Highlights

- Ride up to the top floor of the Tour Montparnasse
- Eat a crêpe
- Visit the masses of bones in the Catacombs
- Play in the Parc Montsouris
- Climb on rocks and rent a remote control boat at the Parc Georges Brassens
- Shop for discount fashions in the Rue d'Alésia

On the esplanade between the Tour Montparnasse and the Montparnasse Train Station there is an old-fashioned **carrousel** that runs just about every day of the year. In the winter the city installs a **skating rink**.

GARE MONTPARNASSE. *Place Bienvenue. Metro: Montparnasse-Bienvenue.*

This train station serves destinations to the west and southwest of Paris. These include Chartres, the Loire Valley, Brittany, Aquitaine, and Spain. Outside, you may notice plenty of crêpe restaurants. These are holdovers from the late 19th and early 20th centuries, when many people from Brittany (where crêpes are king) emigrated to Paris and set up shop near the station. Above the station is a public park called the **Jardin Atlantique**, which has a playground and room to run.

CATACOMBS. *Entrance is at 1, Place Denfert Rochereau (In a building on the SE side of the circle). Metro: Denfert Rochereau. Open 10am-5pm every day except Mon. Ticket booth closes at 4pm. Adults: €7; Youths age 14-26: €5.50; Kids under age 14: free. Note: This visit can be too scary for children under age 10. Also beware that you will exit several blocks south of where you entered. To return to Place Denfert Rochereau, take a right as you exit toward Avenue du General Leclerc. Take a right at the Avenue and continue several blocks north back to the Place.*

The Catacombs are located in some of Paris' old rock quarries, which were dug under the city, as tunnels, to supply the white stone used to build the city's buildings and cobbled streets. The tunnels were dug for hundreds of years until they made up a network that stretched nearly 200 miles.

In the 1780s, central Paris became so crowded that even the cemeteries began to overflow. The decision was made to transfer their contents (more than 6 million skeletons) into some of the abandoned quarry tunnel. These became the Paris Catacombs. During the German Occupation of Paris in World War II, the Catacombs served as the headquarters for the French Resistance fighters.

Today, you can visit parts of the Catacombs and old quarries to see some of the millions of bones that were carefully transferred here and lined up along the walls and ceilings of the tunnels. Personally, I find it dank, dark, and creepy, but it's a big hit with many kids, especially fans of scary movies and the macabre. The visit was recently renovated and expanded.

PARC MONTSOURIS. *Between Boulevard Jourdan, Avenue Reuille, Rue Nansouty, and Rue Gazan. Metro: Porte d'Orléans or Cité Universitaire. Open sunrise to sunset. Entrance is free.*

This large park is located on the southern edge of Paris in what was once a small village, surrounded by windmill-covered hills. Here you will find pony rides, puppet shows, playgrounds, an area for roller blading, and summer concerts in the gazebo.

Nearby is the **Rue d'Alésia**, which features lots of clothing stores, including discounted designer goods.

PARC GEORGES BRASSENS. *Rue des Morillons. Metro: Convention. Open daily, dawn to dusk. Entrance is free.*

Two majestic bronze bulls guard the entrance to the park, as a reminder that this was once the sight of one of Paris' slaughterhouses. Today, there are playgrounds, puppet shows, and a merry-go-round. There are beehives and a garden of scents. There are climbing walls made from stones recycled from old buildings.

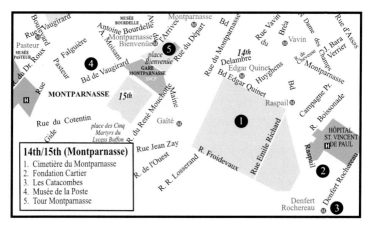

14th/15th (Montparnasse)
1. Cimetière du Montparnasse
2. Fondation Cartier
3. Les Catacombes
4. Musée de la Poste
5. Tour Montparnasse

7. EIFFEL TOWER

This is simply a must-see! No trip to Paris with kids is complete without a visit to the Eiffel Tower.

EIFFEL TOWER. *On the Champs de Mars. Metro: Bir Hakeim. Open daily, 9 am-midnight (last elevator goes up at 11 pm, the stairs close at 6 pm). Rates: Kids under age 3 are free. Elevator to the first level-Adults: €4.80; Children under 12: €2.50. Stairs to levels one and two-Adults: €4; Anyone under 25: €3.10. Elevator to level 2 - Adults: €7.80; Children under 12: €4.30. Elevator to level 3 - Adults: €12; Children under 12: €6.70.*

Note: To avoid long ticket lines during high tourist seasons visit the tower early in the morning or in the evening. Caught midday in a long line?

Don't worry. It's better organized than it looks, and the lines actually move fairly quickly. If your family is active and adventuresome, the line to walk up the stairs is usually considerably shorter than the one for the elevators.

Kids love the Eiffel Tower, and who can blame them? It's big, it's cool, and seen from up close it's surprisingly beautiful. Here's how it works. The Eiffel Tower has three levels. You can take the elevator or walk up the stairs as far as the 2nd level. You must ride a special elevator to reach the 3rd level. One option is to ride the ele-

Eiffel Tower Highlights

• Ride the elevators to the top of the Tower
• Take the stairs down at least one level to see the tower from the inside
• Dine at 58 Tour Eiffel
• Go on a family-friendly bike or Segway tour
• Go on a boat tour down the Seine
• Look for the Statue of Liberty

vator up and take the stairs down from the first or second level. This offers an amazing view of the inner structure of the tower and you can take a break by reading some of the historical interest markers along the way. However, this route is not recommended for very small children or for people with vertigo.

The tower contains a small museum, a replica of Gustave Eiffel's office, a small movie theater, and a post office (mail your postcards from here and they will have a special Eiffel Tower cancellation stamp). In winter, the Eiffel Tower has resurrected an old tradition of having an **ice-skating rink** on the platform of the first level. There is no extra fee to go skating and they will lend you a pair of skates free of charge.

There are two **snack bars** on the tower where you can get pizza, hot dogs, a sandwich, or ice cream. There are also two restaurants: the very expensive **Jules Verne**, and the less fancy 58 Tour Eiffel, scheduled to open March 2009, which offers a great view and an experience kids won't forget

The Eiffel Tower was built to celebrate the 1889 Paris International Exhibition, and the 100th anniversary of the French Revolution. It was designed by **Gustave Eiffel**, an architect/engineer who also designed the interior support skeleton for the Statue of Liberty. Although it is the city's most popular landmark today, many people hated the tower when it was first built. A group of leading artists, writers, and politicians sent an editorial to a major newspaper decrying the project, saying that the tower design looked like a gigantic factory chimney.

Construction of the Eiffel Tower took two years. The day it was finished, March 31, 1889, Gustave Eiffel climbed up the 1,710 steps to the top and raised a French flag from it. Until the Chrysler Tower was built in New York City (1930), the Eiffel Tower was the tallest building in the world.

Originally, each level of the Eiffel Tower was painted a different color, ranging from dark bronze at the bottom to a golden yellow on top. Today it is all one color: light brown. The tower is repainted every 7 years. It takes 25 painters, 40 tons of paint, and nearly a year to finish the job. In 1909, there was talk of tearing down the Eiffel Tower. Then it was discovered to be an ideal spot for a radio-telegraph center. During World War I, the tower housed a military spy center that tracked down enemy agents. The most famous of them was a woman known as Mata Hari, accused of spying for Germany. Ironically, Mata Hari was a familiar face at the Eiffel Tower. Prior to the war, she had been a dancer in the tower's first floor restaurant. After the Liberation of Paris in World War II, there was a nightclub on the Eiffel Tower where American soldiers were welcomed free of charge.

Today, the Eiffel Tower is used by numerous TV and radio stations to emit their signals. It also holds a weather station and devices to measure the city's air quality.

The Eiffel Tower is 320 meters (984 feet) tall. In hot weather it can increase by as much as 6 inches in height due to the expansion of the metal. The Eiffel Tower contains 15,000 pieces of metal and 2.5 million metal rivets. It weighs 9 million kilos (7,000 tons). On a clear day, you can see as far as the Chartres Cathedral (more than 50 miles away) from the top level. On a stormy day, there's a good chance the tower will be struck by lightening. It averages 50 lightening strikes each year.

Lots of people have tried various stunts from the Eiffel Tower, ranging from the catastrophic (e.g., unsuccessful attempts to parachute from the tower or fly an airplane through it) to the funny (e.g., coaxing an elephant up the stairs to the first level) and the daring (e.g., bungee jumping off the second level or walking a tightrope wire from the tower to the Trocadero, across the river).

CHAMPS DE MARS. *Metro: Bir Hakeim or Ecole Militaire. RER: Champs de Mars. Open day and night.*

This park is named for the Roman god of war, Mars, and it marks the spot where the Gauls (early Celtic settlers of Paris) were defeated by Roman invaders in 50 BC. It has been used as a practice field for the nearby Military Academy and the sight of some of the world's first hot air balloon rides. Now it is a quiet park, a favorite spot for skate boarders and roller bladders.

FAT TIRES' BIKE AND SEGWAY TOURS. *Located 3 blocks from the Eiffel Tower at 24, Rue Edgar Faure, Metro: Dupleix. Phone: 01-56-58-10-54. Website: www.fattirebiketoursparis.com/bikes/about-fat-tire/index.shtml or Email: paris@fattirebiketours.com*

This company is American owned and offers English-language tours of Paris via bicycle or Segway. The tours are designed to be fun and not grueling; they stay on flat parts and avoid traffic. It's a great way to see the city. The tours are also very family-friendly, but you may want to call or email in advance to reserve child bikes, child seats, child tandems, or a child trailer.

BATEAUX PARISIENS TOUR BOATS. *Port de la Bourdonnais, at the foot of the Eiffel Tower, Metro:Bir Hakeim. Daily departures every 30 minutes, 10am- 11pm. Price: Adults €9.50; Kids under 12 €4.50. Kid-friendly cruises depart at 1:45 pm and 3:45 pm, Saturday and Sunday. Try also* BATEAU VEDETTES DE PARIS TOUR BOATS. *Port de Suffren (Metro: Bir Hakeim) Hourly rides, 11 am-6pm. Adults: €9; Kids under 12: €4.*

Kids love these boat cruises. It's a great way to see many of the major sights and monuments of Paris, especially if you are jet-lagged or foot sore. The vantage point is unique. The commentaries are in English and French. The regular tour lasts 60 minutes.

STATUE OF LIBERTY. *On the tip of the Isle aux Signes, the small island under the double-decker bridge called Pont de Bir Hakeim.*

This is a small model of the Statue of Liberty that stands in New York harbor. It is a reminder that the statue was a gift from France to the United States and that it was designed by the French sculptor Auguste Bartholdi. Gustave Eiffel (of Eiffel Tower fame) designed the inside support structure for it. The full-size Statue of Liberty arrived in New York in 1885, dismantled into pieces that filled 214 packing crates. It was officially inaugurated on October 28, 1886. At the time, the Statue of Liberty was the tallest (305 feet) building in New York City. The best place from which to see the smaller Paris version of the statue is from a tour boat. You can also see an even smaller version in the Luxembourg Gardens, one in the Museum of Arts and Industry in the Marais neighborhood, or a full-size replica of the statue's torch by the Pont de l'Alma.

PARIS SEWER TOUR AND MUSEUM. (**LES EGOUTS DE PARIS**) *93, Quai d'Orsay. By the Pont de l'Alma. Metro: Alma-Marceau. Open Sat-Wed, 11am-5pm (May-Sept), 11am-4pm (Oct-Apr). Closed Thur and Fri. Beware: the last tickets are sold one hour before closing time. Closed during heavy rains. Adults: €4, Children under 12: €3.*

This is the kind of weird but educational visit that kids (and many adults) really enjoy and remember. Okay, you do have to get used to the smell, but it's not as bad as you might expect. The visit actually offers an interesting glimpse at the underside and mechanics of the city's sewage and water systems. The sewer tunnels cover about 1,400 miles. They run directly under every Paris street, with wider tunnels for broader avenues. Each tunnel is named for the street above it, so that anyone with a road map of Paris can find his or her way. Surprisingly, it takes more than 300 sewer works, engineers, and other specialized staff to maintain this vast and critically important system.

8. LES INVALIDES

The **Invalides complex** (*see photos on page 60*) was built in 1670 by King Louis XIV as a home for wounded war veterans, and the buildings along the eastern side still fill that function. The rest has been transformed into a museum and the final resting place for Napoleon Bonaparte.

NAPOLEON'S TOMB IN THE EGLISE DU DOME. *Invalides complex. 129, Rue de Grenelle. Métro: Invalides, Latour-Maubourg, or Varenne. Combined ticket for tomb, Musée de l'Armée, and Musée des Plans Reliefs. Adults: €8; Kids 12-18: €6; Kids under 12: free.*

The large, golden-domed church in the middle of the Invalides complex was built during the reign of Louis XIV. It was restored in the 1980s, and more than 500,000 pieces of gold leaf were used to bring back the dome's golden luster. The four statues decorating the top of the Dôme represent Hope, Charity, Spirituality, and Religion.

Two of the Invalides' architects, Liberal Bruant and Jules Hardouin Mansart, are buried in the church. So is Marshall Foch, who commanded the allied French, British, and American troops at the end of World War I. But the most famous tomb in the church belongs to Napoleon I.

Who was Napoleon I? Napoleon Bonaparte was born on the island of Corsica. After leading successful military campaigns in Italy, he was elected First Consul of the Republic in 1799. Napoleon established a new constitution for France, a new code of laws, national education system, and reformed the judicial system. He created the nation's leading universities and Academies of Art, Science, Literature, and Engineering. In 1802,

Napoleon was elected Consul for life, and in 1804 declared himself Emperor. He conquered most of Europe, except Britain, but in 1805, he began to suffer military defeats. In 1812 he lost four-fifths of his men in the frozen Russian winter. In

1814, he was forced from power and sent into exile on the Italian island of Elba. Napoleon returned to power in 1815, only to be forced from power once again after his military defeat at Waterloo. He was exiled to Saint Helena, an island in the south Atlantic, where he died.

In 1840, Napoleon's remains were returned to the Invalides with great pomp and circumstance. The remains are contained inside an enormous granite **sarcophagus**. It was a gift from Tsar Nicholas I of Russia, which is ironic since it was Napoleon's unsuccessful attempt to take over Russia that began his downfall. Within the sarcophagus there are 6 coffins, nestled one inside the other like Russian dolls. They are made of iron, wood, lead, lead, ebony, and oak.

> **Les Invalides Highlights**
>
> • See Napoleon's tomb
> • Pick out your favorite suit of armor, find Napoleon's horse, and check out the WWII exhibit at the Military Museum
> • See the 17th century wooden models of towns, bridges, and defense towers at the Musée des Plans Reliefs
> • Admire the statues and have lunch in the gardens of the Rodin Museum
> • Find the movie theater made to look like a Japanese pagoda

Side chapels in the Eglise du Dôme contain the remains of Napoleon's brothers, Joseph and Jerome, and his son, Napoleon II. The adjacent **Saint Louis church** contains a collection of flags that were captured from the enemy during Napoleon's many military campaigns.

MUSÉE DE L'ARMEE (MILITARY MUSEUM). *In the Invalides complex. 129, Rue de Grenelle Métro: Invalides, Latour-Maubourg, or Varenne. Open daily 10am-5pm (winter), 10am-6pm (summer). Combined ticket for tomb, Musée de l'Armée, and Musée des Plans Reliefs. Adults: €8; Kids 12-18: €6; Kids under 12: free. Audioguide is free for those buying a ticket, €1 for kids under 12.*

This Military Museum features exhibits ranging from prehistoric battles to 20th Century World Wars. It is quite interesting, even if you are not a military history buff. The ground floor is filled with suits of armor. The upper floors feature exhibits on the Napoleonic wars, including a display of Napoleon's horse, Vizir. There is a section dedicated to World War I, with lots of (fairly boring) maps and uniforms – the most touching is one from a man in the trenches that is caked with mud.

However, the best part of the museum is its newly renovated section dedicated to World War II. Both children and adults will be moved by its exhibits (conveniently labeled in both English and French). The rooms not

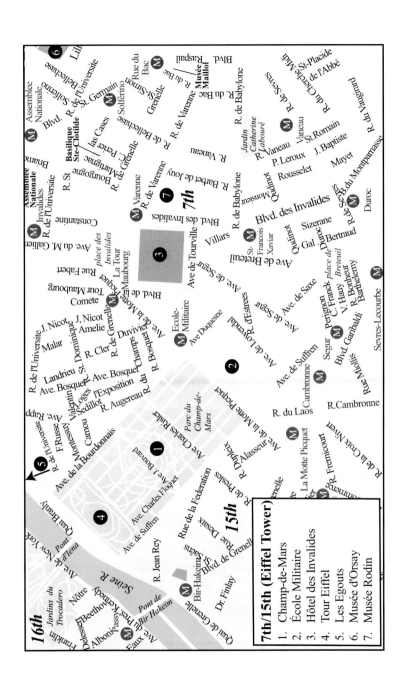

7th/15th (Eiffel Tower)

1. Champ-de-Mars
2. École Militaire
3. Hôtel des Invalides
4. Tour Eiffel
5. Les Egouts
6. Musée d'Orsay
7. Musée Rodin

only show artifacts and films about the fighting and military strategy. They also offer glimpses into the war's effect on ordinary people, including children. The exhibit is organized chronologically and gives a good view of just how many countries and people were affected by WWII.

MUSÉE DES PLANS RELIEFS. *In the Invalides complex. 129, Rue de Grenelle. Métro: Invalides, Latour-Maubourg, or Varenne. Open daily 10am-5pm (winter), 10am-6pm (summer). Combined ticket for tomb, Musée de l'Armée, and Musée des Plans Reliefs. Adults: €8; Kids 12-18: €6; Kids under 12: free.*

This small museum is on an upper floor of the Invalides complex. It presents a collection of made-to-scale wooden models of fortresses, ports, and towns across France. They were prepared for King Louis XIV as part of his strategic defense plans. They were so important that their existence was kept secret for many years.

Parent Tip: The cafeteria in the Invalides complex is pretty Spartan and crowded. If you are visiting during late spring or summer, you may want to head instead to the nearby Musée Rodin gardens for lunch or a snack. There you can enjoy your food in a quiet garden with famous sculptures and plenty of room for kids to move around. ✤

MUSÉE RODIN. *77, Rue de Varenne (Metro: Varenne), not far from the Invalides. Open Tues-Sun, 9:30 am - 5:45 pm (April-September) and 9:30 am - 4:45 pm (October-March). Closed Mondays. There is a nice, outdoor café, open during spring and summer. Adults: €5 for museum and gardens or €1 for tour of only the gardens; Kids under 18: free. Free to all on the first Sunday of each month.*

This is really a gem of a museum. It is small and surrounded by a lovely garden filled with some of Rodin's most famous sculptures. The museum has collections of drawings and sculptures by Rodin, his pal Vincent Van Gogh, and his girlfriend and artistic partner Camille Claudel. It also features excellent temporary exhibits. It is located in the house where Rodin lived and worked.

If you are not up for a museum visit, it is well worth it to pay the small fee to visit the garden. Here, there is plenty of outdoor space for children to run around. There are many of Rodin's most famous works, and there's an excellent café. Just remind your kids not to touch the sculptures.

Some of the major sculptures you'll see in the garden include:

The Gate of Hell: This elaborate, bronze doorway is based on the *Inferno*, a long poem by the Italian writer, Dante. It depicts characters from the poem including *Ugolino* – a crawling man imprisoned for treason and forced to starve to death with his children and grandchildren; *Paolo and Francesca* – caught in the act of kissing and killed by Francesca's husband; *Adam and Eve* – banned from Paradise; and other tortured souls trying to climb their way out of the deepest depths of Hell. Rodin worked on this piece for 20 years. It was commissioned to decorate a Museum of Decorative Arts that was never built (on the site that now houses the Musée d'Orsay).

The Thinker: This large, seated man with his head on one hand is one of Rodin's most famous sculptures. He originally designed it as a small statue for his Gate of Hell, and later turned it into a large statue. It is a portrait of Dante.

The Kiss: Rodin's most popular sculpture was originally a small piece designed for the Gate of Hell. It depicts the two lovers, Paolo and Francesca, shortly before they are discovered and stabbed by her husband.

The Burghers of Calais: This group of six figures commemorates a real story from 1347. Calais, a town on the northern coast of France, had been under siege by the English for nearly a year. To save the town from starvation, the six leading men in the town offered their lives to the English king, Edward III, in exchange for the safety of their townsfolk. The English king accepted, but his wife, Queen Phillippa, was so moved by the burghers' sacrifice that she talked the king into sparing their lives.

Statue of Honoré de Balzac: Rodin's portrait of the famous French author/playwright was commissioned by the Society of Literary Men, led by author Emile Zola. In the end, however, the statue became tangled in larger artistic and political controversies, so the Literary Society refused to accept it.

Here's a tip if your kids think the sculptures are boring. Rodin used the same model (a poor, ragged man who hauled coal for a living) for several of his sculptures, including John the Baptist, one of the Burghers of Calais, one of the damned souls of the Gate of Hell, and the Man with a Broken Nose. Ask your kids if they can find him.

MUSÉE DU QUAI BRANLY (Ethnography Museum) *37, Quai Branly.(Metro: Iena, or Pont de l'Alma). Open 10am-6:30pm daily except Monday. Open until 9:30pm on Thursday. Adults: €8, for general museum entrance. Additional fees for special exhibits. Kids under 18: free. Free to everyone on the first Sunday of each month. Audioguide: €5 for the first person, €2 for any additional persons. There is a special audioguide tour for families in English.*

If you or your kids are fascinated by exotic objects from different cultures, this museum has wonderful ones, such as African drums, North American totem poles. masks from Pacific Islands, Asian costumes, and more (*see photo below*). They are beautifully presented in this new building. The best way to visit the museum as a family is with the family audio-guide tour that lasts less than 2 hours.

If your group is not up for the museum, they may still enjoy the outside of this building. It has jungle-like plants growing on the walls and gardens with ponds, plants, and walkways. There's a nice café in the garden offering breakfast, light lunch, snacks, and a children's menu. It's a great place to stop if you are walking from the Eiffel Tower to the Invalides.

9. LOUVRE

The **Louvre**
and **Tuileries gar-
dens** can be very
intimidating. The
sheer size of the
place (the Louvre
is the biggest mu-
seum in the world)
can be a real turn-
off for children.
The formal layout
of the buildings
and gardens can

feel cold and hostile. Yet, there is much here to delight even the most flat-
footed museum goers. All it takes is a little planning, and knowledge of a
few fun facts and good tips.

LOUVRE MUSEUM. *99, Rue de Rivoli and 34-36, Quai du Louvre.
Metro: Louvre or Palais Royal. Open daily (except Tue), 9am-6pm (until
9:45pm Wed). Closed Tues. Adults: €8.50. On Wed, Thurs entrance is €6 for
adults after 6pm. Kids under 18: free. Free to teachers with ID, to people with
disabilities and their companions. Reduced rates after 3 pm, and entrance is free
on the first Sunday of each month. Audioguide rental: €3. Excellent guidebooks
are available in English for kids and adults in the museum bookstore. Free
strollers and wheelchairs are available from the information desk under the
Pyramid. Note: Hang on to your entry tickets and you will be able to enter and
exit the museum all day.*

Parent Tip: Lines to enter the glass pyramid at the Louvre entrance can
be very long and hot in the summer. It's a little faster if you enter through
the shopping mall, from the steps leading underground by the Arc du
Carrousel or via the metro entrance. Even this method leads to long security
and ticket lines inside. The **quickest way to enter the Louvre** and avoid lines
is to use the little-known **Porte des Lions entrance**. This is in the Southwest
wing of the Louvre, along the Seine, nearly level with the Arch du Carrousel.
Look for the (female) lions on either side of the entrance. ✤

Louvre Area Highlights

- Go on a treasure hunt for your favorite Louvre masterpieces
- Visit the old moat and walls of the medieval Louvre
- Check out the underground shopping mall and US-style food court in the Grand Louvre
- Have lunch on the Louvre's open-air terrace or in an open-air café in the Tuileries
- Stand in the alignment of the Louvre pyramid and Concorde obelisk and check out the views
- Rent a toy sailboat at the central fountain in the Tuileries
- Try out the Ferris wheel in the Fête des Tuileries
- Admire elegant fashions through the ages at the Musée de la Mode
- Play in the Palais Royal gardens and look for its cannon
- See Monet's water lilies in the Orangerie Museum
- Visit the Samaritaine department store and have dinner in the top floor restaurant, Toupary.
- Look at the pet stores along Quai de la Mégisserie
- Draw a picture from the Pont des Arts

To avoid crowds inside, you may want to consider visiting the museum in the late afternoon between 4 and 6 pm or on Wednesday evenings when it's open until 9:45 pm.

The Louvre's history stretches back 800 years. It was first a fort, then a fortified castle, a luxurious palace, and finally a world-famous museum. The first Louvre was built in 1200 by King Philippe Auguste. It consisted of a large, fortified tower built along the city walls at their most vulnerable point: the city's western edge. The purpose of this fort was to protect Paris from the invading English Plantagenets, led by Richard the Lionheart. The early Louvre fortress also was used as a prison, an arsenal to store weapons, and place to safeguard royal treasures.

In 1360, King Charles V transformed the Louvre into a fortified castle with turrets and protective walls. It was occupied by the English for 16 years during the 100 years war with England. In the 1500s, King Francois I rebuilt the Louvre as a Renaissance Palace. His son, Henri II expanded it further, and Henri's wife, Catherine de Médicis added the Tuileries Palace (later destroyed). King Henri IV added the long galleries along the Seine.

In the 1670s, King Louis XIV moved his royal court to Versailles and abandoned the Louvre. In his absence, numerous artists, writers, philosophers, and men of science moved in. Part of the building was made into a museum to show off the royal art collections. Many of the artists living in at the Louvre also exhibited their works in the arcades along the ground level a Fair known as the Foire aux Croutes. (Croute means a crust of bread and is slang for crummy art).

In 1789, King Louis XVI was forced by the revolutionaries to leave the Palace of Versailles and move back to the Louvre. He tried to escape Paris in 1791 with his family, but they were caught and imprisoned. From 1792 to 1793, a guillotine was set up in the middle of the Place du Carrousel. The king was beheaded, and a new museum was officially inaugurated in the Louvre. When Napoleon I came to power, he moved into the Louvre and undertook further expansions and renovations. He also kicked out the last of the artists still living in the building, but added many works of art to the museum's collection from pieces collected during his many military campaigns. Napoleon III also expanded the Louvre with lavish rooms that you can still visit today in the northern wing of the building.

In 1980, President François Mitterand launched a huge project to renovate and expand the Louvre. Architect **I.M. Pei** designed the glass pyramid and underground shopping galleries. The exhibit halls were renovated, and excavations on the eastern side uncovered remnants of the early medieval fortress that was once the original Louvre building. They are now part of the medieval Louvre visit.

Here's a fun fact: To clean the 118 glass triangles and 675 diamond-shaped pieces that make up the Louvre's **Glass Pyramid**, window washers use mountain climbing gear, including ropes, harnesses, and pulleys.

Plan of Approach: The Louvre is a huge museum. A good place to start is with the museum map. It is available where you buy tickets or enter in multiple languages, including English. The map shows where to find some of the museum's most famous pieces. To help you further, here are some **highlights** from different sections of the museum:

Mesopotamia (Richelieu Wing, ground floor): There are two immense bulls with human heads that once guarded the Palace of Sargon, built in 720 BC. Notice that from the front they have two feet, from the side they have four, and if you look from an angle there are five!

Persia (Sully Wing, ground floor): Check out the magnificent tile friezes. One depicts archers and the other a griffin. They are from the palace of the great Persian King Darius, defeated by Alexander the Great in the 5th century BC. Darius' palace also had 72 columns, 21 meters (70 feet) high, topped with two bulls. Two are displayed. Imagine how a whole palace full would have looked.

Egypt (Sully Wing, ground and first floors): The Egyptian galleries take you through different aspects of ancient Egyptian life like food, music, and religion. There are lots of mummies and sarcophagi, even mummies of animals. There are also many small objects from daily life. You will see many statues of Egyptian gods and pharoahs.

Ancient Greece (Sully Wing, ground floor, lower level, and first floor): There are many wonderful Greek sculptures and vases. The most famous statues are the Venus de Milo, still beautiful even though she's missing her arms, and the dramatic Victory of Samothrace. This statue has lost her head, has wings for arms, and has folds in her clothing that seem to be moving in spite of being made of stone. It was built to celebrate a Greek victory on the island of Rhodes and originally stood on a great rock overlooking the sea.

Ancient Rome (Denon Wing, ground floor): You'll see beautiful Roman mosaics and remarkable paintings saved from the walls of villas around Pompeii. They were buried in the ash of the Mount Vesuvius volcano when it erupted suddenly in 79 AD. There are also lovely funeral sculptures.

Medieval period (Sully Wing, lower level): The most fascinating section is the underground exhibit of the medieval Louvre itself, discovered in the 1990s during the museum's renovation. It shows the foundations of the castle, moat, and protective walls built by King Philippe Auguste in 1200. You'll also see a collection of objects that were found during the archeological excavation of the fortress, including a gold helmet belonging to King Charles VI that was thrown into a well by robbers.

Renaissance (Denon Wing, first floor and Richelieu Wing, first floor): The most famous work in this section is Leonardo da Vinci's **Mona Lisa**. There are also many other famous paintings by da Vinci, Raphael, Michelangelo, Donatello, Boticelli, Bellini, and Titian. Don't miss the funny portraits of the four seasons by Giuseppe Archimbaldo (gallery 5). The faces are composed of seasonal fruits and vegetables.

19th century paintings (Denon Wing, first floor and Sully Wing 2nd floor): There are several huge paintings that often captivate children here. Look for the giant paintings of Napoleon I by Jacques Louis David, including the one in which he is crowning his wife, Josephine. Another classic favorite is the Raft of the Medusa by Gericault. This large painting is based on a true story of a shipwreck that left 150 men drifting on a raft for 13 days. Only 15 survived starvation, madness, and cannibalism. Notice, too, Eugene Delacroix's painting of Liberty Guiding the People. It has become a symbol of France. The painting does not actually depict the 1789 Revolution, but rather another popular rebellion in 1830.

Napoleon III's apartments (Richelieu Wing, first floor): These are preserved to reflect the rich gold and red velvet decor of this period. Here you really get a sense for what the Louvre was like as a palace.

TUILERIES GARDENS. *Between Rue de Rivoli and Seine River. Metro: Tuileries, Louvre, or Place de la Concorde. Open daily, sunrise to sunset. Entrance: Free.*

Stretched between the Louvre Museum and the Place de la Concorde is the lovely esplanade of the Tuileries Gardens. If you stroll along the middle lane of the gardens you can see the Glass Pyramid of the Louvre through the Arc du Carrousel in one direction. Then turn and look at the Obelisk in the Place de la Concorde. Notice how it is aligned with the Champs Elysées, Arch de Triomphe, and beyond that the Grande Arche de la Defense 10 kilometers (6 miles) away. The photo opportunities abound.

The name for this garden comes from the French word for roof tiles, tuiles. Before the area became part of the Louvre Palace domain, it housed a roof tile factory, a tuilerie. In the late 1500s, Queen Catherine de Medicis built herself a residence called Tuileries Palace. It was destroyed by fire in 1871, but used to stand in what is now the open section between the two longest wings of the Louvre.

The formal gardens were designed later by Louis XIV's favorite landscape architect, André Le Nôtre. He is also the one who designed the gardens at Versailles.

On the eastern edge of the Tuileries, standing like an entrance gate to the park, is the **Arc du Carrousel**. This triumphal arch was built in an imitation Roman style by Napoleon I to celebrate his military victories. You can see him on top, dressed as a Roman emperor. The golden horses pulling his chariot were stolen from Saint Mark's Cathedral in Venice, during one of Napoleon's Italian campaigns. It was an old tradition: the Venetians had stolen the horses centuries earlier from the city of Constantinople (Istanbul). The Tuileries Gardens are great place to relax after a walk through the Louvre or down the Champs Elysées. There are **playgrounds**, **pony rides**, and **miniature sailboats** for rent at the main fountain. There are also several good **cafés** in the park between the Louvre and the Place de la Concorde, where you can grab a meal or a snack on a nice day. If you are in Paris during the summer or winter holidays, check out the **Fête des Tuileries**. It includes fair rides and games for all ages. A ride up the central Ferris wheel offers one of the best views of Paris.

ORANGERIE DES TUILERIES. *Place de la Concorde, Jardin des Tuileries. Metro: Concorde. Open daily except Tues, 9am-6pm. Closed Tues. Adults €7.50. Kids are free.*

If you are not up to facing the crowds in the more popular Musée d'Orsay across the river, the Orangerie is an excellent alternative. Housed in a former greenhouse, it has had a recent face lift. The museum is rarely crowded, not too big, and features beautiful Impressionist and modern paintings by artists such as Renoir, Cezanne, and Picasso. The most spectacular exhibit includes eight enormous water lily paintings by Claude Monet. They fill two rooms. You may recognize them from the book, *Linnea in Monet's Garden.*

JEU DE PAUME MUSEUM, *1, Place de la Concorde. Metro: Concorde. Open Tues, 12pm-9:30pm; Wed-Fri, 12pm-7pm; Sat-Sun, 10am-7pm. Closed Mon. Entrance fees vary according to the exhibits but generally run around €7 for adults. Kids are free.*

This museum features temporary exhibits of modern and contemporary art. It is housed in a former Jeu de Paume court of the Tuileries Palace. Jeu de Paume was an early form of tennis popular during the Renaissance.

MUSÉE DE LA MODE, MUSÉE DE LA PUBLICITÉ, MUSÉE DES ARTS DÉCORATIFS. *105-111, Rue de Rivoli. Metro: Palais Royal or Louvre. Open Tues-Fri, 11am-6pm (Wed until 9pm); Sat-Sun, 10am-6pm. Closed Mon. One combined ticket allows access to all three of these museums. There are children's programs in French every day during the summer at 10am and 2pm. Adult: €7. Children under 18: Free.*

These museums are lodged in the northern wing of the Louvre. They are small and treat topics that appeal easily to children.

The Musée de la Mode features clothes fashions through the ages, from the Renaissance to Sci-Fi-looking futuristic styles.

The Musée de la Publicité has some wonderful old advertisement posters and TV ads.

The Musée des Arts Décoratifs features every day objects, such as toys, dishes, and furniture from the 13th century to today.

PLACE DE LA MADELEINE. *Metro: Madeleine*

This square is famous for its flower market and fancy food stores, such as Fauchon, Héliard, and our favorite, the Grey Poupon mustard shop. It is also the sight of Paris' most attractive public rest rooms and shoeshine shop. They are underground by the flower market. They were built in the early 1900s in the Art Nouveau style, reflected in the tiles, floors, and restroom doors. Check them out.

AU NAIN BLEU. *5, Boulevard Malesherbes. Metro: Madeleine. Open daily except Sun, 10am-6:30pm.*

Paris' fanciest toy store! Family run for generations, it prides itself on the fact that most of its products are made in Europe.

PALAIS ROYAL GARDENS. *Entrances to the gardens from the Place du Palais Royal, Place de Valois, Rue de Montpensier, and Rue de Beaujolais. Metro: Palais Royal. Open sunrise to sunset. Entrance is free.*

This former royal palace offers gardens where you can relax after a visit to the Louvre. There is plenty of room to run and play. You can also use the gardens as a starting point for a visit through some of Paris' shopping galeries and passages, starting with the **Galerie Colbert** and **Galerie Vivienne**, on the northern side. The courtyard is decorated with modern, black and white columns of different sizes. These were designed in 1986 by artist Daniel Buren and were widely despised when they were first installed. Since then, they have become part of the landscape, and children are allowed to run among them or jump off of them. The arcades of the gardens are lined with cafés, restaurants, and fancy shops, including a lovely toy store and music box shop along the northern edge of the garden. The garden features fountains and tree-lined avenues. In the summer there are temporary sculpture exhibits, outdoor concerts, and plays.

Nestled in a flowerbed on the south side of the Palais Royal gardens is a **small cannon**. It was never used for defense purposes, but had another important role as a timepiece. From 1786 to 1914, it would go off every day at noon, provided the weather was sunny. The canon sits on the line of the Paris Meridian. It was set up so that at midday the sun would pass through an eyepiece and warm up the fuse that shot off the canon. It was restored in 1990. Today this little cannon is set off each Saturday at noon by one of the park's guards.

On the western edge you will see one of Paris' most illustrious theaters, the Comédie Francaise. The famous French playwright, Molière, performed here with his theater company. He even died in the theater after playing the leading role in his play, the Imaginary Invalid.

SAMARITAINE DEPARTMENT STORE. *19, Rue de la Monnaie. Metro: Pont Neuf. Open Mon-Sat, 9:30 am-7 pm (Thurs until 10 pm). Closed Sun.*

This department store is named for a statue of *Jesus and the Good Samaritan Woman* that once decorated a fountain on the nearby **Pont Neuf**. The original building (Shop 2) dates from 1910 and is a beautiful example of the Art Nouveau style of that period. Note the staircase, skylight, and peacock frescoes. You'll find the usual Paris department store array of great stuff, including kids' toys. However, what really makes this store unique is the wonderful view from the top floor restaurant Toupary. In warm weather, you can also enjoy lunch and dinner on the rooftop terrace.

QUAI DE LA MEGISSERIE. *Along the Seine. Metro: Pont Neuf.*

The stretch of this road along the Seine River between the Samaritaine Department Store and Place du Châtelet is filled with pet stores. Along with the usual array of puppies, kittens, birds, and reptiles are more surprising pets, such as roosters, various types of pigeons, and enormous rabbits.

RUE SAINT HONORE. Running parallel to the Rue de Rivoli, this road features an endless array of shops and boutiques. There is something for everyone, ranging from high fashion to Asian noodle restaurants, excellent pastry shops, and goofy souvenirs.

ÉGLISE SAINT ROCH. *296, Rue Saint Honoré. Metro: Tuileries or Pyramides.*
This church offers classical concerts every Tuesday at 12:30pm, often featuring young musicians from Paris' National Conservatory of Music.
PONT DES ARTS. *By the Louvre. Metro: Pont Neuf or Louvre.*
The Pont des Arts was the city's first pedestrian bridge and was also the first to be made of iron. However, it suffered repeated damage from boats and barges during some major floods. Finally, half of the bridge collapsed in 1979. It was rebuilt and reopened in 1984.
The bridge offers lovely views and great photo opportunities. The Pont des Arts is also a favorite spot for painters to set up their easels. Maybe your budding artist will want to give it a try, too.

10. LES HALLES

Author Emile Zola called Les Halles the "Belly of Paris". If other neighborhoods were the spiritual, intellectual, or fashion centers of the city, this was where the serious work of feeding the city took place. Les Halles was for centuries Paris' central marketplace – the realm of butchers and fishmongers.

Today the area has been transformed by modern art and architecture. Urban renewal efforts in the 1970s-80s replaced empty lots and ramshackle buildings with shiny glass and metal constructions. Entire areas have been turned into pedestrian zones, filled with shops, cafés, and art galleries. While you may argue about the architectural merits of these new constructions, your children will enjoy the car-free environment and numerous treats that await them in the belly of the beast that is Paris.

LES HALLES. *Metro: Les Halles.*

From the year 50 AD until 1969, Les Halles was Paris' central marketplace, and the neighborhood was filled with restaurants that offered hearty fare to the neighborhood's workers. In 1969, the wholesale food market, having outgrown this space, was moved to a suburb near Orly Airport. The market buildings were torn down and for a dozen or so years, the place was just a big, empty pit. In the 1980s, the hole was redeveloped as the **Forum des Halles**, featuring a large shopping center, movie theaters, and a metro station complex in three underground levels. There is also an indoor pool called the **Piscine des Halles -Suzanne Berlioux** on the lowest

level. It features palm trees and cacti, bringing a touch of the exotic to the center of Paris. (Porte Sainte Eustache, 10, Place de la Rotonde, Level-3; Metro: Les Halles).

Above ground, there is a big **merry-**

go-round overlooking the Forum. It is the oldest one in Paris and has been in operation since 1872. It is open daily from 11am to 8pm.

The area west of the Forum has been made into a big park. There are walkways, fountains, playgrounds, lawns, and big wide areas well suited for roller blading or tossing a Frisbee. This is also where you will find a large **sculpture of a tilted head and hand** (*see photo on previous page*) by artist Henri de Miller that often fascinates small children. The contrast between its modern style and the Gothic Church of Saint Eustache behind it makes for interesting photo opportunities. To

Les Halles Highlights

• Play in the Jardin des Enfants des Halles, reserved just for kids
• Find the giant sculpture of a head tilted on its side
• Pick out your lunch in the Montorgeuil market street
• Watch the jugglers and other street performers in front of the Pompidou Center
• Check out the fun Stravinsky Fountain
• Look for gargoyles on the Eglise Saint Mérri
• Ride up the glass escalators in the Pompidou Center and check out its Modern Art Museum

the left is a giant sundial. It's curved edges make it popular with roller bladers and skate boarders.

JARDIN DES ENFANTS AUX HALLES. *105, Rue Rambuteau, on the northern side of Les Halles. Hours vary but generally run from 10am-5pm. Cost: €0.5 per child for a 1-hour session.*

This wonderful Children's Garden is reserved for kids ages 7 to 11. Adults are not allowed inside. Instead they drop off their children for a one-hour session. (We recommend sitting in a café in the nearby Rue Montorgeuil and watching the people go by, if you don't know what to do with yourself.) There are gardens, tunnels, mazes, play spaces, and other fun activities. The park is staffed by friendly counselors who supervise group games and individual play. Even if your children do not understand French, they will figure out how to have fun.

MAISON ROUE LIBRE – BICYCLE RENTALS. *1 Passage Mondetour, near angle with Rue Rambuteau. Open daily 9am-7pm. Closed December-January. Cost: €4 for 1 hour, €10 for 4 hours or one full weekday, €15 for one full weekend day.*

Bicycling is very popular in Paris (and all over France) and the city has become very bike friendly. Here, you can rent solid, 3-5-speed bikes to discover the city. You can ask for kids' bikes, kid seats, helmets, and baskets.

You can reserve on line in advance at www.rouelibre.fr/location-velo.php or by calling 08 10 44 15 34.

RUE MONTORGUEIL MARKET DISTRICT. *North of Les Halles. Metro: Les Halles or Etienne Marcel.*

This pedestrian shopping street features an open-air market every day but Monday. There are also excellent food shops, restaurants, and cafés. It's an excellent place to take a break or pick up a snack. Children enjoy checking out the old shop signs that line the streets. Don't miss the giant golden snail above the Escargot Restaurant. There's also a famous pastry shop, called Patisserie Stohrer at #51, that has been around since the days of Marie Antoinette.

FASHION DISTRICT. *Between the Forum des Halles and the Place des Victoires, mainly along the Rue du Jour and Rue Etienne Marcel. Metro: Les Halles or Etienne Marcel.*

If your group includes a fashion slave, you may want to walk up to the Rue du Jour and along the Rue Etienne Marcel to the Place des Victoires, where many big designers have their shops.

POMPIDOU CENTER (ALSO KNOWN AS BEAUBOURG). *Rue Saint Martin and Place Georges Pompidou. Open daily except Tues, 11am-10pm. Metro: Rambuteau or Châtelet/Les Halles. Entrance fees vary for exhibits.*

In the 1960s, the **Beaubourg** neighborhood of Paris was dirty and dilapidated. President Georges Pompidou, a great fan of modern art, launched a program to build a contemporary center for the arts and culture and revitalize the neighborhood. A team of Italian and British architects, Renzo Piano and Richard Rogers, scandalized many people by putting together a multicolored, modern, monstrosity of a building, right in the heart of historical Paris. Their idea was to turn the building inside-out. All the parts that are usually hidden, such as water pipes and electrical supply systems, were not only exposed on the outside but also painted bright colors. Each color has a role: red is for transportation, yellow is for electricity, blue is for air conditioning, and green is for water.

Much of the Pompidou Center's charm is outside (*see photo on next page*). The wide plateau in front of the building features plenty of street performers of various types. Don't miss the wonderful **Stravinsky Fountain** on the south side of the Pompidou Center. It depicts scenes from this modern composer's works, such as the *Sacre du Printemps* (Rights of Spring), *Oiseau de Feu* (Firebird), and *Ragtime*. The brightly colored pieces are by an artist named Niki de Saint-Phalle, and the black ones are by sculptor Jean Tinguely. They spin and spit water to the delight of children and adults alike.

MUSÉE NATIONAL D'ART MODERNE. *Entrance on level 4 of the Pompidou Center. Open daily except Tues, 11am-9pm. Purchase tickets on the ground level. Adults: 10-12 € depending on dates; Kids under 18: free. Free to all on the first Sunday of each month.*

This museum has an important collection of modern and contemporary art. The contemporary section (level 4) is filled with things to interest young children. Here they will find all sorts of wild and wacky paintings and sculptures. There is a reconstructed shop covered with recycled bits turned into art. There are wonderful models of futuristic buildings designed in the mid-20th century. There are examples of Op-Art. It's a good reminder for children that art can be fun and does not need to be intimidating. The modern art collection (on level 5) has works by the greats, such as Matisse, Leger, Picasso, Rouault, Delaunay, Kandinsky, and Calder. There is a whole section dedicated to Dada and Surrealism, including a reproduction of Andre Bretons' studio.

ÉGLISE SAINT MÉRRI. *76, Rue de la Verrerie. Metro: Châtelet.*

This large, flamboyant Gothic-style church is especially notable for its wonderful gargoyles. You can get a good view of them outside from the square by the Pompidou Center that has the wacky Stravinsky Fountain. The church also has impressive 16th century stained glass windows and a 13th century bell (thought to be the oldest in Paris). The composer Saint-Saëns (who wrote the Carnival of the Animals) played the organ here. There are free concerts on weekends.

11. MARAIS

This section of town was once covered with nothing but marshy fields (marais means marsh in French) running along the northern edge of the Seine River. Today, the Marais is a lively area, and a favorite among Parisians and tourists alike. The small, cobbled streets are full of colorful shops, young designer stores, and interesting eateries (including excellent Jewish delis and bakeries). There are numerous museums that appeal to kids' interests: toys (**Musée de la Poupée**); inventions (**Musée des Arts et Métiers**); history and gore (**Musée Carnavalet** and **Musée d'Art et d'Histoire Juive**); wackiness (**Musée Picasso**); and Magic (**Musée de la Magie et de la Curiosité**).

PLACE DES VOSGES.

This square originally housed a royal palace and gardens. In the late 1500s it was redone to include fancy apartment buildings. Author Victor Hugo, who wrote *Les Miserables* and the *Hunchback of Nôtre Dame* lived in one, which has been turned into a small museum. Notice the buildings

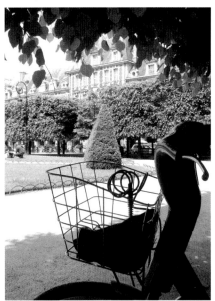

around the square. They seem to be made of red bricks, but if you look closely you'll see that they are actually made of stone that is covered with a thin layer of false bricks. The square has playground areas and is a nice place to sit and relax (*see also photo on page 85*).

VILLAGE SAINT PAUL–THE SOUTHERN MARAIS (Situated between Metro: Saint Paul and Metro: Pont Marie)

This "village" used to contain a royal palace, gardens, and even a collection of wild animals. Today, it has a little park, called the **Jardins**

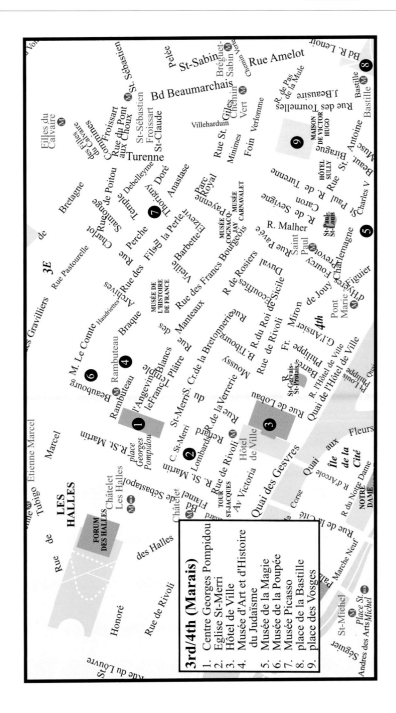

3rd/4th (Marais)

1. Centre Georges Pompidou
2. Eglise St-Merri
3. Hôtel de Ville
4. Musée d'Art et d'Histoire du Judaïsme
5. Musée de la Magie
6. Musée de la Poupée
7. Musée Picasso
8. place de la Bastille
9. place des Vosges

de Saint Paul (through some archways off of the Rue Saint Paul, near the Seine) where you can see a fairly large section of the old fortress wall that used to protect the City of Paris in the late 1100s and earl 1200s. There are even guard towers and plenty of open space to let children run free or enjoy a snack while parents look in on the windows of the antique boutiques that line the archways.

MUSÉE DE LA CURIOSITÉ ET DE LA MAGIE (MUSEUM OF MAGIC). *11, Rue Saint Paul (Metro: Pont Marie or Saint Paul). Open Wed, Sat, Sun, 2pm - 7pm. Adults: €9; Kids: €7.*

Note: Kids love this little museum. Beware, however, that its hours are quite limited. Without careful planning, you may end up facing a locked door and disappointed travel companions.

This is great fun for anyone who enjoys a good magic show. The museum features optical illusion tricks, automates, and old-fashioned carnival games dating from 1800 to 1950. There are also live magic demonstrations, much of which you can understand even if you don't know a word of French. To round out the visit there is a shop full of magic tricks and paraphernalia.

THE JEWISH QUARTER.

Walk along the **Rue des Rosiers** and surrounding streets and you are in the heart of Paris' Jewish Quarter. This is a great place to stop for a meal, pick up a picnic to eat in the Place des Vôsges, or grab a snack. At **Jo Goldenberg's** (corner Rue des Rosiers and Rue des Ecouffes) you can stop for a sit-down meal or go to the deli counter for a familiar array of kosher meats, chopped liver, bagels and lox, potato salad, and so forth. You'll also find Middle-Eastern eateries along the Rue des Rosiers run by North African Jews, and some excellent Jewish pastry shops. In the narrow **Rue Pavée** – said to be the first paved road in Paris – check out the remarkable

Marais Highlights

- Search for optical illusions and see fun tricks at the Museum of Magic
- Pick out a Jewish pastry in the Rue des Rosiers
- Tour the Doll Museum
- Look for wacky animals at the Picasso Museum
- See models of Paris, the guillotine, and a ballroom fit for a queen at the Musée Carnavalet
- Follow the footsteps of Nicholas Flamel and search for the secrets of the Sorcerer's Stone
- Admire the inventions at the Musée des Arts et Métiers
- Go ice skating (in winter) in front of the Hôtel de Ville.

facade of the Synagogue at #10. It is the work of the Art Nouveau architect Hector Guimard, famous for having designed Paris' metro entrances.

MUSÉE D'ART ET D'HISTOIRE DU JUDAISME (**MUSEUM OF JEWISH ART AND HISTORY**). *71, Rue du Temple. Metro: Rambuteau or Hôtel de Ville. Open Mon-Fri, 11am to 6 pm and Sun 10 am to 6 pm. Adults: €6.10; Kids under 18: free.*

This museum celebrates not only Jewish history and religion, but also the cultural and artistic contributions of Jews in Paris. The museum features exhibits describing everyday life, religious festivals, and the coming together of two traditions: Sephardim and Ashkenazi. There are paintings by Marc Chagall and Amadeo Modigliani. There is also a pretty café and nice boutique. The gardens were originally designed by Louis XVI's favorite landscaper, André LeNôtre.

HÔTEL DE VILLE (**PARIS CITY HALL**). *Place de l'Hôtel de Ville. Metro: Hôtel de Ville.*

This is Paris' City Hall. The building is very ornate and decorated with statues representing different French cities. The square in front of the Hôtel de Ville used to be the sight of public executions, lively markets, workers' strikes, and other festivities. Now it features exhibits, activities, and during winter months, an **ice-skating rink**. In late June, it is the starting and end point of the city's 5-mile **café servers' race**. Waiters and waitresses run through the streets of Paris in their work clothes (no running shoes) carrying a full tray of drinks. It's quite impressive!

CENTRAL MARAIS. *Metro: Saint Paul or Chemin Vert.*

A walk up the Rue Vieille du Temple, Rue Pavée, and along the Rue des Francs Bourgeois takes you past shops filled with funky gadgets, cartoon characters, or clothing by hip designers.

When you are ready for more sight-seeing, you face the choice of three terrific museums:

MUSÉE CARNAVALET. *29, Rue de Sévigné. Métro: Saint-Paul or Chemin-Vert. Open Tues-Sun, 10am to 3:40 pm. Closed Mon. Entrance to the permanent collections is free, but there is a fee for special exhibits.*

The Musée Carnavalet is devoted to the history of Paris, from prehistory through the early 20th century. Although this may sound stuffy, you might be surprised at how many of the objects can arouse your child's curiosity and imagination. There are wooden canoes made by prehistoric fishermen and discovered along the Seine when construction was underway for the new Parc de Bercy. There is a room filled with old shopkeepers' signs. Have fun guessing what kind of trade they represented. There are models and maps of Paris through the ages. There's a set of locks from the

Bastille prison (ask the guard to give you a demonstration), a portrait of Dr. Guillotin who designed the guillotine, and a chess set that King Louis XVI played in prison before his execution. There's the cradle in which Napoleon Bonaparte slept as a baby. There are replicas of a 16th century room, a room during the Revolution, and Marcel Proust's bedroom. There is a jewelry store and a ballroom from the Hotel Wendell guaranteed to delight any fan of Cinderella. To finish the visit, the gift shop offers nice games, books, and souvenirs.

MUSÉE PICASSO. *Hôtel de Salé, 5, Rue de Thorigny. Metro: Saint Paul. Open Wed-Mon, 9:30am-5:30pm. Closed Tues. Adults €8.50. Kids under 18: free. Free to all on the first Sun of each month.*

This museum contains a huge collection of works by Pablo Picasso, whose long career lasted from 1894 to his death in 1973. Born in Malaga, Spain, Picasso spent much of his younger artistic life in Paris and later life in Provence. The pieces are organized chronologically, taking you through different periods of the artist's style: blue, rose, cubism, surrealism.

Young children may not get excited about the influence of African art on Picasso, his experiments with planes, or the fundamentals of cubism. But they do respond well to the humor and wackiness of many of the pieces – sometimes more than adults. Kids also enjoy hunting for depictions of children (e.g. Harlequin Boy, Girl Jumping Rope) and animals (e.g. crouching cat, bicycle goat). Don't be afraid to move at the pace of a short attention span. There's a lot here and some of the best is saved for the last galleries. The reward at the end of the journey is a lovely café and interesting gift shop.

The building that houses the Picasso Museum was once a private mansion known as the **Hotel de Salé** (Hotel of Salt). In spite of this name it was neither a hotel nor filled with salt. Instead it was a fancy residence. The salty part comes from the fact that this building's first owner was in charge of collecting the royal tax on salt.

MUSÉE DE LA POUPÉE. *located in the Impasse Berthaud, just off the Rue Beaubourg (Metro: Rambuteau). Open Tues-Sun, 10am-6pm. Closed Mon. Adults: €7; Kids and Youth age 12-25: €5; Kids 3-11: €3. Kids under 3: free.*

This charming little museum is nestled in a lane, just half a block from the back of the Pompidou Center. It has a collection of dolls dating back to the mid-1800s and up through the 1960s. They are arranged with accessories and furniture to reflect the time period in which they were made. There are also two rooms devoted to temporary exhibits, often set up around fun themes like the history of the Barbie doll or plastic squeeze toys. The museum has a gift shop with doll accessories and dollhouse furniture. There is also a repair shop that can offer estimates of the age and value of collectors' dolls.

Many of the dolls in the Musée de la Poupée have faces of a type of porcelain called **biscuit**. Do they look like they are made of dough? Actually, the name comes from the fact that the porcelain is cooked twice: *bis* = twice, *cuit* = cooked.

THE NORTHERN MARAIS – FOLLOWING THE FOOT-STEPS OF NICOLAS FLAMEL.

Do you have any Harry Potter fans in your midst? Do they remember how Harry, Hermione, and Ron searched the school library for clues about Nicolas Flamel during their first year at Hogwarts? Here's your chance to hunt him down yourself, and maybe discover the secrets of the Sorcerer's Stone.

Nicolas Flamel was a real person, born in Pontoise (town west of Paris) in 1330. He was a bookseller who set up shop in Paris near the Place des Innocents. It is said that one night, Flamel dreamt that an angel appeared to him with a mysterious book, saying that some day he would discover its secrets. A few days later, a stranger walked into Flamel's shop with the exact book from his dream. It was about alchemy and supposedly held the secret of creating the sorcerer's stone which could change ordinary metal into gold and guarantee eternal life. Flamel studied the book for years. Then in 1382, he claimed to have successfully turned mercury into gold. He did it again in 1386. Was it true? Who knows? What is certain is that Flamel did become a wealthy man. Though he and his wife continued to live modestly, they became generous benefactors, financing the building of 14 hospitals, 3 chapels, 7 churches, and several houses. Legend has it that Flamel also discovered the secret to eternal life. Records suggest that he died in 1417 though some will argue that he and his wife, Pernelle, are still alive today. His tombstone is on exhibit in the Cluny Museum.

For your Flamel tour, start at the **Tour Saint Jacques**, located just off the Place du Châtelet. This Gothic-style bell tower is all that remains of a church called Saint Jacques de la Boucherie. The church was built in 1523 for the butchers and tanners who worked in the nearby Les Halles (Paris' former central market). One of its most regular and generous patrons was Nicolas Flamel, who lived nearby. Most of the church was destroyed during the French Revolution, but the bell tower was saved.

The Tour St. Jacques was also the starting point in Flamel's day for the religious pilgrimage to St. Jacques de Compostelle (Saint James the Apostle of Compostella) in Spain.

Since 1891, the Tour Saint Jacques has served as a weather station for Paris. The tower holds meteorological instruments to measure the air quality, pollution levels, and other readings.

From the Tour Saint Jacques, if you head due north you will find a little pedestrian street (one block west of the larger pedestrian street, Rue Saint Martin). Look up at the street sign. This is the **Rue Nicolas Flamel**. Notice that the first cross street you meet is called the **Rue Pernelle**, named for Flamel's wife. They had an apartment near here, and their bookshop was only a few blocks away.

Here you may want to stray a bit from Nicolas Flamel to admire the Eglise Saint Mérri, visit the Stravinsky Fountain, check out the Pompidou Center, or visit the Doll Museum.

The trail of Nicolas Flamel resumes up the Rue Beaubourg (heading north). Take a right when you reach the old, narrow **Rue de Montmorency**. You have just stepped back into medieval times. Notice the house at #51. It was built in 1407 by Nicolas Flamel and is said to be the

oldest house in Paris. He built it as one of his many charitable acts and as a place to house the poor. Tenants were given free room and board. In exchange they were asked to live an honest life and offer a prayer each day for Flamel and his wife. The ground floor of the building had shops that were rented out to help cover the costs of feeding and housing the tenants. Today, the ground floor features a restaurant called the **Auberge Nicolas Flamel**. It offers a friendly lunch menu that includes kids' meals.

MUSÉE DES ARTS ET MÉTIERS. *60, Rue Réaumur (Metro: Arts et Métiers). Open Tues-Sun, 10am-6pm (Thurs. until 9:30 pm). Closed Mon. Adults: €6.50; Kids are free. Free to all on Thursday evenings and on the first Sunday of each month. Audioguides: €5. The museum is handicap accessible and free to individuals accompanying persons with disabilities.*

This museum is just four blocks up the Rue Beaubourg from Flamel's house in the Rue Montmorency. The museum is chock full of scientific and artistic inventions, like the first calculator (1642), telegraph (1794), and automobile (1770). The exhibit rooms are airy and well done. There are numerous interactive computer stations to explore different sections. Much of the fun, however, comes from seeing models of early airplanes, drawbridges, and skyscrapers. There are early measuring tools, cameras, and bicycles. You'll see Volta's battery and Watt's steam engine. There's Edison's phonograph and Foucault's pendulum.

In the final room of the museum, a converted chapel, you'll see large-scale models of the Statue of Liberty (including a full-size replica of her thumb), the first autobus, early airplanes, and the Vulcain motor used in the French space shuttle, Ariane.

QUARTIER DU TEMPLE. *(Around the Square du Temple. Metro: Arts et Métiers or Temple).*

This neighborhood is named for the Templar Knights, an order founded in 1169, whose headquarters were located in this neighborhood. The Templars were both monks and knights, and they were famous for being highly skilled and disciplined fighters. They participated in the Crusades and guarded the king's troops. Aas their fame and fortune grew they became seen as a threat to both the king and the church. In 1307, they were declared to be heretics, and members were hunted down.

Today, the Temple neighborhood is the city's garment district. The **Carreau du Temple**, near the Square du Temple, is a covered market hall full of new and used clothing. It is a favorite spot among teens to look for clothing, especially bargain-priced leather jackets.

12. BASTILLE

On July 14, 1789 the storming of the **Bastille Prison** marked the launch of the French Revolution. Ever since, the neighborhood has maintained a reputation for feistiness. For many years, the Saint Antoine neighborhood east of the Bastille was home to woodworkers and craftsmen. Many of them made up the core of those ready to revolt against repressive governments, both in 1789 and during later rebellions.

In the 1980s, this area became home to artists, young designers, and cybercafés seeking less expensive living and retail space. Today, the old mingles with the new around the Bastille. Small woodworking shops sit next door to new internet cafés. An old train route has been converted into suspended gardens. Houseboats still pass slowly through the locks of the city's canals, and a new park welcomes strollers to their banks.

PLACE DE LA BASTILLE. *Metro: Bastille.*

The Bastille was originally a military fort. It was built in the 1370s to protect the eastern edge of the city from invaders. The fort's walls were 5 feet thick, and built to resist attack. Over time, they proved to be more useful at keeping people in than out, and the Bastille was transformed into a prison.

By the 1700s, most of the people shut inside the Bastille had been sent there by royal decree. Some were political prisoners. Others were there by request of their family members, who appealed to the king to lock away troublesome relatives; for example, someone who was spending too much money, causing embarrassment, or otherwise in the way. By 1789, the Bastille was seen as a symbol of royal tyranny to many Parisians. So it was here that they launched an attack on the prison on July 14, which started the French Revolution. The prisoners were freed and the building was set on fire. Eventually, some of the stones were recovered and used to build the Pont de la Concorde. One enterprising businessman gathered up stones and other remnants of the building to sell as souvenirs. He even carved some into miniature copies of the Bastille Prison. You can see examples of these at the Musée Carnavalet.

Bastille Highlights

- Hunt for traces of the old Bastille prison
- Walk, bike, or rollerblade above the crowds along the Promenade Plantée
- Take a ride on a canal boat
- Check out the exotic foods and spices at the Place d'Aligre Street Market

If you visit the Place de la Bastille today, you'll see an outline of the old prison on the pavement in the middle of the Place. A plaque at #4, Rue St. Antoine marks where the entrance was. The Bastille metro station (line 5) has an exposed fragment of the prison's foundation.

The tall column you can see today in the middle of the Place de la Bastille is called the **Colonne de Juillet** (July Column – *see photo on previous page*). The statue on top represents Liberty.

PROMENADE PLANTÉE. *Access from numerous stairs and elevators along the Avenue Daumesnil and Rue du Sahel. Metro: Bastille, Gare de Lyon, Daumesnil, Bel-Air, or Porte Dorée. Entrance is free.*

The Promenade Plantée is a lovely park planted along a 4 kilometer stretch of an old railroad line. It offers nice views with flower-lined paths and gardens. It is a great place for families, since there are no cars or streets to cross. In some sections of the park the paths split into two: one is reserved for walkers and people pushing strollers, and the other reserved for bikes and rollerbladers.

About midway along, the Promenade Plantée passes through a large park called the **Jardin de Reuilly**. It features wide green lawns, playgrounds, and a giant sundial. This park also has a public swimming pool, called the **Piscine de Reuilly** (13, Rue Hénard, Metro: Montgallet).

VIADUCT DES ARTS. *Under the Promenade Plantée, Along Boulevard Daumesnil. Metro: Bastille or Gare de Lyon.*

The Viaduct des Arts is located under the Promenade Plantée is . It is made up of graceful, brick archways that have been converted into art studios, designer stores, craftsmen's workshops, computer stores, and restaurants.

CANAUXRAMA (CANAL TOUR BOAT RIDES). *Near #50, Boulevard de la Bastille. Metro: Bastille. (Tel. 01.42.39.15.00). Daily departures at 9:45 am and 2:30 pm. Weekend and Holiday rates €13 for everyone, regardless of age. During the week, Adults: €14; Kids 6-12: €8; Under 6: free.*

Canal tour boats leave from the Port de l'Arsenal for a 2 hour 40 minute tour up the Canal Saint Martin to the Parc de la Villette, where you can go visit that park's spectacular playgrounds and Science Museum. There is a special sound and lights show as you go through the tunnel under the Place de la Bastille.

ROLLERS ET COQUILLAGES. *Nomades Store. 37, Boulevard Bourdon. Metro: Bastille. Free kid-friendly group outings meet in front of the store every Sunday, 2:30-5:30 pm.*

The Nomades store will outfit your whole family (ages 7 and up) with rental roller blades, helmets, and pads. Then you can join the group Rollers et Coquillages Sunday afternoons for a 3-hour ride along Paris sidewalks and parks. If you prefer to go on your own, take your skates and head for the Promenade Plantée. There you will find smooth, flat paths. Some of them are specially reserved for rollerblading.

PARIS À VELO C'EST SYMPA. *37, Boulevard Bourdon, Metro: Arsenal, Tel. 01 48 87 60 01. Be sure to call ahead to make sure that the kids' equipment you may need will be available.*

This is just one of many shops where you can rent bicycles, helmets, and other equipment for a nice cycling tour in Paris. The Bastille neighborhood offers several excellent routes that keep you well away from traffic. The **Promenade Plantée** has special paths reserved for bikes and roller blades. There are also bike paths north of the Place de la Bastille along the **Saint Martin Canal**. On Sundays during the year, and every day from July 15-August 15, the parkways along the Seine River are closed to motorized traffic. Here you can enjoy some of Paris' best sights at a leisurely bicycling pace.

PLACE D'ALIGRE MARKET. *Place d'Aligre. Between Rue de Charenton and Rue du Faubourg Saint Antoine. Metro: Ledru Rollin. Open 9am-1pm Tues-Sun. Closed Mon.*

This square contains both a covered market, originally constructed in 1777, and street vendors that spill onto the side streets. It features very interesting and exotic types of foods, including plenty of Caribbean and North African specialties. You also can find used clothes and flea market items, here. It is a colorful and exotic experience (*see photo on next page*).

GARE DE LYON. *Cour L. Armand. Metro: Gare de Lyon*

This train station services routes going to the south of France, the Alps, and Italy. It was built in 1895, as part of the massive construction projects for the Paris Exhibition of 1900. The large clock tower is decorated with statues representing Paris and Marseilles. There are 40 murals inside the station representing many of the cities and towns along the routes served by the station.

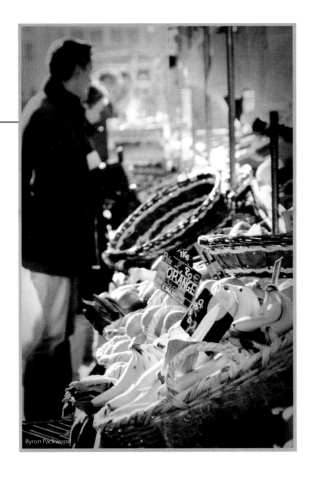

13. BERCY

In the 1990s, Bercy was transformed from an area filled with empty wine warehouses to a lovely new park and shopping district. During the construction, workers stumbled across several 7,000-year old dugout canoes. These once belonged to the people who fished and hunted along the marshy banks of the Seine during prehistoric times.

Modern Bercy has much to offer children. There is a great park filled with gardens, bridges, a maze, and play areas. Family-friendly stores and restaurants round out the visit in a pedestrian section that makes you feel as though you have left the bustle of the city for a quieter village.

PARC DE BERCY. *Along the Seine in Eastern Paris, between Boulevard de Bercy and BercyExpo. Metro: Bercy or Cour Saint Emilion. Entrance is free.*

The Bercy Park is filled with wide expanses where children can run, explore, and discover. It features a variety of small gardens. One is a vegetable patch tended by children. Others include a vineyard, a botanical garden, a garden of scents, and a wonderful maze that kids love to run through. There are ponds, large grassy areas, some very old trees, and small bridges. There are little buildings that house temporary exhibits or gardening workshops. The alleyways are named for famous wine regions.

On the northern side of the Bercy Park, at 51, Rue de Bercy, is a remarkable building designed by architect Frank Gehry. It was originally built to house the American Center, which had moved from its old space in Montparnasse. For decades it had featured art exhibits, dance, and theater productions to promote Franco-American cultural exchanges. Unfortunately, the

Bercy Highlights

- Try to figure out how they mow the grass growing up the sides of the Bercy Sports Arena
- Go through the maze, see what's growing in the childrens' garden, and throw crumbs to the ducks in the Bercy Park
- Have a snack and enjoy the shops along the pedestrian zone of Bercy Village

American Center went bankrupt shortly after moving to its new building. Now the building houses a **Museum of Cinema**, open Saturdays and Sundays, 10am-8pm.

On the eastern edge of the Bercy park is a new development called **Bercy Village**. It includes a pedestrian section filled with kid-friendly shops, restaurants, and cafés. There is a large movie complex called **Ciné Cité**. It often plays kid-friendly films, including American ones in English.

14. BOIS DE VINCENNES

The **Bois de Vincennes** borders the eastern edge of Paris. Like the Bois de Boulogne, it is a remnant of the large ring of forests that once encircled the city, when it was known as Lutetia. Once the domain of kings, the Bois de Vincennes is now a favorite among Parisian families when they need a breath of fresh air. It features large woods, lakes, bike trails, a big zoo, a small farm, a castle, a museum, a tropical garden, terrific playgrounds, a horse racing track, and even a baseball field.

CHÂTEAU DE VINCENNES (**CASTLE**). *Metro: Château de Vincennes or RER Vincennes Station. Open daily 10am-5pm (winter), 10am-6pm (summer). Adults: €7.50; Kids: free.*

Here is your chance to see a real castle, complete with fortifications and a giant donjon tower. Vincennes Castle was originally constructed more than 800 years ago, and was used pretty much through the 19th century. Highlights include the donjon tower (or keep), 17th century palace rooms, the gothic Holy Chapel, and the walk around the defense walls.

PARC FLORAL. *By the Esplanade du Château and Route de la Pyramide. Metro: Château de Vincennes. Then take bus # 112 or walk about 10 minutes. Open daily 9:30am-6pm. Adults: €1; Kids 6-18: €0.50; Kids under 6: free. Ask for the map and the program to free "Pestacles" performances at the entrance. There is a little white train that has stops all around the Parc Floral.*

This park is a real treat for kids and families! When you first walk in you are greeted by several different gardens. There are flower gardens, pine gardens, and a garden of four seasons that blossoms all year. If you head towards the left, you come to a small museum that features exhibits on the ecosystems around Paris and a butterfly garden. If you keep going past the crêpe restaurant and big pond, you'll come to the children's section. It features wonderful playgrounds, complete with castles and climbing webs. There also are some really fun activities, such as pedal-powered horse chariots, race cars, and a hilarious mini boat ride for babies, for which you will need to purchase tickets. They are organized according to age and size. Look at the horizontal bars at the entrance. They indicate the minimum and maximum heights for each ride.

Bois de Vincennes Highlights

- Visit the Vincennes castle
- Try out the playgrounds and fun rides in the Parc Floral
- Rent a rowboat and paddle around the lake
- Go to the Foire du Trone Fair

The park features several eateries, ranging from light fare at the crêpe restaurant to a full (and still family-friendly) meal in the big restaurant by the pond.

There are two theaters in the park. One features a **marionette show**. The other has live performances and concerts.

If you enjoy **miniature golf**, don't miss the one in this park. Each hole features one or several of the major monuments of Paris. Can you get your ball through the Eiffel Tower or up the Montmartre hill? See if you can recognize all the sights. Hint: the course is laid out as if it were a big map of the city.

RENTING BICYCLES. Bikes are a great way to explore and enjoy this vast park. You can rent bicycles at the **Lac des Minimes** (*Tel. 01 30 59 68 38*); **Lac Daumesnil** (*Tel. 01 47 47 76 50*); or the **Bicyclub** in the Parc Floral (*Tel. 01 47 66 55 92*).

LAC DES MINIMES, *on the northeastern side of the Bois de Vincennes, RER: Fontenay sous Bois* and LAC DAUMESNIL, *on the western edge of the park, near Metro: Porte Dorée.*

Both of these lakes were artificially created and decorated with fake islands and grottos. They are very pretty. You can rent rowboats or paddleboats, or just watch the ducks and swans float by.

FOIRE DU TRONE. *In the Bois de Vincennes, near the Lac Daumesnil. Metro: Porte de Charenton. During the summer months.*

In the 9th century, monks used to hold a fair on this spot every year. Here we are, over 1,000 years later, and the tradition continues. The Foire du Trône is held every year, between Easter and the end of May. The fair is named for the thrown (trône) that once stood in the Place du Trône (now called Place de la Nation) in honor of the marriage of King Louis XIV and Marie-Therese. There are plenty of thrill rides, merry-go-rounds, carnival games, food, and other amusement park attractions.

15. CHAMPS ELYSEES & CONCORDE

The **Avenue des Champs Elysées** is one of the most famous avenues in the world. It was named for the Elysian Fields of Greek mythology, where heroes get to go after they die. Today, the Champs Elysées is more of a shopper's paradise. A popular old French tune describes it this way: "Whether it's sunny or rainy, midnight or midday, there's something for everyone on the Champs Elysées."

With its wide, tree-lined sidewalks, the Avenue des Champs Elysées also follows the perspective formed by the Louvre, Tuileries Gardens, Place de la Concorde and Arc de Triomphe. Lovely vistas and photo opportunities abound.

ARC DE TRIOMPHE. *Place Charles de Gaulle-Etoile. Access to the arch through the metro or underground passageway from the Champs Elysées. Do not attempt to cross the traffic circle. Metro: Charles de Gaulle/Etoile. Museum and viewing platform open daily, 9:30am-11pm (April-September); 10 am-10 pm (October-March). Adults: €7, Kids ages 12-25: €4.50. Kids under 12: free.*

The Arc de Triomphe (*see photo above*) graces the center of the Place Charles de Gaulle-Etoile and the top of the Champs Elysées hill. It is directly in line with the Louvre, Arch du Carrousel, and Concorde Obelisk to the east. To the west it is aligned with the modern, Grande Arche de la Défense. The perspective offers great photo opportunities.

The Arc de Triomphe was built by Napoleon I to celebrate his military victories. It was meant to look like an ancient Roman triumphal arch, only bigger. Work on the project began in 1809. When Napoleon was

Area Highlights

• Climb up to the top of the Arc de Triomphe
• Go shopping or look at car showrooms along the Champs Elysées
• See Paris' oldest puppet show
• Watch the rats go through their maze at the Palais de la Découverte
• Have your photo taken on the Pont Alexandre III
• Imagine living inside one of the statues on the Place de la Concorde
• Play in the Parc Monceau

ousted from power in 1814, the arch was still unfinished. It was finally completed in 1836.

Napoleon was not the first to think of building a monument on this hilly crossroad. Fifty years earlier, King Louis XV had plans drawn up for a monumental elephant to be built on this spot. It was meant to be as big as a palace with fancy rooms, staircases, and fountains that would pour out of the elephant's trunk. Too bad it was never built, but you can see drawings of it in the small museum inside the Arc.

For over a hundred years, the Arc de Triomphe has been one of the most recognizable monuments of Paris, and it has come to represent a symbol of patriotism and national glory. Great funeral and military parades have taken place up and down the avenue. In 1920, the ashes of an unknown soldier killed in World War I were laid to rest under the Arc de Triomphe. A memorial flame was placed to mark the spot in 1923. It is re-lit every day at 6 pm.

The sides of the Arc de Triomphe are decorated with battle scenes. The most famous depicts a woman representing Liberty who is guiding the troops to victory. It is called *La Marseillaise*, which is the name of France's national anthem. There are also sculptures representing Peace and Triumph.

You can visit the inside of the arch and climb up the 284 steps to the top. The entrance is inside one of the legs of the arch. There is a small museum and a roof top terrace that offers terrific views of the city.

CHAMPS ELYSÉES. *Stretches from the Arc de Triomphe to the Place de la Concorde. Metro: Charles de Gaulle-Etoile, George V, Franklin Roosevelt, Champs Elysées-Clemenceau, or Concorde.*

In the early 16th century, Queen Marie de Médicis ordered that the marshy fields west of her Tuileries Palace be drained and transformed into a tree-lined promenade. It was named the Cours de la Reine (Queen's Course). In 1667, King Louis XIV asked his favorite landscape architect, André Le Nôtre, to redesign the area. In 1709, the course was renamed Champs Elysées.

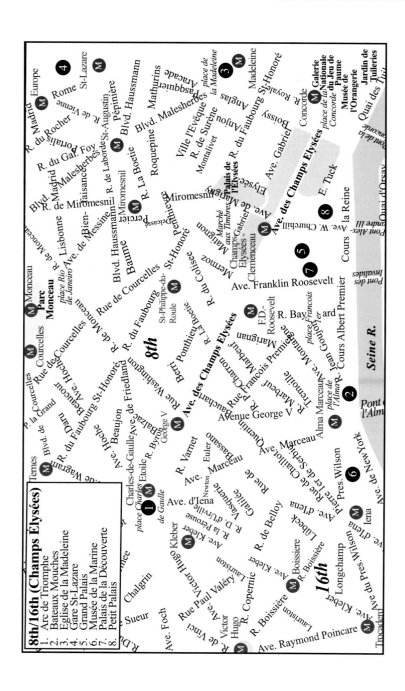

8th/16th (Champs Élysées)
1. Arc de Triomphe
2. Bateaux Mouches
3. Eglise de la Madeleine
4. Gare St-Lazare
5. Grand Palais
6. Musée de la Marine
7. Palais de la Découverte
8. Petit Palais

For many years, much of the Champs Elysées path was lined with houses, cafés, and cabarets. Cows grazed in nearby fields. In 1814-1815, invading Russian and Prussian troops camped out in the fields and gardens along the Champs Elysées, leaving the place a wreck. In the 1830s, the Champs Elysées started to undergo a massive facelift. Gardens were rebuilt. Sidewalks, fountains, and gas street lamps were added. Famous architects were hired to build fancy dance halls, theaters, circuses, restaurants, and mansions.

By 1900, the Champs Elysées had become Paris' most fashionable address. It was lined with luxury shops and cafés, and filled with elegant folks dressed in their finest clothes. The avenue's popularity was boosted even more with the completion of the first subway line in 1902. This line still runs directly under the Champs Elysées, from the Place de la Concorde to the Arc de Triomphe.

As you walk up and down either side of the Avenue des Champs Elysées, you will encounter a wide mix of shopping opportunities. There are occasional reminders that this avenue was once the heart of high fashion, with designer and high-end boutiques. There are gourmet eateries, like Fouquet's that continue to attract French movie stars. Mixed in with these are more familiar-looking American imports, such as Planet Hollywood, Virgin Records, Disney Store, and the ubiquitous Mac-Do (as the French call MacDonalds). There are several, large movie theaters, often featuring the latest Hollywood hits. To catch one in English, ask if it is in *version originale*. The *version française* will be dubbed in French.

If you enjoy checking out the latest models of European cars, there are several showrooms on either side of the avenue. The Renault showroom on the south side of the features a small exhibit of older models.

Below the Rond Point des Champs Elysées, where the avenue intersects with Avenue Gabriel and Avenue Matignon, is the oldest **marionnette show** in Paris (on the left as you face the Place de la Concorde). The main character, Guignol, has been delighting audiences young and old on this spot since 1818. Shows take place daily during summer holidays (Wed, Sat, Sun during the school year) at 3pm, 4pm, and 5pm. Cost: €3.

Close by, at the lower end of the Champs Elysées, also on the left as you face the Place de la Concorde, is the Carée Marigny. This is where Paris' **stamp collectors** have been meeting to talk, buy, and sell their stamps for more than 125 years. Open every Thurs, Sat, and Sun.

The house of the French President, called the **Palais de l' Elysée**, is by the Rond Point. It is a former royal palace, built in 1718.

PALAIS DE LA DECOUVERTE (SCIENCE MUSEUM). *On the western side of the Grand Palais, along the Avenue Franklin Roosevelt. Metro: Champs Elysées/Clemenceau. Open: Tues-Sat, 9:30 am-6 pm, Sun, 10 am-7 pm. Note: the ticket offices shuts down 30 minutes before closing time. Closed Mon. Adults: €7. Kids: €4.50. Supplement for the planetarium show: €3.50. Planetarium shows at 11:30am, 2pm, 3:15pm, 4:30pm (also at 5:45 Sat, Sun, and during school holidays).*

The Palais de la Découverte (Palace of Discovery) started out as a temporary exhibit for the 1937 Universal Exposition in Paris. It featured the latest scientific discoveries and techniques. The exhibit was such a hit that it was made into a permanent science museum, with lots of hands-on experiments and demonstrations. However, some are hard to figure out if you don't read French. The Ecole des Rats is fun; watch rats push levers, open doors, and find their way through a maze to food. The static electricity exhibit will make your hair stand on end. You also can take a voyage into the center of a cell in the human biology section, or a virtual trip into space at the planetarium.

GRAND AND PETIT PALAIS. *Facing each other on the Avenue Winston Churchill by the Pont Alexander III (Metro: Champs Elysées-Clemenceau). The Petit Palais is open daily except Mon, 10am-5:40pm. Hours for the Grand Palais vary according to different temporary exhibits.*

The Grand and Petit Palais were both built of glass and metal for the Paris Exhibition of 1900. Today, the Petit Palais features French art from the Renaissance through the 19th century, including nice impressionist paintings. The Grand Palais is used for blockbuster temporary exhibits on everything from Ancient Egypt to contemporary cartoons. They both make a great backdrop for family photos.

PONT ALEXANDRE III. *Between the Invalides and the Grand Palais. Metro: Invalides or Champs Elysées-Clemenceau.*

Another great photo opportunity, this is Paris' most elaborately decorated bridge. It was started 1897 to commemorate a new alliance between France and Russia and finished in time for the Paris Exposition of 1900. The first stone was laid by Czar Nicholas II of Russia, and the bridge is named for his father. On either side in the middle of the bridge are two statues representing the Seine and the Volga Rivers. At each end are statues of the mythical Greek winged horse Pegasus. They are covered in real gold leaf, as are many of the decorations on the bridge. The lamp posts were added in 1925. Their globes are made of hand-blown glass.

PARC MONCEAU. *Along Boulevard de Courcelles. Metro: Monceau. Open daily 7am-10pm (summer), and 7am-8pm (winter).*

This park was developed in 1787, with lots of naturalistic features such as little rivers, water falls, woods, boulders, and artificial grottos. There are exotic touches such as a Chinese pagoda, an Egyptian pyramid, ruined Greek columns (*see photo below*), and a Nomad's tent. There is a fine playground and plenty of room for kids to play. The Parc Monceau also is home to the biggest tree in all of Paris. It is an Oriental Sycamore. At its widest, the tree's trunk measures more than 7 meters (23 feet) in circumference.

PLACE DE LA CONCORDE. *Metro: Concorde.*

This square was originally called Place Louis XV since it was started during his reign. Following the French Revolution, it was briefly renamed Place de la Revolution, and it was here that the guillotine was placed which was used to behead King Louis XVI, his wife, Marie Antoinette, and another 1,000 or so others.

The tall **obelisk** in the center of the Place de la Concorde was a gift from Egypt to recognize the contributions of the French archaeologist Champollion, who deciphered the secret to understanding hieroglyphics. The obelisk was from the Temple of Ramses II in Luxor where it was used to measure the sun's shadows. It dates from the 13th century BC. It took two years to transport the obelisk from Luxor to Paris. The obelisk still functions as a sundial. Look for the markings on the ground and see where the shadow of the monument's point hits them; that tells you the time.

There are two large fountains on the Place, representing river and maritime navigation. There are also eight large female statues. These represent some of France's main cities: Marseilles, Lyon, Lille, Strasbourg, Bordeaux, Nantes, Rouen, and Brest. In the late 1800s, people lived inside the bases of these statues. Note the small doors and windows.

16. OPÉRA, GRANDS MAGASINS & GRANDS BOULEVARDS

This area is much more fun than you might think. Visiting the Opera house may sound stuffy but is like visiting a big palace. Nearby, there are fabulous department stores and plenty of uniquely Parisian adventures along the Grands Boulevards. See map on page 106 to get oriented.

PALAIS GARNIER OPERA HOUSE. *Place de l'Opéra (Metro: Opéra). English language tours of the Opera House, including basements and backstage, are offered Wed, Sat, Sun at 11:30am and 2:30pm (winter), and daily at 11:30am and 2:30 pm (summer). Adults: €12; Kids 10-25: €9; Kids under 10: €6. You can also tour the grand staircase, performance hall, and museum on your own. Adults: €8; Kids: €4.*

Although the idea of taking children to the Opera House may strike you as absurd, we were surprised at how much our boys and other kids around us enjoyed visiting the building. To them it offered all the glitter and adventure of a real palace. For a treat, take a guided tour (in English). It includes visits to grand staircase, *Grand Foyer*, performance hall, and mysterious lower levels, including the underground lake. You'll hear about the famous Phantom and some of the other secrets held within the magnificent bowels of this monumental building. There is also a small museum with a collection of costumes, set designs, and other articles from famous operas and ballets.

By the way, you may also want to bring your children to a show here. It's a major venue for ballet and other dance performances.

**BRENTANO'S BOOK-
STORE.** *37, Avenue de l'Opera.
Metro: Opera or Pyramides. Closed
Sun*

If you or your children have
run out of reading materials, this
is a good place to stop. Brentano's
is an American bookstore that has
been around for over 100 years. It
offers a huge selection of English-
language books on two floors. It
has a large children's section and
hosts a children's book club (in
English).

**GRANDS MAGASINS–
DEPARTMENT STORES.**

Opéra Area Highlights

• Go behind the scenes and into
the basements on a tour of the
Opera House
• Check out the toys and other
cool stuff in the Grands Magasins
• Have lunch on top of the
Galeries Lafayette
• See a real fashion show
• Discover Paris' shopping
galleries and passageways
• Visit the Musée Grévin wax
museum

Le Printemps, *64, Boulevard Haussmann. Metro: Havre-Caumartin or
Auber. Open Mon-Sat, 9:30 am-7 pm (Thurs until 10pm), Closed Sun.*

Galeries Lafayette, *40, Boulevard Haussmann. Metro: Chaussee d'Antin.
Open Mon-Sat, 9:30 am-6:45 pm, (Thurs until 9 pm), Closed Sun.*

Paris invented the first department store and still shows the rest of the
world how to do them well. The Printemps and Galeries Lafayette chains
have stores throughout the city and across France. However, the Boulevard
Haussman stores are the best. The buildings themselves are quite beautiful.
There are elaborate, art-nouveau style skylights, stairways, and decorations. Each one has a top floor caféteria. The Galeries Lafayette also has a
nice rooftop café open in warm weather. The views of the Opera and other

rooftops of Paris
are spectacular.

Inside these
stores, you'll find
fantastic toy sec-
tions with play
areas for smaller
tots. Of course
there are many
fashions, per-
fumes, and cos-
metics to choose
from. If you need
gifts for folks back

home, don't miss the souvenir and gourmet food sections. You will also see plenty of electronics and video games. Remember, however, that French appliances function on a 220 volt current, whereas those in the US are made for 110 volts. You can purchase an adapter to compensate, or opt for those that are battery powered. Note that French televisions, DVDs, and videos function on a different standard than those in the US. Finally, remember that if you purchase a computer or video game in France, it will likely be in French.

If you are in Paris during the winter holidays, don't miss the lights and decorations along the **Boulevard Haussman**. The window displays are wonderful.

If you are in Paris in August or early September, take your children to see the "Back to School" section of the Grands Magasins. It's fun to compare the French version of school supplies with those back home. Besides, a Parisian pencil case, agenda, or portfolio can make a nice souvenir or gift for friends and teachers.

If your child is a fashion critic or budding clothing designer, you can check out the latest fashion trends up close at the Galeries Lafayette Store. Free 1-hour fashion shows take place every Tuesday at 11 am (all year), and Fridays at 2:30 pm (April-October).

GRANDS BOULEVARDS. *East of the Opera, including Boulevard des Capucines, Boulevard des Italiens, Boulevard Montmartre, Boulevard Poissonière, and Boulevard Bonne Nouvelle. Metro: Richelieu Drouot, Grands Boulevards, and Bonne Nouvelle.*

These boulevards were once the sight of a protective wall built to defend the city from its enemies. Later they were lined with high class cafés and theaters. In the 19th century, the Grands Boulevards became more bohemian and home to a lively theater and music hall scene. They also are the setting of paintings by Maurice Utrillo and Edouard Manet .

Today, the Grands Boulevards feature theaters, cinemas, shops, and American-style eateries. In fact, if you are homesick for American food, this is where you can find some familiar names and menus (e.g., TGI Fridays, Hard Rock Café, Ben and Jerry's, the ubiquitous McDonalds).

If you are going to be in Paris for New Year's Day, don't miss the parade down the Grands Boulevards. It comes complete with floats, giant balloons, clowns, the works!

SHOPPING GALLERIES AND PASSAGES. *Running perpendicular to the Grands Boulevards with entrances on Boulevard des Italiens and Boulevard Montmartre. Metro: Richelieu Drouot.*

These are the best feature of the Grands Boulevards. Long before there were shopping malls, Paris had its indoor shopping galleries and passages.

These were built in the second half of the 19th century to offer Parisians a chance to shop protected from the elements and street traffic. There were over 100 of them across the city. Many were elaborately decorated with fancy skylights, tile floors, columns, and statues. Some had motifs from Egypt or Ancient Rome. Today, there are about 20 galleries and passages that are still open to the public. They remain one of the city's best shopping treats. The ones near the Grands Boulevards have much to please kids of all ages. There are stores featuring comic book characters, dollhouse furniture, teddy bears, and hip clothing. There are also nice cafés and irresistible pastry shops. So make like a 19th century Parisian and stroll through the shopping galleries away from the traffic, bad weather, and general bustle of the big city.

The first set of passages you will come to if you are arriving from the Avenue de l'Opéra is at #5 Boulevard des Italiens. It is called the **Passage des Princes**, and should not be missed. The whole place was recently renovated and transformed into a "Village of Toys."

As you reach the Boulevard Montmartre, you will encounter two sets of passages, facing each other across the boulevard. At #10 Boulevard Montmartre, on the north side of the street, you can enter the **Passage Verdeau**. It is filled with fun shops, including the biggest collection of dollhouse furniture and other miniatures in the city. It has an excellent pastry place, a shop that sells rocks and minerals, and one of the oldest cane stores still in existence. This passage also contains a charming hotel (Hotel Chopin) and has Paris' wax museum (see below). Once you reach the end of the Passage Verdeau, cross the small side street to enter the **Passage Jouffroy**. Here there are excellent tearooms, used book stores, and shops. It then leads to the Rue Cadet which has a very nice outdoor market.

On the south side of the Boulevard Montmartre, across the street from the Passage Verdeau, is the **Passage des Panoramas**. This one was developed by an American businessman. It was originally decorated with giant circular paintings called panoramas. It was also the first passageway to be lit with gas lamps. The Passage des Panoramas has several parallel galleries, like a tic-tac-toe board. It eventually leads to the Rue Vivienne. If you follow the Rue Vivienne several blocks south to #6, you will come to the **Galerie Vivienne**. In here don't miss the wonderful toy shop called Si Tu Veux, featuring games, toys, teddy bears, and costumes. The Galerie Vivienne leads right into the **Galerie Colbert**. Both of these galleries have recently undergone a facelift and are very pretty. The Galerie Colbert has a wine paraphernalia store with a remarkable array of corkscrews.

MUSÉE GRÉVIN (**WAX MUSEUM**). *10, Boulevard Montmartre. Also opens onto the Passage Verdeau. Metro: Grands Boulevards. Open daily 10am-6pm. Adults: €17; Kids 6-14: €10; Kids under 6: free.*
This museum originally featured wax characters designed by Marie Gresholtz-Tussaud, the same woman who set up Madame Tussaud's Wax Museum in London.

Today, the wax museum's figures include famous actors, sports figures, politicians, historical figures, and even French chefs. Some are staged to represent historical events, including gory scenes from the French Revolution. These are a big hit with kids.

Most of the Grévin museum's wax figures are dressed in clothes that actually belonged to the people they represent. In fact, the designers start with the clothes and model the wax figures to fit into them. The hairpieces are made of real hair and placed in softened wax one strand at a time. Some of the wax figures (mostly politicians) have been stuck with pins and needles by people who believe in voodoo magic.

LE GRAND REX. *1, Boulevard Poissonière. Metro: Bonne Nouvelle or Grands Boulevards. Self-guided, 50-minute tours offered every 5 minutes, 10 am-7 pm, Wed-Sun during the school year and daily during the summer. Ask for an English version. Adults: €9.80; Kids 6-12: €8. You can get a combined ticket for the visit + a movie for an additional €5 per person. Note: the visit includes dark hallways and special effects that may scare smaller children.*

The Grand Rex is a beautiful, grand, art-deco style movie theater built in 1932. It has welcomed many movie stars over the years and still has twinkling stars that shine from the ceiling of the main theater. You can go for a movie or opt for a self-guided backstage tour (ask for an English headset). The tour, called *Les Etoiles du Rex* (Stars of the Rex), takes you up a glass elevator behind the giant screen. If there is a movie playing, you will catch a glimpse of it from the back. The tour introduces you to cartoon and real movie legends, shows you special effects, lets you feel and hear surround sound at its fullest, and shows films clips of the Rex's history. You even take part in a mini-movie production. At the exit, you can purchase a video of your own movie or buy photos that have been snapped by a candid camera during your tour. Giggles guaranteed.

PARIS STORY. *11, Bis Rue du Scribe. Metro: Opera. Open daily, 9am-7pm. Adults: €10; Kids 6-18: €6; Kids under 6: free. Shows daily on the hour, 10am-6pm.*

Two-thousand years of Paris' history, legends, and monuments are told in this hour-long panoramic film. Headphones available in 12 different languages, including English.

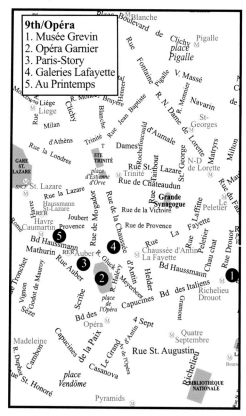

GARE SAINT LAZARE (**TRAIN STATION**). *Place du Hâvre.*
Metro: Saint Lazare.
This is the oldest of Paris' train stations, built in 1837. The Gare Saint
Lazare is where you come if you need to catch a train for Giverny and other
parts of Normandy. There are also trains for England (through Dieppe,
other British-bound trains go from the Gare du Nord). The station has a
hotel called Le Terminus. It was built for the Paris Exposition of 1889.
You may recognize the Gare Saint-Lazare from Impressionist paintings of it by **Edouard Manet** (whose art studio was nearby at #58, Rue de
Rome) or by **Claude Monet** (who used to catch the train here to reach his
house in Argenteuil and later at Giverny). Outside, in front of the station
are two funny modern sculptures. One is called l'Heure de Tous (Everyone's
Time). It is composed of pile of clocks. The other, called Consigne à Vie
(Baggage Check for Life) is a pile of suitcases. Both were created in the
1980s by the artist Arman.

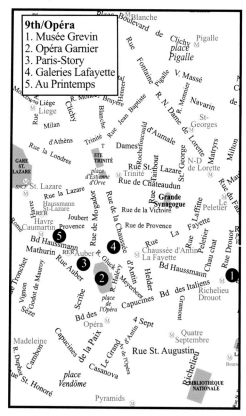

17. TROCADERO

If you want a photo of your family in front of the Eiffel Tower, the **Trocadéro terrace** is a must stop for you. It is on a hill, directly across the river from the Eiffel Tower, flanked by two rows of golden statues.

This neighborhood is also the sight of several wonderful museums, a lovely shopping street, and an informal memorial to the late Princess Diana.

The **Place du Trocadéro** is named for a Spanish Fort that was captured by the French in 1823. A magnificent museum was built on the Trocadéro hill for the Paris International Exhibition of 1878. It looked like the Taj Mahal in India. It was torn down and replaced with the current Palais de Chaillot (the two curved buildings surrounding the Trocadéro) for the Paris Exhibition of 1937.

MUSEE DE LA MARINE. *Palais de Chaillot. 17, Place du Trocadéro. In the same building as the Musée de l'Homme. Open Wed-Mon, 10am-5:50pm. Ticket office shuts down 30 minutes before closing time. Closed Tues. Adults: €5. Kids: Free. Audioguide: €5. A kid's guide with games (in French) is available free of charge at the entrance.*

Trocadero Highlights

• Have your photo taken with the Eiffel Tower in the background
• Check out Napoleon's golden boat and other amazing ships at the Musée de la Marine
• Watch the roller-bladers and fountains in the Trocadéro Gardens
• Go window shopping along the Rue de Passy
• See Monet's Impressionist paintings at the Musée Marmottan
• Take a boat tour and find the statue of the Zouave

This is a must-see for anyone big or small who likes boats of any kind. The museum has a remarkable collection of large ship models designed for King Louis XIV. There are also models of Columbus' Santa Maria, famous cruise ships, submarines, and many others. You can see a full-size replica of Napoleon's imperial boat. There are live demonstrations by people who make or repair ship models. Special exhibits cater to kids' tastes, with topics such as pirates or ships featured in the Adventures of Tintin.

The TROCADERO GARDENS were created for the 1937 Paris Exhibition. The statues lining the fountains celebrate joy and youth. The fountains are very impressive when the *canons* (big jets) are turned on. These gardens have become a favorite rendez-vous spot for roller-bladers. You can watch them perform their stunts, framed by the majestic view of the Eiffel Tower. The gardens contain playgrounds and plenty of space for running around. There is a big, double-decker carrousel at the bottom of the hill.

PASSY NEIGHBORHOOD. *Southwest from the Place du Trocadéro, down the Rue Franklin to the Place de Costa Rica, and Rue de Passy. Metro: Passy.*

This is a very chic neighborhood. The Rue de Passy is a great street for window-shopping, particularly if you favor classic fashions (known in French as Bon Chic, Bon Genre). Think preppy with a French flair. The nearby Rue de l'Annonciation has a lovely outdoor market. It is a nice place to pick up a picnic lunch or some delicious pastries for a snack.

Also in this neighborhood is a statue of **Benjamin Franklin** and a street that bears his name. This statue commemorates the fact that Franklin lived in the nearby Rue Raynouard when he was America's Ambassador to France. In 1776, Franklin successfully persuaded the French King Louis XVI to help support the American War of Independence. It was a good move – without the support of the French navy, French troops, and French General Lafayette, the Americans would not have won. Franklin returned to Paris to negotiate the peace treaty recognizing America's independence from Britain.

MUSÉE MARMOTTAN – MUSÉE MONET. *2, Rue Louis Boilly. Metro: La Muette. Open Tues-Sun, 10am-5:30pm. Closed Mon. Adults: €7. Kids ages 8-25: €4.50. Kids under 8: free.* This is another fun stop for any child who enjoyed the book, *Linnea in Monet's Garden.* It is an excellent place to see some of the most important examples of Impressionist art. It is rarely crowded and a good alternative if you are not up to facing the crowds at the Musée d'Orsay. The permanent collection includes 65 paintings by **Claude Monet** that were donated by his son, Michel. This is where you can see Monet's *Impression, Soleil Levant* (Impression, Sunrise) that gave Impressionism its name (*see photo on next page*). The museum also features works by Monet's friends, Renoir, Sisley, Berthe Morisot, Pissarro, and Gauguin. They were part of his private collection. The museum's upper floors contain medieval art objects and furniture from the time of Napoleon I.

Parent Tip: After a tour of the Musée Marmottan head for a break in the **Jardin du Ranelagh**. It is located behind the museum, across the street. There are playgrounds, roller-bladers, pony rides, a puppet theater, and an antique merry-go-round. ✤

PONT DE L'ALMA. *Between Place de l'Alma and Place de la Résistance, Metro: Alma Marceau*

This bridge was built by Napoleon III and named for one of his successful battles in the Crimea in 1854. It is famous for its statue of a **Zouave soldier,** used to measure high water points. Boatmen know that if the Seine's water rises as high as the Zouave's waist during periods of flooding, it is not safe to navigate under the bridges. During the Great Flood of 1910, the Seine's waters rose all the way up to the Zouave's chin.

Who is the Zouave? In 1830, a group of Zouaoua tribesmen from the hills of Algeria and Morocco joined the French army as an auxiliary battalion. Their uniform was based on their brightly colored traditional clothes, including a red sash, blue vest, baggy pants, and red fez (a brimless cap with a tassel). Called Zouaves, they were brave and well trained. They developed a reputation as dashing daredevils. The Zouaves remained an important part of the French military up to World War I.

On the Place de l'Alma side of the bridge there is a full-size replica of the golden torch that sits atop the Statue of Liberty in New York Harbor. The torch sculpture was turned into an informal memorial to Princess Diana, whose fatal car accident occurred in a nearby tunnel.

BATEAUX MOUCHES (**TOUR BOAT RIDES**). *Pont de l'Alma. Right Bank. Metro: Alma Marceau. Daily departures at 11am, 11:30am, 12:15pm, 1pm, 2pm, 3:15pm, and every 30 minutes from 4-10pm. Adults: €10; Kids 4-12: €5; Under 4: free. Lunch cruises at 1 pm feature both adult and a kid's menu. Adults: €50; Kids under 12: €25. (Note: Although there are also evening dinner cruises, they are formal affairs and not recommended for children.)*

Always a welcome treat, the Bâteaux Mouches boat rides offer a unique view of many of the city's major monuments and bridges. Regular tours last one hour. There are commentaries in French and English. The lunch tour lasts 2.5 hours. Either is a great way to rest weary feet or recover from jet lag. It is also the best vantage point from which to admire the Zouave statue on the Pont de l'Alma and the small replica of the Statue of Liberty on the Ile Aux Cignes.

18. MONTMARTRE

The name Montmartre conjures up images of Bohemian artists, accordion players, and Amélie Poulain. Perched atop one of the tallest hills in Paris, this village-like neighborhood has preserved its cobbled streets, little houses, even a vineyard and two windmills. There is much to enchant both adults and children here. So climb to the top of the hill and enjoy the wonderful views and secrets hidden among the winding streets of this village on a hill.

Montmartre is fun to visit on foot if you don't mind walking, hills, and cobble stones. If you are pressed for time or not up to walking, you can hop on the tourist train, called **Montmartretrain**, for a 40 minute tour. Pick it up at the Place Pigalle or in front of the Sacré Coeur (Adults: €3.50 one way or €5 round trip; Kids: €2.50 one way or €3.50 round trip). There is also a public bus that runs through the neighborhood, called the **Montmartrebus**. For the price of one metro ticket, you can ride in a circle through Montmartre and past many of the major sights. The Montmartrebus has stops at the Place des Abesses and along many side streets.

GOING UP TO THE SACRÉ COEUR CHURCH. From the square at the bottom of the Montmartre Hill, below the Sacré Coeur, you face several choices for reaching the top. You can opt for the lovely staircases that wind their way up in front of you. You can choose the slightly straighter stairs that run up the hill on both the right and left sides. Or you can head to the left and

Montmartre Highlights

- Ride the funicular up the Montmartre hill
- Check out the view from the Sacré Coeur
- Have your portrait done at the Place du Tertre
- Find the Montmartre vineyards
- Look for the man who could walk through walls
- See Montmartre's two remaining windmills
- Admire the Art Nouveau subway entrance and church on the Place des Abesses
- Retrace the footsteps of the saint who carried his chopped off head up the hill
- Take a ride on the Montmartrain tourist train.

take a ride on the **funicular**. For the price of a regular metro ticket, you can glide up the hill on this diagonal train track. The ride is fairly short, and some parts take place in tunnels. However, the view when you are out in the open is fun, and kids love it.

BASILIQUE DU SACRÉ COEUR (BASILICA OF THE SACRED HEART). *Place du Parvis Sacré Coeur. Metro: Anvers or Château Rouge. Open daily: 9am-6pm. Entrance to the church is free, but you must pay to visit the crypt or to climb up to the top of the dome. Adults: €4.50; Kids: €2.50.*

One of the most recognizable sights on top of the Montmartre hill is the giant white Basilique du Sacré Coeur. The church is made of a special type of limestone that bleaches itself every time it rains. This explains why the Sacré Coeur looks so white and bright. In contrast, the inside of the church is quite dark. You can climb up to the top of the dome for a magnificent view of Paris and the surrounding area. There is also an excellent view from the terraces in front of the church. The belfry contains the largest bell in the world. It weighs 20,000 kilos (19 tons) and is 8 feet in diameter.

The small cobbled streets west of the Sacré Coeur take you into the heart of old Montmartre.

PLACE DU TERTRE (*see photo on page 117*). *One block west of the Sacré Coeur Basilica. Metro: Abesses or Lamarck Caulaincourt.*

In the 1880s, many of the old buildings in the center of Paris were torn down as part of the period's great urban renewal projects. Low-income Parisians fled to the outskirts of the city, including to the Montmartre neighborhood. At the time, Montmartre was like a small village with narrow streets, fields, vineyards, and windmills. There were also cafés and dance halls, such as the famous Moulin Rouge. Until World War I, the area

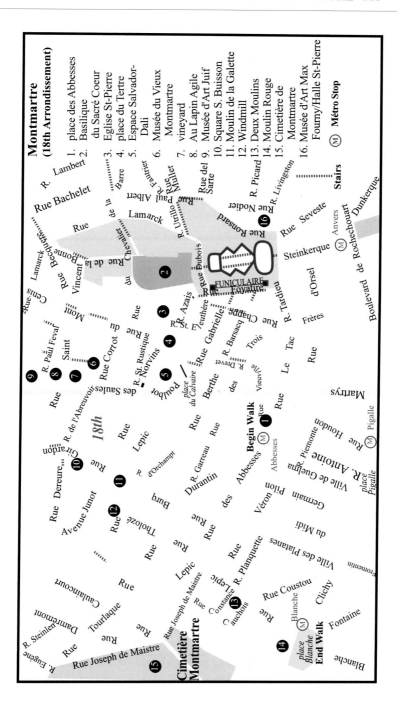

Montmartre
(18th Arrondissement)

1. place des Abbesses
2. Basilique du Sacré Coeur
3. Eglise St-Pierre
4. place du Tertre
5. Espace Salvador-Dali
6. Musée du Vieux Montmartre vineyard
7. Au Lapin Agile
8. Musée d'Art Juif
9. Square S. Buisson
10. Moulin de la Galette Windmill
11.
12. Windmill
13. Deux Moulins
14. Moulin Rouge
15. Cimetière de Montmartre
16. Musée d'Art Max Foumy/Halle St-Pierre

Ⓜ **Métro Stop**

attracted many starving artists, musicians, and writers who flocked here to live the bohemian life. Some of their names included painters Henri Toulouse-Lautrec, Paul Cézanne, Auguste Renoir, and Pablo Picasso; composers Hector Berlioz and Jacques Offenbach; and poets Henrich Heine and Guillaume Apollinaire.

The Place du Tertre does its best to keep alive the spirit of Montmartre's artistic heyday. It still resembles a village square surrounded by shade trees, shops, and small houses. Here you can purchase reproductions of the works of Montmartre's famous painters as well as other souvenirs. You can also support today's generation of starving artists who display their works in the Place or may offer to do your portrait. It is a fun place to grab a bite in a café and soak in the artistic atmosphere. If you have budding artists in the family, they may want to pull out the paper and drawing supplies for some artistic inspiration of their own.

The nearby **Place du Calvaire** offers a great view of the city, and has a small museum dedicated to the surrealist paintings of **Salvador Dali** that some kids really enjoy.

EXPLORING SIDE STREETS. The area by the Sacré Coeur and Place du Tertre can get quite crowded during high tourist season. Luckily, you don't have to go very far into the side streets of Montmartre to escape the crowd and enjoy the quieter charm of the neighborhood.

If you take the Rue des Saules from the Rue Norvins, Rue Saint Rustique, or Rue Cortot you will run into several Montmartre landmarks. Three restaurants were famous hangouts for artists such as Cezanne, Toulouse-Lautrec, and Renoir. They include the **Auberge de la Bonne Franquette**, **La Maison Rose**, and the **Lapin Agile**. To the right, as you go down the Rue des Saules is the famous **Montmartre vineyard**. Each year

on the first Saturday in October, the grapes are picked, then taken to the basement of the district's town hall to be pressed, aged, and bottled.

Along Rue Lepic, you'll come across Montmartre's two windmills, the **Moulin Radet** and the 600-year old **Moulin de la Galette** (*photo at left*). They are all that remain of the 30 or more that used to dot the Montmartre hillside.

At the Place Marcel Aymé you will come across an odd **statue of a man walking through a wall**. It depicts a character from a novel by Marcel Aymé. The novel is a story about a man named Dutilleul who discovers he can walk through walls, and uses this skill to become a burglar.

The **Place Emile Goudot** features a building called the **Bâteau Lavoir**, which is full of art studios. This is where artists Pablo Picasso, George Braque, and Juan Gris lived when they were experimenting with a new style of art called cubism.

Further down the hill still is the pretty **Place des Abesses**. This square is notable for its beautiful metro entrance. The glass awning is one of only two left that were designed in the Art Nouveau style by Hector Guimard. There is also an Art Nouveau style church across the street called Eglise Saint Jean de Montmartre.

FOLLOWING THE TRACES OF SAINT DENIS. *This path takes you through Montmartre, from the Pigalle Metro, up the Rue des Martyrs, Rue Yvonne Le Tac, past the Place Emile Goudeau, Moulin Radet to the Square Suzanne Buisson.*

Saint Denis was the first Bishop of Paris. He is also the patron saint of France. There are different stories about who he really was. Some versions say he was Greek, others that he was from Rome. In either case, he was sent to Paris to spread the word of Christianity around 250 AD, during the Roman occupation of Gaul. He was evidently very good at his work. Along with his two companions, Rustique and Eleuthère, Denis converted many people to Christianity. This made the Roman Emperor furious. He wanted his subjects to worship the Roman gods. The Emperor sent troops to Paris to stop the Christians. Roman soldiers arrested Denis, his companions, and many other Christians throughout the city. Denis and his companions were tortured and sentenced to death. According to the legend, the night before the execution was scheduled to take place, Christ (or in some versions a group of angels) appeared to Denis in his jail cell to give him Holy Communion.

The next day Denis, Rustique, and Eleuthère were marched up Mount Mercury (now known as Montmartre) to be executed in front of the temple of Mercury. However, the impatient Roman guards took matters into their own hands and beheaded the three prisoners well before they reached the top of the hill. According to the legend, while Rustique and Eleuthère fell to the ground, Denis picked up his head and continued walking up the hill. He washed the head off in a fountain, then walked another six kilometers (4 miles) until he reached the house of a holy woman named Catulla. Denis handed her his head, then collapsed. Catulla had him buried near her house. Today it marks the spot of the great Saint Denis Cathedral, located north of Paris in a suburb called Saint Denis.

You can retrace the footsteps of Saint Denis as a way to enjoy some of the sights of Montmartre. Start at Metro: Pigalle. Walk one block east to the Rue des Martyrs and take it north, up the Montmartre Hill. This is supposedly the path that was taken by Denis and his companions on their way to the execution. When you reach the end of the street, take a right into the Rue Yvonne Le Tac. At #11, you will come to the Chapel of the Martyrs. This supposedly marks the spot where Denis, Rustique, and Eleutère were beheaded. In the 7th century, this chapel was considered to be a place of asylum. Any criminal who made it inside the building could seek refuge and pardon.

Next, go back down the Rue Yvonne Le Tac the way you came, until you reach the Place des Abbesses (described above). Climb up the Rue de Ravignan, admiring the Place Emile Goudeau and Bâteau Lavoir along the way. Turn left into the Rue Norvins, past the Place Marcel Aymé (described above) with its sculpture of the man who could walk through walls. Take the Rue Girardon to the **Square Suzanne Buisson**. This pretty garden features a fountain and a statue of Saint Denis with his head in his hands. It is supposed to mark the spot where Denis rinsed off his head before continuing his journey north. It is also a nice place to play or relax in the shade, if you need a break from walking uphill.

To follow the rest of Saint Denis' path, you would need to go another four miles north and east from this spot. This would take you beyond Paris and into the suburb of Saint Denis to the great Saint Denis Basilica. This magnificent, gothic cathedral is well worth a visit. It contains the tombs of the French kings. You don't actually have to walk the whole way. There is an excellent subway station, called Basilique de Saint Denis that you can get to from the Pigalle or Anvers metro, by changing and heading north at the Place de Clichy metro stop.

To continue your tour of Montmartre, meanwhile, go past the Place Dalida and up the Rue de l'Abreuvoir to the Rue de Saules, where you can admire the Montmartre vineyard, Maison Rose, and Lapin Agile. A hike back up the Rue de Saules gets you to the Rue Cortot and to the Place du Tertre. Then head for the Sacré Coeur. You can ride the funicular down the hill or opt for the stairs. At the bottom, kids will enjoy the fancy **merry-go-round**.

GARE DU NORD TRAIN STATION. *Located south and east of Montmartre, on the Rue Dunkerque. Metro: Gare du Nord.*

This station serves trains going to and from northern France as well as Belgium, the Netherlands, Scandinavia, and trains bound for Britain through Lille (including the Eurostar that goes through the Chunnel).

GARE DE L'EST TRAIN STATION. *Located just a few blocks south and east of the Gare du Nord, on the Place du 8 Mai 1945. Metro: Gare de l'Est.*

This is where you come to catch trains bound for eastern France, Germany, Switzerland, and Austria.

RUE DU PARADIS. *Located one block south and west of the Gare de l'Est. Metro: Gare de l'Est.*

This interesting street is lined with crystal and porcelain shops. It makes for fun window shopping. At # 30 Bis Rue du Paradis there is a neat little museum, called the **Musée Baccarat**. This place absolutely glitters with chandeliers and crystal.

19. LA VILLETTE

It's a little hard to imagine that this massive urban park with its modern museums and structures used to be just a little village. But that is where the name, Villette (small village) comes from. Originally a Roman hamlet on the road to Belgium, **La Villette** took on greater importance in the 1800s, when it became the home of Paris' main slaughterhouse. When that work was moved to the suburbs in the 1970s, a massive new plan was devised to transform the site into a series of public parks, museums, and entertainment halls.

The result is a huge green space, dotted with gardens, waterways, playgrounds, and architectural "follies." There is much to spark the interests and joys of children here, starting with the magnificent science museum, leading through a slide shaped like a dragon, across a canal, all the way to an excellent Museum of Music.

CITÉ DES SCIENCES ET DES INDUSTRIES (**SCIENCE MUSEUM**). *Parc de la Villette, 30, Avenue Corentin Cariou. Metro: Porte de la Villette. Open Tues-Sun, 10am-6pm (Sun, until 7pm). Closed Mon. Adults: €8; Kids 7-12 yr: €6. Kids under 7: free. Planetarium: additional €2 with museum ticket.. Argonaute submarine: €3 or free with ticket for the museum. Audioguide rental: €1.50.*

This "Science City" is made to spur your child's curiosity and natural urge to touch and experiment. To get the most out of it and avoid language barrier frustrations: rent the audioguide, available in English.

The museum is very interactive with sections on sound, optical illusions, health, the ocean, geology, stars and galaxies, plants, volcanoes, and virtual reality. There are plenty of computer opportunities as well as activities like trying out a helicopter engine, seeing how the gears of a car work, checking out a racing bike prototype, or designing a puzzle.

The Cité des Sciences also contains a **planetarium** and a lower level cafeteria that features its own **aquarium**. Outside, you can take a self-guided tour (with free audioguide) through the Argonaute **submarine**. It will give kids an appreciation for the claustrophobia of life on board.

LA GÉODE IMAX MOVIE THEATER. *Next to the Argonaute submarine and Cité des Sciences et des Industries. Open Tues-Sun. Closed Mon. Shows projected every hour from 10 am to 9 pm. Adults: €10.50; Kids and Students under age 25: €9. Ask for English-language headphones.*

La Villette Highlights

• Explore the human body, the ocean, the solar system, or virtual reality at the Cité des Sciences
• See an IMAX movie at La Géode
• Visit a real submarine
• Play on a giant dragon slide
• Bounce, pedal, get sprayed with water, and play in the delightful gardens of the Park
• Go on a canal boat ride
• Check out the ancient instruments and many musical sounds at the Musée de la Musique

This theater is already cool just from the outside, where its mirrored spherical surfaces reflect the sky and passers-by. Inside it shows 3-D IMAX movies. You are literally surrounded by images that transport you under the sea, into outer space, back to the dinosaurs, etc. It's so realistic that it is not recommended for children under age 3 or women who are more than 6 months pregnant.

Note: Want to avoid a stiff neck at La Géode? Try the theater's top row seats.

LE CINAXE. *From the Géode, this theater is around the Cité des Sciences building, on the left. Buy tickets at the Géode box office. Open Tues-Sun, 11am-5pm. Closed Mon. Shows projected every 15 minutes. Adults: €6; Kids: €5.*

Get ready to shake, rattle, and roll. The seats of this theater are mounted on a platform that sends you lurching and laughing along with the crazy ride being projected on the movie screen. It is not recommended for kids under 4, pregnant women, people with heart problems, epileptics, and people with fragile backs or necks. For the rest, it's 15 minutes of wacky fun.

JARDIN DU DRAGON (**PLAYGROUND**). *Near the Cité des Sciences et des Technologies, on the south side.*

This dragon is irresistible if you are a kid. It contains a giant slide plus several smaller ones that offer plenty of opportunities to climb and squeal.

BIG PLAYGROUNDS. *Near the Grande Halle, along the path called Galérie de la Villette. If you are coming from the dragon or science museum, you will need to take the bridge across the Canal de l'Ourcq.*

Technically, this area is known as the **Jardin des Vents** (Garden of Winds), **Jardin des Dunes** (Garden of Dunes), and **Jardin des Miroirs** (Garden of Mirrors). To a kid, and anyone who is young at heart, it is really a giant playground. These gardens are filled with clever and delightful activities. Large sections (divided by age groups) are covered with moon-bounce type surfaces where kids can jump to their hearts' content. They are connected by wobbly sidewalks. Watching you try to negotiate these will be guaranteed to make the rest of the family laugh. Kids also love trying out the pedal-powered windmills that they can manipulate with their hands or feet. There are mini-mountains to climb and a garden filled with mirrors.

OTHER GARDENS. *In the Parc de la Villette.*

In the vast 3-kilometer stretch – about 2 miles – between the Porte de la Villette side of the park and its Porte de Pantin entrance, you will find several interesting little gardens. They are full of charm and surprises. The

Jardin des Equilibres features games where kids try out their skills of balance. The **Jardin de Bambous** is like walking through a bamboo forest. The **Jardin de la Treille** (Trellis Garden) has 90 small fountains decorated with trellises of climbing vines and plants. The **Jardin des Frâyeurs Enfantines** (Garden of Childhood Fears) takes you through dark paths filled with strange music and sounds of the forest. The **Jardin des Brouillards** (Garden of Fog) sprays you with jets of mist on warm days.

There are also two wide fields, called **Prairies**, where kids can run, kick a ball, and generally let loose. The benches, lampposts, trash cans, and other park furniture were designed by Philippe Starck. During July and August, the Triangle Prairie is transformed into a free, outdoor movie theater.

Once you are near the canals at La Villette, keep a sharp eye on active toddlers. There are no railings along the water's edge.

PARIS CANAL BOAT RIDE. *Dock near the bridge crossing the Canal de l'Ourcq by the Jardin des Brouillards (Garden of Fog). Metro: Porte de Pantin. Tel. 01 42 40 96 97. One-hour rides depart hourly. A 3-hour ride all the way to the Seine departs at 2:30pm and arrives at the Musée d'Orsay at 5:30 pm. Adults: €16; Kids 12-25: €13; Kids 4-11: €9; Under 4: free.*

Enjoy a ride through Paris' canals and locks from the Canal de l'Ourcq. A 1-hour trip takes your through part of the canals and back again. It is ideal for younger children. A 3-hour trip goes all the way through the canals to the Seine River and over to the Musée d'Orsay. For kids who love boating, it's a great thrill. You go through locks and tunnels, and see some of Paris' most famous sights. Reserve in advance during high tourist season. The tours sell out quickly.

CANAUXRAMA CANAL BOAT RIDES. *Depart from 13, Quai de la Loire on the Bassin de la Villette. Metro: Jaurés. This is 4 metro stops down from Porte de Pantin, past the Canal de l'Ourq and at the southern end of the Bassin de la Villette. Phone: 01 42 39 15 00. Departures at 9:45 am or 2:45 pm. Tours last 2hrs 40min. Adults: €15; Students and Seniors: €11; Kids 4-12: €8; Kids under 4: free.*

These boats take you down through the canals and locks from the Bassin de la Villette to the Place de la Bastille. The ride is long for short attention spans, but for those who enjoy boats, the passages through tunnels and locks are fascinating. The sights along the way take you through some truly Parisian neighborhoods and under picturesque foot-bridges. You'll feel like you've stepped onto the set of *Amélie Poulain* or any other charming Parisian film. Bring along a picnic. Reserve in advance, during high tourist season.

MUSÉE DE LA MUSIQUE. *In the Cité de la Musique building, 221, Avenue Jean Jaures. Metro: Porte de Pantin. Open Tues-Sun, 10am-6pm. Closed Mon. Adults and Kids: €8.*

This is a very interesting museum for any child who plays a musical instrument or enjoys music. It offers not only lots to see, but also many sounds. The exhibits are easy to follow and enjoy thanks to the free headsets (available in English) supplied at the entrance. There are also live presentations by musicians demonstrating all types of different instruments from around the world.

Outside the museum, you can refuel at the **Café de la Musique**. It is conveniently situated facing the Place de la Fountaine aux Lions, which offers plenty of car-free space to run while kids wait for their food.

20. BOIS DE BOULOGNE

This huge park fills most of the western edge of Paris. There are gardens, playgrounds, lakes, and museums. It is here that you can find Paris' only campgrounds, two equestrian centers, two hippodromes, and the Roland Garros stadium, which hosts the French Open Tennis competition each year in May.

JARDIN D'ACCLIMATATION. *Entrance at intersection of Boulevard des Sablons and Avenue du Mahatma Gandhi on the N edge of the park. Walk from Metro: Sablons or take the free train from Metro: Porte Maillot. Open daily, 10am-6pm (until 7pm, Jun-Sep). Adults and Kids 3-18: €2.50; Kids under 3: free. People with disabilities: free. Ask for a free map at the entrance.*

This garden is full of rides and activities for kids of all ages. It's a little old-fashioned but that's part of the charm. For example, the bouncing horse course will remind you of Mary Poppins. There's also a petting zoo and farm, a hall of funny mirrors, and a free puppet show. There are several large playgrounds, organized by age group. The park also has a bowling alley and poney rides. There are two small museums, the **Explor@Dome** science museum and the **Musee National des Arts et Traditions Populaires** that presents elements of rural life from different regions of France.

BIKE RENTALS. These are located across from the main entrance to the Jardin d'Acclimatation. There are special bike lanes and paths throughout the Bois de Boulogne. It's a great way to enjoy the park.

PRÉ CATALAN. *In the middle of the Bois de Boulogne, off the Allée de la Reine Marguerite, at the same level as the Lac Inférieur.*

This area features big grassy fields and some ancient trees.

There is also a lovely **Shakespearean garden** with plants and herbs that are mentioned in the Bard's plays. From May to October the garden becomes an open-air theater, featuring works by Shakespeare. These are often performed in English by British theater companies.

LAC INFERIEUR AND LAC SUPERIEUR. *Towards the middle of the Bois de Boulogne on its eastern side. Near the Porte de la Muêtte. Metro: Avenue Henri Martin.*

The Lac Supérieur is the smaller of these two lakes. Its most interesting feature is that fact that on warm afternoons, you can rent a remote-controlled toy powerboat to play with on the lake. On the Lac Inférieur you can rent full-sized rowboats. For a nominal fee, you can also take the ferry to the lake's main island.

The Bois de Boulogne has two horse-racing tracks. The **Hippodrôme de Longchamp**, which features thoroughbred races and poney rides for little tikes, is located on the SW side of the Bois, along the Route des Tribunes. Free buses run from Metro: Porte d'Auteuil. Races start at 2pm. The **Hippodrôme d'Auteuil**, located on the SE side of the Bois, along the Route des Lacs features steeple-chase races. There are pony rides and a kids play area. Metro: Porte d'Auteuil.

There is a public swimming pool, with both indoor and outdoor pools, called **Piscine d'Auteuil**, on the Rue des Lacs de Passy and Allée des Fortifications. Metro: Ranelagh.

ROLAND GARROS TENNIS STADIUM. *2, Avenue Gordon Bennett. On the southern edge of the Bois de Boulogne. Metro: Porte d'Auteuil. You can purchase tickets for the French Open: Tel. 01 47 43 48 00 or www.frenchopen.org.*

This red-clay tennis stadium is named for a French pilot who was the first aviator to fly solo across the Mediterranean Sea. It hosts the annual French Open Tennis Tournament in May. This is a real treat for tennis fans, old and young.

21. DAY TRIPS!

Versailles

A fancy palace, spectacular gardens, musical fountains, and fireworks: this is Louis XIV's Château de Versailles. Come taste of the luxury and splendor that was life at court during the reign of the France's Sun King.

VERSAILLES PALACE. *Place des Armes, in Versailles, 20 kilometers southwest of Paris. By car take highway A13 towards Rouen to exit Versailles-Château. By public transportation take RER line C-line to Versailles Rive Gauche station (this station is only a few blocks from the Palace). The Palace is open Tues-Sun, 9am-6:30pm (May-Sep), 9am-5:30pm (Oct-Apr). Closed Mon. The pricing system in the palace is complicated and confusing. It varies depending on which parts you want to see. The king's apartments are a separate visit from the rest of the palace. If you go to Entrance A, you can opt for a combined ticket, including the king's rooms, queen's rooms, and Hall of Mirrors (Galerie des Glaces). Adults: €9; Kids: free. The audioguide (highly recommended) is €3.*

Parent tip: To avoid summer crowds, you may want to do the visit backwards. Start with the park and gardens. Have lunch by the Grand Canal. Go for a boat or bike ride. Save the palace for the late afternoon. The western light will be filling the Hall of Mirrors and the crowds will be thinner. �֍

The palace of Versailles was originally built by King Louis XIII as a small hunting lodge. Louis XIV had already planned to expand Versailles when he saw Nicholas Fouquet's palace at Vaux-le-Vicomte. Fouquet's palace was so splendid that the king had him arrested. Officially,

Fouquet was imprisoned for using state funds for his own luxurious life style. Unofficially, his main crime was to have dared to outshine the Sun King. Louis XIV immediately hired Fouquet's architect Le Vau, painter Le Brun, and landscape designer Le Nôtre to make him an even grander palace at Versailles.

The builders and designers had their work cut out for them at Versailles. The land was marshy and unstable. Workmen had to bring in mountains of earth to build up the land. Fully grown trees were uprooted and replanted to make a forest, many of them dying along the way. A long and complicated system of pipes, pumps, and windmills was installed to drain the swamps and bring water for a grand canal and the multitude of fountains set up to decorate the gardens.

Louis XIV moved into the new palace in 1682. He made his whole court move from Paris to Versailles with him. It was a good way for the king to show his absolute power and keep an eye on members of his court. He loved to organize elaborate parties and festivities. Louis XIV filled his palace and gardens with musicians, writers, painters, acrobats, and other entertainers. Even the canals were filled with elaborately decorated boats for the amusement of the king and his court. The gardens were decorated with statues and fountains. In spite of all the installations, there was never enough water to run all of the fountains at one time. So when the king took a stroll through the gardens, workmen would whistle back and forth to signal which fountains to turn on and off along the king's path.

The new palace was built to be large, imposing, and extravagantly decorated. It included 700 rooms and 67 staircases. There were over 2,000 windows and 6,000 paintings. The chandeliers, throne, and some of the furniture were made of solid silver. Gold gilding (a thin layer of solid gold paint) covered much of the wall and ceiling decorations. Gold thread was woven into the wall coverings. There were 5,000 pieces of furniture and decorative objects.

Versailles was one of the first royal palaces to be permanently furnished. Prior to that, most furniture was moved along with the king each time the royal court went from one palace to another. After the French Revolution of 1789, all the furniture was sold to the highest bidder. The paintings and antiquities were sent to the Louvre. The silver and metal pieces were melted down. The books were transferred to the national library. The palace was turned into a museum and never again served as a royal residence.

VERSAILLES GARDENS. *Open daily from sunrise to sunset, except during stormy or extreme weather. Entrance to the gardens is free except during special events like the Grandes Eaux Musicales or Fêtes de Nuit.* There are over 50 fountains decorating the gardens around the

Versailles Palace. Many refer to Greek and Roman mythology:

The **Bassin de Latone** is named after a character in mythology who was seduced by the god Zeus and gave birth to Apollo and his twin sister Diana, goddess of the hunt. One day Latone took her children to have a drink from a spring in a land called Lycia. The locals teased and insulted her. Latone called for Zeus' help. He exacted revenge on the Lycians by turning them into frogs and lizards, which now decorate this fountain.

The **Bassin d'Apollon** is a huge fountain featuring Apollo driving his magnificent golden chariot, pulled by four horses, across the sky (*see photo on page 125*). The figure of Apollo was meant to remind his subjects of Louis XIV's power and splendor.

On the north side of the palace is another spectacular fountain, the **Bassin de Neptune.** This is where the Nuits d'Eté shows are held (see below). You can recognize Neptune, god of the seas, by his trident (three-pronged spear).

Hidden among the plants and alleyways is another great fountain. It represents **Enceladus,** a mythical Greek giant who tried to climb Mount Olympus and overthrow Zeus, king of the gods. Zeus sent down a barrage of stones to hold him back. In this fountain you can see the golden figure of Enceladus partially buried under the huge rocks.

The **Bassin du Dragon** at the end of the Allée de l'Eau is not based on Greek or Roman mythology but is still a delight. Here you will see statues of little children riding on swans and fighting off a big dragon. The jet coming from the dragon's mouth can shoot up nearly 30 meters (over 90 feet).

GRAND CANAL. *In the Versailles Gardens.*

In the days of Louis XIV, this canal was filled with golden boats – even a special gondola from Venice. Some of the boats carried musicians who entertained the king and his guests as they ambled round the water. Today, you can rent a more modest rowboat. Though less fancy than the king's, it will still offer nice views of the Palace and gardens.

BICYCLE RENTALS. *Two locations: 1) at the vehicle entrance to the park, on the Boulevard dela Reine; and 2) in the park, by the Grand Canal. Open daily 10am-6:30pm. Closed in December and January.*

These bike rental spots offer a large supply of bicycles, including kid-sized ones and child carriers. It is a great way to explore the vast park around the palace and make your way to the Trianons or Hameau de la Reine. There are plenty of car-free lanes, so you won't have to worry about traffic. Just watch out for the little tourist train that makes the rounds between palace, Grand Canal, and Trianons.

GRAND TRIANON, PETIT TRIANON, HAMEAU DE LA REINE. *On the Versailles grounds, north and west of the Palace. Access from the Avenue du Trianon, Petit Canal, Allée de la Reine, or Allée des Deux Trianons. Open daily 9am-6:30 pm (May-Sep), 9am-5:30 pm (Oct-Apr). Adults: €7; Kids: free.*

These three outbuildings were built as royal residences. The Grand and Petit Trianon were designed as retreats where the king could escape from the royal court from time to time. The Grand Trianon is still used today to house visiting dignitaries. The Hameau de la Reine was built for Marie Antoinette, the wife of Louis XVI. She would go there dressed up as a milk maid and pretend to be in a small country village, surrounded by a real working farm. There is still a small farm here.

GRANDES EAUX MUSICALES. *Sat-Sun during the summer at 11 am and 3:30 pm. Adults: €6; Kids: 10-18: €4; Kids under 10: free.*

This show emulates the festivities at Versailles during Louis XIV's reign when the fountains would dance to the concerts by Lully and other baroque composers. The king would invite his guests to stroll among the gardens as different fountains became animated to the music. Today, the music is piped in, but the effect is still lovely.

FETES DE LA NUIT. *By the Neptune Fountain on N side of the park. Sat evenings in Jul, Aug, Sep at 10:30 pm. Seats range from €10-40. Kids under 8: free.*

In Louis XIV's day, the gardens were filled with musicians, dancers, plays, and other forms of entertainment. The Fêtes de la Nuit give you a taste of this. There are characters dressed in period clothes. There is plenty of music, and the fountains are on in full force. It's quite spectacular. At the end of the show there is a magnificent fireworks display.

LITTLE TRAIN. *Starts from the Palace (N-side terrace), with stops at the Grand Canal, Petit Trianon, and Grand Trianon. Adults and Kids 12 and up: €5.50; Kids 3-12: €3; Kids under 3: free.*

The little train is always a favorite with kids, especially if they are tired of being on their feet. It takes you from the palace to the royal residences and on to the Grand Canal. Hang on to your tickets and you will be able to get on and off all day.

CARRIAGE RIDES. *Start from the Palace (N-side terrace, near the little train). Available Tues-Sun. Closed Mon. Adults: €6.50; Kids: €5.50.*

Hop on board one of the horse drawn carriages for a charming tour of the grounds and park. Your kids will be delighted.

Giverny – Monet's House

Venture just an hour west of Paris along the Seine River and you come to the lush, green, rolling hills of Normandy. The region is famous for its apples, creamy butter, and camembert cheese. This is where Claude Monet had a house and wonderful garden so filled with color it will make you feel like you've walked right into an Impressionist painting.

CLAUDE MONET'S HOUSE AND GARDENS. *Rue Claude Monet, in Giverny, 80 kilometers (50 miles) west of Paris. By car, follow the directions for the A13 highway toward Rouen (via the Pont de Saint Cloud on the west side of Paris) to the Bonnières exit, then the D201 to Giverny. By train, go from the Gare Saint Lazare to Vernon, 45 minutes away. From the Vernon train station you can catch a bus, take a taxi, or rent bikes for the 5 kilometer (3 mile) ride to Giverny. There are also tour bus trips to Giverny from Paris. Contact Paris-Vision (Tel. 01 42 60 30 01) or Cityrama (Tel. 01 44 55 61 00). Claude Monet's house and gardens are open daily, Apr-Oct, Tues-Sun, 19:30am-6pm. Closed Mon and Nov-Mar. Adults: €5.50 (house and gardens), €4 (gardens only); Kids 12-18: €4, Kids 7-11: €3 (house and garden); Kids under 7: free.*

"It's just like in the book!," exclaimed a 6-year-old friend on one of our trips to Claude Monet's house in Giverny. Sure enough, if you've seen the book *Linnea in Monet's Garden* by Christina Bjock and Lena Anderson, you'll recognize Monet's pink house, his art studio, the big garden filled with flowers and alleyways, the Japanese footbridge, and the pond full of water lilies. Children love this place, even if they have never heard of Linnea, Monet, or Impressionism. They can't resist the urge to explore the garden paths, hide behind gigantic flowerbeds, and listen to the gobble gobble of the white turkeys. See if they can find the underground passageway to the water lily pond. Do they recognize the Japanese Bridge from his paintings? How about the little green rowboat?

Monet's house offers a glimpse of daily life in the home of a great painter. You'll see the original furniture, decorations, and dishes. There's also one of Monet's art studios, his reading room, and his bedroom. There are lots of Japanese prints on the walls from which he drew inspiration. You can also see how Monet's love of color extended to the inside of his house. Bright blues and yellows dominate throughout the entire house. Don't forget to look out the windows for nice views of the gardens.

At the end of your visit, you'll find Linnea, copies of water lily paintings, and other souvenirs in the gift shop. This was formerly Monet's big studio. Today it is an excellent place to pick up gifts for folks back home.

MUSEE D'ART AMERICAIN (MUSEUM OF AMERICAN ART). *99, Rue Claude Monet, in Giverny. Open Apr-Oct, Tues-Sun, 10am-6pm. Closed Mon. Closed Nov-Mar. Adults: €5.50;Students, Seniors, and Teachers: €4; Kids 12-18: €3; Kids under 12: free. Free to all on the first Sun of the month. Audioguide: €1. The museum offers painting classes for children and adults in July and August.*

In the 1890s, as Monet's fame and that of other French Impressionist painters spread, many American painters came to live in Giverny and the surrounding area. This relatively new museum, built in the 1990s, showcases their work. The permanent collection features paintings from 1870 to 1920. Temporary exhibits embrace themes such as depictions of trains in Impressionist paintings or views of the Seine. The museum is bright, airy, and not terribly big – excellent qualities for a kid-friendly visit. There is a nice café and a terrific gift shop featuring a good kids' section.

Theme Parks

If you or your child's idea of a real vacation isn't complete without life size cartoon characters or thrill rides don't worry.

DISNEYLAND PARIS. *Located 32 kilometers E of Paris in the town of Marne-la-Vallee. By car, take highway A4 towards Nancy-Metz to exit 14. The parking lots are huge. Don't forget where you've left your car, and be prepared to hike 10-15 minutes to the park entrance. By public transportation, take the RER line A4 commuter train to the Marne la Vallee- Chessy stop. You can also take a special shuttle bus to the park from either Orly or Charles-de-Gaulle airports. Buses leave every 45 minutes. High-speed TGV trains also service the Marne-la-Vallee station from many major French cities. Open year-round, 9am-11pm (July-Sept) 9am-8pm (Fall, Spring), 10am-8pm (Nov-Dec). Entrance costs vary depending on time of year, and whether you purchase a one or several-day pass. Passes can be purchased at many Metro/RER stations, FNAC stores, Virgin Megastores, and Galeries Lafayette department stores. Further information and special discounts are available online at www.disneylandparis.com*

If you've never had a chance to go to the American Disney theme parks or want to compare the French and American ones, here's your chance. Disneyland Paris is hugely popular with Europeans, including French families. They look on it as a way to get a big dose of American culture without having to cross the Atlantic or give up red wine with lunch.

Just like in the American parks, Disneyland Paris features a Main Street with its afternoon parade of Disney characters and Sleeping Beauty's castle. There are sections (Fantasyland)

designed for younger kids and others (Adventureland, Discoveryland, Frontierland) that feature rides for older kids. Walt Disney Studies is located next to the Disneyland park.

Not surprisingly, Disneyland Paris gets very crowded during the summer tourist season. Your best bet during this time is to arrive early, as the park is opening, and head straight for the most popular rides. Another strategy is to wait until the end of the day to try the favorite sections, when many people are leaving or watching the Main Street Parade. You can also obtain a Fast-Pass for the most crowded rides. These are available by the entrance and give you a specific time when you can go to a particular ride. You will then get to bypass the long line and go through the much shorter Fast-Pass line.

PARC ASTERIX. *Located 35 kilometers N of Paris, near Charles de Gaulle Airport. By car, take highway A1 north to the Parc Asterix exit, located between exits 7 and 8. By public transportation, take RER line B3 from Paris to the Charles de Gaulle/Roissy station where you can catch the Parc Asterix shuttle bus that leaves every 30 minutes. You can purchase a combined RER-Park Entrance tickets for a discount at RER stations in Paris. High-speed TGV trains from across France also stop at the Charles de Gaulle/ Roissy Station, where you can catch the Parc Asterix shuttle. Open daily, April-August and every weekend in Sept-Oct, 10am-6pm (Mon-Fri), 9:30am-7pm (Sat-Sun and daily in August). Adults: €31; Kids 3-12: €23; Kids under 3: free. The nearby hotels offer special family rates for lodging plus park entrance. Strollers and wheelchairs are available in the park free of charge. Baby changing station and place to warm up bottles located under the big rock with Asterix on top.*

Note: Due to its proximity to the Charles de Gaulle/Roissy Airport, you may want to save a visit to Parc Asterix for the end of your trip. You can visit the park on the day before your flight home (there are places to check your bags at the park entrance). Spend the night at a hotel near the park or near the airport, and catch your flight out the next day. It's a great way to combine fun and convenience.

If you want to see a truly French theme park, this is the place! Parc Asterix is based on the popular French comic book characters **Asterix** and **Obelix**. Their (very funny) adventures are set in the 1st century BC, during the Roman Occupation of Gaul (France). If you've seen any of the comic books, you'll really enjoy recognizing the characters and buildings from the stories. If you haven't seen the books, you'll want to after this visit (Note: they are available in French, English, and numerous other languages). We love this park not only because we are big Asterix fans, but also because it is a more manageable size than Disneyland Paris, yet still offers plenty of fun.

Parc Asterix is divided into several sections, starting with Gaul, Classical Rome, and Ancient Greece. Then you pass through time to Medieval France, the Renaissance, and on to 19th century Paris. There are plenty of activities for kids and adults of all ages. There are some great thrill rides, including a huge wooden roller coaster, plenty of loop de loops, and a bobsled ride. There are several different boat rides, ranging from a steep roller coaster one to a hilarious bumper boat ride on the River Styx. There are also lots of funny rides, playgrounds, merry-go-rounds, automates, and shops. You can also take in any number of shows. Examples include a dolphin show in Ancient Greece, a Three Musketeer sword fight in Medieval Paris, a mystery about thieves stealing the Mona Lisa, a magic show in Gaul, and acrobats in the Roman Amphitheater.

Since this is France after all, there are plenty of eateries throughout the park, ranging from a little crêpe hut in the Gaul village to full restaurants by the Medieval and Renaissance sections. There are family-friendly hotels near the park with shuttle service to the park and to the Charles de Gaulle/ Roissy airport.

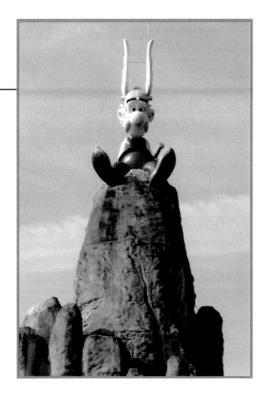

22. BEST FAMILY SLEEPS & EATS

Paris has many lovely hotels. You can count on their being clean and well kept. However, be warned that the rooms are often much smaller than the ones you find in hotel chains in the U.S. The ones listed here have been chosen for their location, charm, and family-friendliness. The prices noted here reflect official listings – you can often get a better bargain by looking for deals on line.

In terms of restaurants, you will find that most are very happy to cater to kids and families (provided they are reasonably well behaved). If you want something simple, you may want to opt for a café or some of the chains listed here. This selection reflects a variety of options and palates to help all of your group enjoy French food.

Apart'hotel Chains

The apart'hotels combine the freedom and space of an apartment with hotel services such as laundry and concierges. Apartments come as efficiencies that sleep 2-4, 1-bedroom apartments that sleep 2-4, and in some cases a 2-bedroom apartments that sleep 4-6 people. The apartments are clean, modern, and efficient.

Generally, the living room has a two-person sleeper sofa (sometimes two day beds), color TV with cable or satellite channels, small stereo, phone, and table. Bedrooms have either double beds or two twins. You can ask for a crib or extra bed. The bathrooms come equipped with a hair dryer. The kitchen has a refrigerator, microwave oven, stovetop, coffeemaker, dishwasher, and all the necessary utensils. Bed and bath linens are provided.

CITADINES APART'HÔTEL***. This chain has numerous locations throughout the city. Rates range from €130-280 per night depending on size and location:

Hotels Red, Restaurants Blue

In this chapter, the hotel names are in red, and the restaurants/dining selections are in blue!

Saint Germain des Prés, 53 ter, Quai des Grands Augustins, 75006 Paris. Metro: Saint Michel. Tel. 01 44 07 70 00; Fax 01 44 07 29 50. Email: resa@citadines.com. Studios and 1-bedrooms.

Jardin des Plantes-Austerlitz, 27, Rue Esquirol, 75013 Paris, Metro: Campo Formio or Place d'Italie. Tel.01 56 61 5400; Fax 0145 86 59 76; Email: resa@citadines.com. Studios and 1-bedrooms. **Bastille and Marais,** 37, Boulevard Richard Lenoir, 75011 Paris, Metro: Bréguet Sabin or Bastille. Tel. 01 53 36 90 00; Fax 01 53 36 90 22; Email: resa@citadines.com. Studios and 1-bedrooms. **Bastille and Promenade Plantée,** 14-18 Rue de Chaligny, 75012 Paris. Metro: Reuilly Diderot. Studios, 1-bedrooms, 2-bedrooms.

Les Halles, 4, Rue des Innocents, 75001 Paris. Metro: Les Halles. Tel. 01 40 39 26 50; Fax 01 45 08 40 65; Email: resa@citadines.com. Studios and 1-bedrooms.

Louvre, 8, Rue Richelieu, 75001 Paris. Metro: Palais Royal-Musée du Louvre Tel. 01 55 35 28 00; Fax 01 55 35 29 99. Email: resa@citadines.com. Studios and 1-bedrooms.

Montparnasse, 67, Avenue du Maine, 75014 Paris. Metro: Gaite or Vavin or Montparnasse. Tel. 01 53 91 27 00; Fax 01 43 27 29 94; Email: resa@citadines.com. Studios and 1-bedrooms.

Montmartre, 16, Avenue Rachel, 75018 Paris. Metro: Blanche. Tel. 01 44 70 45 50; Fax 01 45 22 59 10. Email: resa@citadines.com. Studios and 1-bedrooms.

Opéra-Drouot, 18, Rue Favart, 75002 Paris. Metro: Opéra. Tel. 01 40 15 14 00; Fax 01 40 15 14 50. Email: resa@citadines.com. Studios, 1-bedrooms, duplexes.

Opéra Vendôme Préstige, 2, Rue Edouard VII, 75009 Paris. Metro: Opéra, Auber, or Madeleine. Tel. 01 40 06 56 00; Fax 01 40 06 96 50. Email: resa@citadines.com. Studios, 1-bedrooms, 2-bedrooms.

Eiffel Tower, 132 Boulevard de Grenelle, 75015 Paris. Metro: La Motte Piquet Grenelle or Cambronne. Tel. 01 53 95 60 00; Fax 01 53 95 60 95. Email: resa@citadines.com. Studios and 1-bedrooms.

Trocadéro, 29 bis, Rue Saint Didier, 75016 Paris. Metro: Trocadéro or Victor Hugo. Tel. 01 56 90 70 00; Fax 01 47 04 50 07. Email: resa@citadines.com. Studios, 1-bedrooms, 2-bedrooms.

Place d'Italie, 18, Place d'Italie, 75013; Metro: Place d'Italie. Tel. 01 43 13 85 00; Fax 01 43 13 86 99; Email: italie@citadines.com. Studios and 1-bedrooms.

République, 75 bis, Avenue Parmentier, 75011 Paris. Metro: Parmentier or République. Tel. 01 55 28 08 20; Fax 0143 14 90 30. Email: resa@citadines.com. Studios and 1-bedrooms.

PIERRE ET VACANCES***. This chain offers 3 locations. Rates range from €180-250 per night depending on size and location:
Montmartre: 10, Place Charles Dullin, 75018 Paris, Tel. 01 42 57 14 55; Fax 01 43 54 48 87; Email: montmartre@pierreetvacances.com. Studios, 1-bedrooms, 2-bedrooms.

Bercy, 1-7 Cours du Minervois, 75012 Paris. Metro: Cour Saint Emilion. Tel. 01 53 02 11 00; Fax 01 53 02 11 10. Email: paris@pierreetvacances.com. Studios and 1-bedrooms.

Buttes Chaumont, 3-5 Cours du 7ième Art, 75019 Paris. Metro: Buttes Chaumont or Botzaris. Tel. 01 53 38 24 24; Fax 01 53 38 24 00; Email: butteschaumont@pierreetvacances.com. Studios, 1-bedrooms, 2-bedrooms.

Family-friendly Restaurant Chains
BÎSTROT ROMAIN: These restaurants offer good food at a great price. Adult menus offer ample options, such as salads, appetizers, well-garnished main courses, and tasty desserts – including vast quantities of chocolate mousse. Kids get crayons and an activity sheet. A kids menu proposes a choice of lasagna, chicken nuggets, or hamburger; unlimited supplies of French fries or pasta; chocolate mousse or ice cream; and a drink – all for €10. Adult menus are about €20.
Champs Elysées - 26, Avenue des Champs Elysées, 75008; Metro: Franklin Roosevelt, near the Rond Point des Champs Elysées.
Champs Elysées -122, Avenue des Champs Elysées, 75008; Metro: George
Les Halles - 30, Rue Saint Denis, 75001; Metro: Châtelet; near Les Halles and Pompidou Center
République – 17, Place de la République, 75003, Metro: République
Opéra - 2, Rue de la Chaussée d'Antin, 75009; Metro: Chaussée d'Antin; near the big department stores.
Gobelins – 64, Avenue des Gobelins, 75013, Metro: Gobelins

Parent Tip: You'll find red meats much less cooked in France than in either England or the US. Even if you ask for it well done, "*bien cuit,*" it will be pretty red. For children, you may want to specify very well done, "*très bien cuit.*" ✤

HIPPOPOTAMUS RESTAURANT AND GRILL. This family-friendly chain specializes in grilled meats including beef, chicken, lamb, and even ostrich. You can also opt for salads or vegetarian dishes. Kids get a fun sheet and crayons. The €8 kid's menu offers a salad; choice of burger, fish sticks, or chicken nuggets; fries; ice cream or chocolate mousse; and a drink. Adult menus range in price from €16-30 depending on how many courses you want to include. Early bird specials offer a 30% discount for meals ordered between 2:30 and 7:30 pm.

Les Halles, 29, Rue Berger, 75001; Metro: Les Halles

Opéra, 1, Boulevard des Capucines, 75002; Metro: Opéra

Bastille, 1, Boulevard Beaumarchais, 75004 Paris; Metro: Bastille

Latin Quarter, 9, Rue Lagrange, 75005; Metro: Maubert Mutualité

Montparnasse, 119, Boulevard Montparnasse, 75006; Metro: Vavin

Montparnasse, 68, Boulevard Montparnasse, 75014; Metro: Montparnasse

Montparnasse, 12, Avenue du Maine, 75015 Paris; Metro: Montparnasse

Champs Elysées, 6, avenue Franklin Roosevelt, 75008, Métro: Franklin Roosevelt

Champs Elysées, 20, rue Quentin Bauchart, 75008; Métro: George V

Champs Elysées, 42, Avenue des Champs Elysées, 75008; Metro: Franklin Roosevelt

Arc de Triomphe, 46, Avenue de Wagram, 75008; Metro: Ternes

Bercy, Cour Saint Emilion-Bercy Village, 75012; Metro: Cour Saint Emilion

Aquaboulevard (aquatic and sports center), 4, Rue Louis Armand, 75015; Metro: Balard

La Défense, 2, Place de la Défense; Metro: La Défense-Grande Arche

OH! POIVRIER! This chain offers warm and cold gourmet sandwiches, as well as salads, burgers, and quiches. The ingredients are fresh and vary with the seasons. Prices are reasonable, €10-20 per platter. There is an €8 kids menu with a choice of sandwiches or pasta, drink, and dessert.

Montparnasse, 143, Boulevard Raspail, 75006 Paris, Metro: Vavin, near intersection of Boulevard Raspail and Boulevard Montparnasse

Montparnasse, 2, Avenue du Maine, 75015; Metro: Montparnasse, near the train station.

Opéra, 2, Boulevard Haussman, 75009; Metro: Chausée d'Antin or Richelieu Drouot

Aquaboulevard (aquatic and sports center), 4, Rue Louis Armand, 75015; Metro: Balard

AMERICAN CHAINS. You will find several familiar American restaurant and snack chains in Paris, including the ubiquitous **McDonalds** (or Mac Do as the French call it); **TGI Fridays**, 8, Boulevard Montmartre, 75009, Metro: Grands Boulevards, **Hard Rock Café**, 14, Boulevard Montmartre, 75009, Metro: Grands Boulevards; **Chicago Pizza Factory**, 5, Rue de Berri, 75008 Paris; Metro: George V; *Tel. 01 45 62 50 23*; **Planet Hollywood**, 78, Avenue des Champs Elysées, 75008, Metro: George V; and **Baskin Robbins Ice Cream** (numerous locations around the city). These are familiar and predictable.

Ile de la Cité & Ile Saint Louis

LES FOUS DE L'ILE, *33, Rue des Deux Ponts, 75004 Paris, Metro: Pont Marie. Tel. 01 43 25 76 67; Open Tues-Fri for lunch and dinner, Sat for dinner only, Sun for lunch. Closed Mon.*
This restaurant has an artsy décor and offers nice daily specials and delicious pastries. Dinner selections run from €16 to €35. You can also go for afternoon tea and snacks or for Sunday brunch.

LE FLORE EN L'ILE, *42 Quai d'Orleans, 75004 Paris, Metro: Pont Marie. Tel. 01 43 29 88 27. Open daily, breakfast, lunch, and dinner.*
This is a good spot to stop for Berthillon ice cream (see below), a snack, or a full meal. The outdoor tables offer a great view of the back of Notre Dame Cathedral and the Seine River.

GLACES BERTHILLON, *Main store: 31, Rue Saint Louis en l'Isle, 75004 Paris, Metro: Pont Marie; Open Wed-Sun, 10am-8pm. Other stands open more regularly throughout the Ile Saint Louis.*
This is some of the best ice cream in Paris. Although the scoops are small, they are bursting with flavor. The tough part is picking among the wide selection, including flavors such as vineyard peach, black currant, mirabelle (yellow plum), pain d'epice (spice cake), poire william (pear liquour), and wild strawberries.

Latin Quarter

HÔTEL DES GRANDES ECOLES***, *75, Rue du Cardinal Lemoine, 75005 Paris. Tel. 01 43 26 79 23; Fax 01 43 25 28 15; Email: Hôtel.Grandes.Ecoles@wanadoo.fr; www.hôtel-grandes-ecoles.com; Metro: Cardinal Lemoine or Place Monge; Rates: €115-140 (doubles), additional bed: €15; breakfast: €9; parking: €30.* This is one of our all-time favorite Parisian hotels. It offers the best of both worlds: a quiet country lane-type atmosphere, nestled in the heart of the lively Rue Mouffetard neighborhood and Latin Quarter. You are close to major sights, with easy public transportation access to the rest of

the city. Yet, you are off the main roads in a quite corner with a lovely garden. The rooms are distributed among several 3-story buildings. Five of the double rooms are large enough to fit 1-2 extra beds comfortably, and in some there is even a large curtain to separate the adult bed from the kids. When the weather is nice you can eat breakfast or have an afternoon drink on the terrace.

HÔTEL DES ARÈNES***, *51, Rue Monge, 75005 Paris; Metro: Place Monge or Jussieu; Tel. 01 43 25 09 26; Fax 01 43 25 79 56; Email:hôteldesarenes@wanadoo.fr; Rates: €90 (double); €140 (triple). Children under 5 stay with parents at no extra cost. Children ages 5-12: €30 supplement. Buffet breakfast: €10 (free for kids).*

This hotel overlooks the gardens and ruins of the former Roman Arena, built in the 1st century AD. Make sure to get rooms on the Arena side and not on the street, which can be very noisy. The location is excellent: in the Latin Quarter near the Jardin des Plantes, Rue Mouffetard market street, and an easy walk to Nôtre Dame Cathedral. The rooms, though not huge (this is Paris, remember), are efficient and comfortable. Although there are no family suites, you can ask for a triple or for adjoining doubles that can be made into a suite.

HÔTEL DU LEVANT***, *18, Rue de la Harpe, 75005 Paris; Metro: Saint Michel; Tel. 01 46 34 1100, Fax 01 46 34 25 87; http://peprso.clubinternet.fr/hlevant; Email: hlevant@club-internet.fr; Rates: €118-160 (doubles); €165-220 (triples); €220-240 (quadruple); €300-315 (4-5 person suite). Rates include the buffet breakfast or continental breakfast in the room.*

This hotel is a real gem, especially considering its location in such a central, touristy spot. It is very family-friendly and has been run by the same family for four generations. They take great pride in keeping it clean, tastefully decorated, and up to date. It is situated on one of the pedestrian side streets near the Place Saint Michel. The rooms are quite pretty and several are well-designed to accommodate a family of four or five. Most of the rooms are air-conditioned. The ones on the top floor are especially charming.

HÔTEL RÉSIDENCE HENRI IV***, *50, Rue des Bernardins, 75005 Paris; Metro: Maubert Mutualité; Tel. 01 44 41 31 81; Fax 01 466 33 93 22; Email: reservation@résidencehenri4.com; Rates vary according to the season and special deals: €175 (double room); €190 (2 person apartment); €220 (3 person apartment); €250 (4-person apartment). Buffet breakfast: €11.*

This handsome hotel combines convenience and quiet in a great location. The hotel is set back from the main road on a nice little square. It feels intimate, because there are only 7 rooms and 7 apartments. Each features high ceilings, with decorated friezes and moldings, that give the place a feeling of elegance. The apartments feature 2 rooms, plus a kitchenette with a refrigerator, microwave, stovetop, and utensils.

HÔTEL LE JARDIN DE CLUNY (**Best Western**)***, *9, Rue du Sommérard, 75005 Paris; Metro: Maubert Mutualité or Cluny-La Sorbonne; Tel. 01 43 54 22 66; Fax 01 40 5103 36; www.bw-paris-hôtels.com/jardin/ ; Email: hôtel.decluny@wanadoo.fr; Rates: €180-200 (double); €370 (family suite).However you may get a significant discount booking early, on-line. Buffet breakfast: €14.*

This hotel combines old features with modern comforts. Although you are in a very central location, the hotel is on a small side-street and away from the noise of the main avenues. The rooms are well-appointed, air-conditioned, and efficient. There are only 2 rooms on each floor, so you can comfortably rent two adjacent doubles to accommodate a family of four. Some rooms are reserved for non-smokers. There is a pretty garden courtyard in the middle of the hotel. For breakfast you can eat in your room or head downstairs to the Louis XIII style dining room. It features vaulted stone ceilings and copies of the Woman with a Unicorn tapestries that you can see in the nearby Cluny Museum.

HÔTEL MERCURE PARIS LA SORBONNE***, *14, Rue de la Sorbonne, 75005 Paris; Metro: Cluny-La Sorbonne; Tel. 01 56 24 34 34; Fax 01 56 24 19 60; Email: H2897@accor-hôtels.com; Rates: €200 (double); €240 (triples); €280 (duplex-quadruple). Buffet breakfast: €15.*

Tucked away in the heart of the Latin Quarter, across the street from the historic Sorbonne University, this hotel welcomes families with bright, modern rooms. There are several large enough to fit a family of 4. Each features air-conditioning and the usual 3-star amenities of satellite TV, hairdryer, safe, and minibar. You are a stone's throw from the Cluny Museum and Luxembourg Gardens. At the end of a day of touring you can sit back and relax with a cold drink in the cafés of the charming Place de la Sorbonne around the corner from this hotel.

HÔTEL RÉSIDENCE LE VERT GALANT***, *41-43, Rue Croulebarbe, 75013 Paris; Metro: Place d'Italie or Les Gobelins; Tel. 01 44 08 83 50; Web: www.vertgalant.com; Rates: €90-110 (double); €100-130 (double with kitchenette). Extra bed: €10. Garage: €10. Buffet breakfast: €8.*

This is a very nice little hotel. It is a little off the beaten track. However, you still have excellent bus and metro access to all the major sights. What's more, there is a lovely public park across the street with excellent playground facilities. You are also only a few blocks away from the Butte aux Cailles indoor/outdoor public swimming pool. One room is equipped for individuals with disabilities. Many of the rooms open onto the hotel's private garden, as does the breakfast room. The larger rooms feature fully equipped kitchenettes. The owners also run an excellent restaurant, located next door. Called l'Auberge Etchegorry, it features delicious Basque specialties from southwestern France. It is located in a building that used to house a popular cabaret, frequented by author Victor Hugo (*Les Misérables* and *Hunchback of Nôtre Dame*). Menus range from €20 to €40.

HÔTEL DES TROIS COLLEGES**,*16, Rue Cujas, 75005 Paris; Metro: Luxembourg or Cluny; Tel. 01 43 54 67 30; Fax 01 46 34 02 99; Email: hôtel@3colleges.com; Rates: €70-110 (single); €90-120 (double); €125-145 (triple). Continental breakfast: €8.*

This is a really nice hotel, conveniently located near the Luxembourg

Gardens and Cluny Museum. It's remarkably quiet and discreet, considering you are in the heart of Paris' Latin Quarter. The welcome is very warm, and the rooms are bright and cozy. The largest ones are on the top floor. They are under the rafters and offer great views of the rooftops of Paris. On the lower floors, you can opt for two double rooms across from each other at the end of the corridor.

HOTEL SAINT JACQUES**, *35, Rue Des Ecoles, 75005 Paris, Metro: Maubert-Mutualité. Tel: 01 44 07 45 45. Fax: 01 43 25 65 50.*

www.paris-hotel-stjacques.com. Rates: €137-144 (double); €168-176 (triple). Breakfast €10.

This is a very friendly hotel in a great Latin Quarter location. The building is in a former mansion, and the owners have taken pride in restoring many of the original details, including ceiling paintings and door details. The rooms have high ceilings and big windows. The upper floors offer terrific views of the rooftops of Paris, Nôtre Dame Cathedral, and the Panthéon.

HÔTEL AU ROYAL CARDINAL**, *1, Rue des Ecoles, 75005 Paris; Metro: Cardinal Lemoine or Jussieu; Tel. 01 46 33 93 62; Fax 01 44 07 22 32; Rates: €98-121 (double); €135 (triple); €140 (quadruple). Breakfast: €6.*

This hotel is more affordable than most in this neighborhood and offers 8 triple rooms and 2 quadruples. The rooms are a little cramped and don't have that nice, updated feel that you find in higher end hotels. Still, you get a functional room, with soundproofed windows, TV, safe, and a hairdryer. Some even have a little balcony overlooking the street. The service is very friendly, and the location is very convenient – in the heart of the Latin Quarter, and a short walk to Nôtre Dame.

HÔTEL MARIGNAN*, *13, Rue du Sommérard, 75005 Paris; Metro: Maubert Mutualité or Cluny-La Sorbonne; Tel. 01 43 54 63 81; Fax 01 43 25 16 69; www.hôtel-marignan.com; Rates: €90 (double w/private bathroom); €110 (triple w/private bathroom); €130-150 (quadruple/quintuple with private bathroom). Extra bed: €20. Rates include breakfast. Note: They do not accept credit cards.*

This hotel feels like a youth hostel. It will take you back to the days when you bummed around Europe with a backpack on your back. The friendly owners, a Franco-British couple, are happy to help you get around the city, lend you a guidebook, or give advice. The hotel offers a free washer and dryer – a real luxury when you are traveling with kids – and access to a communal kitchen and dining area. The rooms have a hostel-like feel to them, too, with plaid bedspreads and cheap, utilitarian furniture. Some of the rooms do not have private bathrooms, so you have to share the ones in the hallway. The family-size rooms, however, have private facilities that were recently renovated. The hotel is located in the heart of the Latin Quarter, on a quiet side street.

HÔTEL ESMERALDA*, *4, Rue Saint Julien Le Pauvre, 75005 Paris; Tel. 01 43 54 19 20; Fax 01 40 51 00 68; Metro: Saint Michel or Cluny/La Sorbonne; Rates: €115-125 (double); €130 (triple); €145 (quadruple). Continental breakfast: €8. Note: This hotel does not accept credit cards!*

This is the same Hôtel Esmeralda as the one featured in the book *Linnea in Monet's Garden*. It's old, funky, and full of charm if you don't mind a certain amount of shabby gentility and a small staircase. You get exposed beams and old stones. The rooms are small but the price is hard to beat in such a wonderful location. You are directly across from Nôtre Dame Cathedral, around the corner from Shakespeare and Company English Language Bookshop, and in the heart of the Latin Quarter. Some of the rooms have a view of Nôtre Dame. There is a park across the street with room for kids to run.

BRASSERIE BALZAR, *49, Rue des Ecoles, 75005 Paris; Metro: Cluny – La Sorbonne; Tel. 01 44 07 14 91; Open daily.*

This is a classic, Parisian institution that has been welcoming French intellectuals from the nearby Sorbonne for ages. There are tall ceilings, big mirrors, and a 1930s style feel. Underneath their somewhat cold, professional exterior, the waiters are actually quite friendly to kids. The restaurant has joined the Flo Brasseries chain of high-end restaurants, which means the food is traditional and reliable. There is a big aquarium to distract bored children. There is a special kids menu. Count on spending €32-45 per person for adults.

MARTY, *20, Avenue des Gobelins, 75005; Tel. 01 43 31 39 51; Metro: Les Gobelins or Censier Daubenton.*

This is a big, traditional Parisian brasserie with beautiful mahogany wood features and a décor from the 1920s. The food is excellent. The specialty is fish and seafood, but there are also plenty of meat and poultry alternatives. There is a €15 kid's menu. The €35 menu includes appetizer, main course, and dessert. Eating à la carte runs about €45 with beverages.

RESTAURANT LA MOSQUÉE, *39, Rue Geoffroy Saint Hilaire, 75005 (across from entrance to Jardin des Plantes); Metro: Place Monge.* Walk through the entrance of this restaurant and you'll feel like you've been transported to a Moorish Palace. It is decorated with white walls, carved wood, and beautiful blue and green tiles. The seats are covered with plush pillows and the tables composed of enormous, brass platters. The menu offers North African specialties such as couscous, brochettes (shish kabobs), tajines (stews), and brick (ground meat and egg fried inside a turnover made of phillo pastry). Main courses range in price from €10-25.

If you are only searching for a snack after visiting the Jardin des Plantes and Natural History Museums, check out the lovely tea room next to the restaurant. Here you get sweet mint tea served in a glass or chilled drinks, along with baklava and other North African pastries (each for €2). On warm days, you can eat in the garden surrounded by flowers, fig trees, and fountains.

LES DÉLICES D'APHRODITE, *4, Rue de Candolle; Metro: Censier Daubenton, Tel. 01 43 31 40 39. Open Mon-Sat.* There are plenty of mediocre Greek restaurants in the Latin Quarter. This is one of the good ones. The ingredients are fresh and carefully chosen, including classics such as tzatziki, tarama, and moussaka. There is a special lunch menu for €18. You can get a plate of assorted Greek appetizers for €18. Dinners run €25-30.

JARDIN DES PÂTES, *4, Rue Lacépéde; Metro: Place Monge. Tel: 01 43 31 50 71* Located right by one of the entrances to the Jardin des Plantes, this restaurant offers a wide variety of types of pasta and pasta dishes. It's all organic and many of the choices are vegetarian. Dinners run about €20.

LE VOLCAN, *10, Rue Thouin (near Place de la Contrescarpe), 75005 Paris. Metro: Cardinal Lemoine or Place Monge; Tel. 01 46 33 38 33; Open daily for lunch and dinner.* In a neighborhood where restaurants tend to come and go, this one has been around for ages. You won't get anything fancy here, but you will get good basic food, such as onion soup, steak and fries, chicken breast in cream sauce, and *confit de canard* at a good price. There are also selections of Greek and Nordic foods. The menus offer an appetizer, main course, and dessert for €10, €15, and €25.

Light Fare
PIZZA PEPPA BELLA, *25, Rue Francisque Gay, 75006; Metro: Saint Michel (small side street 1 block south of Saint Michel Fountain); Open daily for lunch and dinner.*

This restaurant makes assorted pizzas in a wood-burning oven. They may or may not be the best in Paris as a sign in the window claims, but they are pretty good. There are also numerous pasta dishes to choose from. The price is certainly right, especially in this touristy neighborhood. Pizzas and pasta dishes run €12-16. There is a €16 lunch menu that includes pizza, pasta, or the daily special plus a drink. The daily special is €10. For €20, you can get an appetizer, pizza, and dessert. You can order pizzas to take out if you want to have a picnic by the Seine or in the Luxembourg Gardens.

CAFÉ DESCARTES, *1, Rue Thouin, 75005. Tel. 01 43 26 17 70. Metro: Place Monge.*

This place offers good salads, sandwiches, and other typical café fare at the top of the Ste. Genevieve hill. It is around the corner from where Ernest Hemingway lived when he wrote his classic autobiographical story of living in Paris, *An Immoveable Feast*. You are in walking distance of the Rue Mouffetard, Institut du Monde Arabe, and Arenes de Lutèce.

MAVROMMATIS, *47, Rue Censier, 75005; Metro: Censier Daubenton.*

Located just around the corner from the Rue Mouffetard market street, this is a great place to pick up take-out Greek food. There are creamy dips and spreads, freshly stuffed grape leaves, grilled shish kabobs, and other Greek delights.

LES COMPTOIRS DE LA TOUR D'ARGENT, *2, Rue du Cardinal Lemoine, 75005 Paris. Metro: Maubert-Mutualité or Cardinale Lemoine.*

If you would like a touch of the luxury of dining at the famous Tour d'Argent restaurant (located across the street) without having to endure the cost and endless courses, drop in here. The ready-made foods are prepared with the same art and finesse as the ones in the restaurant.

TEA CADDY, *14, Rue Saint Julien le Pauvre, 75005 Paris; Metro: Maubert Mutualité, Cluny/La Sorbonne, or Saint Michel; Tel. 01 43 54 15 56; Open noon-7pm, Closed Tuesdays.*

This little restaurant offers light fare, including breakfast, at affordable prices. There are salads and scrambled eggs; hot dogs and grilled sandwiches; salmon torte and eggs Florentine. For a snack, you can try the scones, muffins, toast, and pastries.

JADIS ET GOURMANDE, *88, Boulevard Port Royal, 75005 Paris; Metro: Port Royal.*
This shop is filled with chocolates that not only taste wonderful but also look beautiful. There are chocolate pianos, chocolate coins, and chocolate letters that you can pick to spell out the names of your loved ones. There are also creatively attractive gift boxes that are bound to be a hit with folks back home.

Light Fare along the Rue Mouffetard
Along with wonderful market offerings, there are many places to pick up a light meal or snack along this lively street:
LE PAIN QUOTIDIEN, *138, Rue Mouffetard, 75005 Paris; Metro: Censier Daubenton.*
This is part of a Belgian chain that has opened their wonderful bakery/restaurants all over Paris and the world. There are all kinds of breads and spreads to put on them, along with sandwiches, salads, and other light meal items.
STEFF, LE BOULANGER, *123, Rue Mouffetard, 75005; Metro: Censier Daubenton.*
This bakery is known for its wonderful breads, made the old-fashioned way and sometimes filled with nuts, raisons, or olives. The plain old baguette is delicious, too. It's also a good place to pick up a sandwich and pastry.
LES PANETONS, *113, Rue Mouffetard, 75005; Metro: Censier Daubenton.*
This bakery, along with its sister pastry shop next door, **Le Moule à Gateaux**, uses plenty of butter to make mouth-watering pastries and desserts. The croissants are deliciously puffy, and get my vote for the best around. You can also get fresh sandwiches, quiches, and breads. The cakes and pies are out of this world.
SHANGHAI EXPRÈSS, *105, Rue Mouffetard, 75005; Metro: Censier Daubenton.*
I had to include this little Asian deli, because it never fails to win high praises from kids. You can choose from a wide assortment of grilled skewers, steamed dumplings, and dishes such as cashew chicken or sweet and sour pork.
LA MAISON DES TARTES, *67, Rue Mouffetard, 75005; Metro: Place Monge.*
This shop specializes in both sweet and savory types of pies, with a wide assortment of quiches and fruit tarts.

GELATI D'ALBERTO, *45, Rue Mouffetard, 75005; Metro: Place Monge. Open daily in the summer, noon-midnight. Closed Mondays in Spring and Fall. Closed November-February.* The owner of this shop, Alberto, has been written up in numerous newspapers and magazines for daring to set up an Italian ice cream shop in the middle of Paris. It has been a big success. It seems that people can't resist his rose-shaped scoops of strawberry, wild currant, or even Nutella flavored ice cream.

Saint Germain des Près & Musée d'Orsay

HÔTEL DES MARRONNIERS***, *21, rue Jacob, 75006 Paris; Metro: Saint Germain des Près or Mabillon; Tel. 01 43 25 30 60; Fax 01 430 46 83 56; www.hotel-marronniers.com; Rates: €130-190 (double); €200-220 (triple); €240 (quadruple). Buffet breakfast: €12 downstairs or €14 rooms service.*

This hotel is located in the heart of Saint Germain des Près. To reach the entrance, you walk through a little courtyard filled with flowers and chestnut trees. Since it is set back from the street, the rooms are nice and quiet. The bathroom is stocked with Roger Gallet soaps. Some rooms have a view of the Saint Germain church. After a warm welcome at the front desk you proceed to your room, which can only be described as… unforgettable! It's hard to tell whether you've just stepped into the royal bedroom of the king's palace, or onto the theatrical set of some silly farce. Each room has a main color theme (like RED! or BLUE!). The decorators have had no fear of using an abundance of matching fabrics and wallpaper (even on the ceilings).

HÔTEL LEFT BANK – SAINT GERMAIN (**Best Western**) ***, *9, Rue de l'Ancienne Comédie, 75006 Paris; Metro: Odeon; Tel. 01 43 54 01 70; Fax 01 43 26 17 14; Email: lb@paris-hôtels-charm.com; book.bestwestern.com/bestwestern/priceAvail.do; Rates: €270-280 (doubles);*

€270-330 (triple). One child under 12 is free with 2 paying adults. Rates include buffet breakfast.

This hotel offers charm and a great location. It is situated in the heart of Saint Germain des Près. It is around the corner from the Rue de Buci street market, not far from the Luxembourg Gardens and Cluny Museum. You can walk to Nôtre Dame Cathedral, the Musée d'Orsay, or the Louvre. The rooms feature exposed wooden beams and antique furniture, and they are decorated in warm red and golden tones. From the upper floors there are beautiful views of the rooftops and church towers of Paris. Some of the adjacent double rooms can be set up as a 2-room suite.

HOTEL PERREYVE**, 63, Rue Madame, 7006 Paris. Tel. 01 45 48 35 01. Fax. 01 42 84 03 30. perreyve@clubinternet.fr Rates: €119.

The big advantage of this hotel is its location in a quiet side street right near the Luxembourg Gardens. The rates are also quite reasonable for this neighborhood. There is one triple room or you can choose two doubles next door to each other.

POLIDOR, 41, Rue Monsieur le Prince, 75006; Metro: Cluny – la Sorbonne or RER: Luxembourg; Tel. 01 43 26 95 34; Open daily for lunch and dinner.

This restaurant has been around for over 150 years and continues to provide good food at a reasonable price in a friendly atmosphere. You sit at big, family-style tables covered with red-checkered table clothes. The food is traditional French fare, paté, hâchis parmentier (ground beef with mashed potatoes), boeuf bourguignon (beef stew), ham and lentils, stuffed cabbage, salmon steak, and more. There are dinner menus for €22 and €32. Daily specials run €11-15. There are two down sides. They do not accept credit cards, and the restroom is the old-fashioned hole in the ground style.

LA TABLE D'AUDE, 8, Rue de Vaugirard, 75006 Paris; Metro: Odeon or RER: Luxembourg. Open Tues-Fri, Closed in August.

This jolly restaurant caters to every age group. It offers specialties from southwestern France, and is most famous for its cassoulet – a casserole composed of white beans, sausages and pork meats, and vegetables. Dinner runs €30-40.

RESTAURANT DU MUSÉE D'ORSAY, Level 2 of the Musée d'Orsay; Metro:Solférino; Open Tues-Sun, for lunch, 11:30am-2:30 pm. Thurs, open for dinner. Tea and snacks offered from 3pm-5:30pm. Closed Mon.

If your child has never eaten in a fancy restaurant this might be a good place to start. The soaring ceiling, big mirrors, and golden details recall the days when Orsay was a train station with a luxury hotel and dining room.

Yet it is family friendly, so it's a good place for kids to practice their good restaurant behavior. The lunch menu includes a main course and dessert for €16.50. The kid's menu offers a choice of ham or fish, plus ice cream and a drink for €8. Thursday evenings, when the museum is open late, there's a dinner menu for €42.

Note: The Musée d'Orsay also has a nice (though often crowded) café on Level 5, called the **CAFÉ DES HAUTEURS.** There are sandwiches, quiches, salads, and snacks for afternoon tea. It offers a remarkable view of the reverse side of one of the building's giant clocks. A snack bar is located on Level 6.

CAFÉ MINOTTI, *33, Rue de Verneuil, 75007 (Metro: Solférino); Open daily for lunch and dinner.*

This airy, friendly restaurant is a great place to stop after hours of wandering through the Musée d'Orsay or Saint Germain neighborhood. Legend has it that the Three Musketeers lived down the street. If they were around today, they would undoubtedly approve of this restaurant. The food is very fresh and delicious. The secret here is good, basic ingredients that change regularly to reflect the seasons. For example in summer you might choose the chilled ratatouille or melted goat cheese salad. There are simple omelets, sandwiches, and pasta dishes to please kids' tastes. The chef will adapt a selection to your child's tastes, too. Menus range from €27-33.

LE CAFÉ DES LETTRES, *53, Rue de Verneuil, 75007; Tel. 01 42 22 52 17; Metro: Solferino; Closed Sun. evening.*

This Swedish restaurant is filled with books and decorated with paintings by young, local artists. It is in the same building as the *Maison des Lettres* where writers and Nobel Laureates come to meet. In nice weather you can eat in the outdoor courtyard, well away from street noise and traffic. The menu features plenty of smoked salmon, herring, and shrimp. There are also salads, sandwiches, and our kids' favorite: Swedish meatballs. On Sunday, there is a smorgasbord brunch from 12 to 4 pm. Main courses a la carte run between €15-30. Daily specials at €15 and €20. Sunday brunch is €25.

Light Fare

GRANDE EPICERIE IN THE AU BON MARCHÉ DEPART-MENT STORE, *22, Rue de Sèvres, 75007 Paris. Metro: Sevres-Babylone; Open Mon-Sat.*

On the ground level of this historic department store (the first in the world) you will find a huge assortment of gourmet foods. There are several deli and bakery counters where you can get prepared foods. There are also plenty of packaged delights for a snack or to take home as gifts. While you are here, take your children to the 3 Hiboux section in the basement. It is filled with kids' crafts, games, and toys.

POILÂNE, *8, Rue du Chèrche Midi, 75006 Paris; Metro: Saint Sulpice or Saint Germain des Près; Open Mon-Sat.*

This may be the most famous bakery in Paris, thanks to Lionel Poilâne's dark, round bread. You can get open-faced sandwiches on Poilâne bread in many fancy cafés around the city, but here you get it straight from the oven. The pastries and other varieties of bread are also excellent.

PETIT HONG KONG, *1 Rue Haute Feuille, 75006 Paris. Metro: St. Michel*

This is one of many Asian delis that you see all over Paris. It gets a mention here because of the convenient location, wide choice, and fact that it is a hit with kids. You can eat in or take out and have a picnic in the nearby Luxembourg Gardens.

PIERRE HERMÉ, *72, Rue Bonaparte, 75006 Paris. Metro: Mabillon or Saint Sulpice.*

A good address, especially known for its exotic ice cream flavors, such as lime with basil.

CHRISTIAN CONSTANT, *37, Rue d'Assas, 75006 Paris. Metro: Rennes.*

Another great address with irresistible pastries and a wide selection of delicious ice creams.

Montparnasse

HÔTEL DELAMBRE*, *35, Rue Delambre, 75014 Paris; Metro: Vavin or Edgar Quinet; Tel. 01 43 20 66 31; Fax 01 45 38 9176; www.delambre-paris-hotel.com; Email: hôtel@hôteldelambre.com. Rates: €90-180, depending on the room and available specials; buffet breakfast: €11 (free for kids under 12).*

This is a great little hotel. It is located in the heart of the Montparnasse neighborhood, with easy access to metro and buses. There are some wonderful rooms for families. We liked the L-shaped mini-suite on the top floor, under the gables with lovely views of the rooftops of Paris. There are also some nice adjoining double rooms on the lower floors. They are in short supply, however, so be sure to reserve well in advance of your trip. As an added convenience, there is a Laundromat next door to the hotel.

HÔTEL JARDIN LE BRÉA***, *14, Rue Bréa, 75006 Paris (Metro: Vavin or Nôtre Dame des Champs). Tel. 01 43 25 44 41; Fax 01 44 07 19 25; Email: brea.hôtel@wanadoo.fr; Rates: €162-222. Buffet breakfast: €13 (downstairs) or €15 (room service).*

This pretty hotel is located in the heart of Montparnasse and is only a 5-minute walk from the Luxembourg gardens. The lobby and rooms are decorated with taste and warm, Provençal colors. The rooms are divided into standard and superior categories, with the superior ones being a bit larger. All of them were renovated in the late 1990s, and they feature new bathrooms and air-conditioning. The rooms with two twin beds are definitely bigger than the ones with a double bed. There is a nice sunroom and attractive breakfast room. The Rue Bréa in which the hotel is located is lined with wonderful kids' stores.

A LA VILLA DES ARTISTES (Best Western)***, *9, Rue de la Grande Chaumière, 75006 Paris; (Metro: Vavin) near intersection of Boulevard Montparnasse and Boulevard Raspail; Tel. 01 43 26 60 86; Fax 01 43 54 73 70; www.villa-artistes.com. Rates: €159-220 for doubles or triples. Buffet breakfast: €11.*

This pretty hotel is very popular with American families. Maybe it's because the parents spent their Junior Year Abroad days in Reid Hall, 1 block away. Perhaps it's the combination of comfort and convenient location: you are in Montparnasse, surrounded by artists' studios, and a 5-minute walk to the Luxembourg Gardens. Yet you are set back from the hustle and noise of the nearby avenues. The hotel takes its name Villa des Artistes seriously. It helps promote contemporary painters with exhibits of their works. It is also decorated with reproductions of paintings from many of Montparnasses' great early 20th century painters. The rooms are separated into standard and deluxe categories. The main difference is that the deluxe rooms are air-conditioned and a bit bigger. There is a pretty little outdoor garden with a fountain where you can eat breakfast in warm weather.

HÔTEL DAGUÈRRE***, *94, Rue Daguèrre, 75014 Paris; Metro: Gaité or Denfert Rochereau; Tel. 01 43 22 43 54; Fax 01 43 20 66 84; Email:*

paris@hôteldaguerre.com; Rates: €85 E (single); €110 (double); €120 (3-person suite). Buffet breakfast: €11.

This hotel recently had a face lift. It is located down the street from a little toy store (Les Cousins d'Alice) and a few blocks from the part of the Rue Daguèrre that is reserved for pedestrians and an open-air market. You are a bit off the beaten path here, but close to Montparnasse, the Catacombes and numerous subway and bus lines. The hotel owners offer a warm welcome to families. The rooms are small, but nice, and you can ask for an extra bed.

RESTAURANT WADJA, *10, Rue de la Grande Chaumière, 75006 Paris; (Metro: Vavin); Tel. 01 46 33 02 02; Closed Sun all day and Mon lunch.*

I must confess that I used to eat here in my starving student days when the tables were set family style, and the waiters greeted you by tossing a big chunk of bread directly onto the table. Since then, the place has gone more upscale. Now you get things like salad with stingray; roasted chicken with olive polenta; and rhubarb pie. But the secret to its continued popularity is still the same: offer good food at a reasonable price. Menu prices range from €14 to €47. Each month, the restaurant features specialties from a different region of France.

LA COUPOLE, *102, Boulevard Montparnasse, 75014, Metro: Vavin or Montparnasse. Tel. 01 43 20 14 20. Open daily 8 am-1 am.*

This is a big, classic Paris icon. It was once a favorite haunt of the artists, writers, and dancers who made Montparnasse such an artistic haven

– Man Ray, Josephine Baker, Marc Chagall, Pablo Picasso, Ernest Hemingway, and many others whose spirit still lingers. The dining room columns are decorated with paintings in an early 20th century modern art style. It is quite kid-friendly and popular with families. Anyone celebrating a birthday gets a special tribute from the waiters, who turn down the lights and emerge from the kitchen singing Happy Birthday. The food is classic and reliable. The fixed priced menus are €18 for lunch and €35 for dinner, including a small carafe of wine. The kids' menu is €16 and includes a special kiddie cocktail, choice of main fish or meat-based dish, and choice of several desserts.

LA PATACRÊPE, *19, Rue Daguèrre, 75014 Paris; Metro: Denfert Rochereau; Tel. 01 43 20 20 79; Open daily except Monday evening; Menu: €10.*

This nice crêperie is located in a courtyard off of the pedestrian market street, Rue Daguèrre. It is decorated with pretty Breton paintings and ceiling fans. The menu offers an ample range of salads and crêpes, with a nice terrace for warm weather meals. You are far away from traffic, so restless children can move around safely between courses.

TY BREIZ, *52, Boulevard de Vaugirard, 75015 Paris; Metro: Montparnasse or Pasteur. Open for lunch and dinner. Closed Sun-Mon, and in August.*

This is reputed to be the best crêpe restaurant in Paris. It's also very family-friendly. It's also easy on the budget, count on €10-20 per person.

MAX POILANE, *29, Rue de l'Ouest, 75014. Metro: Gaité. Open Mon-Fri, 10-7.*

The Poilâne family has become famous for its delicious country-style bread. Here you can try it with a variety of hot and cold sandwiches. There are also salads and other snacks.

LES BONBONS, *6, Rue Bréa, 75006 Paris. Metro: Vavin. Closed on Mondays and in August.*

You'll feel like a kid in a candy shop!

Eiffel Tower & Champs de Mars

EIFFEL PARK (**Best Western**)***, *17 Bis, Rue Amélie, 75007 Paris; Metro: La Tour Maubeuge; Tel. 01 45 55 10 01; Fax 01 47 05 28 88; Email: reservation@eiffelpark.com; www.eiffelpark.com; Rates: €125-200 (double).Breakfast: €12.*

This hotel is situated in a nice, quiet street in the tony residential section of the 7th arrondissement. It is close to the Eiffel Tower and Invalides. You can go to the Pont Alexandre III and cross the Seine towards the Champs Elysées. The rooms are bright and airy. Each one is decorated differently, but tastefully. They are all air-conditioned. The upper floor rooms have lovely views over the rooftops of Paris. There is a cozy breakfast room, or you can eat on the terrace in nice weather. Some of the adjacent double rooms can be connected and made into a 2-room suite.

ALTITUDE 95, *Level 1, Eiffel Tower; Metro: Bir Hakeim or RER: Champs de Mars – Tour Eiffel; Tel. 01 45 55 20 04; Open daily for lunch and dinner.[Note: You should make a reservation if you are visiting during high tourist seasons. You can either call ahead or make a reservation at the Altitude 95 kiosk at the foot of the tower. With a lunch or dinner reservation, you can access the tower's elevators without having to stand in line for tickets.]*

This is the less formal and less expensive of the Tower's restaurants. It's worth going just for the view and the experience!! Unfortunately, Altitude 95 has been under renovation, and as of the printing of this book is scheduled to reopen March 20, 2009. In the past the food was good, and the service was very kid friendly. Let's hope that part doesn't change. It's certainly worth a try.

Invalides

HÔTEL DE TURENNE**, *20, Avenue de Tourville, 75007 Paris; Metro: Ecole Militaire, Invalides, or La Tour Maubeuge; Tel. 01 47 05 99 92; Fax 01 45 56 06 04; Email: hôtel.turenne.paris7@wanadoo.fr; Rates: €80-90(double); €110 (triple). Continental breakfast: €8.*

This very affordable hotel offers a friendly welcome in a cozy atmosphere. The rooms are small and not luxurious, but they are quite pleasant – some even have a view of the Eiffel Tower. The owners are happy to accommodate families, adding a bed to one of their larger rooms, or offering adjoining rooms with a common door. The hotel is located between the Eiffel Tower (and its large Champs de Mars park) and the Invalides and Rodin Museum in a very pleasant residential area. There are plenty of metros and buses to take you all over the city.

HÔTEL LE PAVILLON**, *54, Rue Saint Dominique, 75007 Paris; Metro: Latour Maubeuge or Invalides; Tel. 01 45 51 42 87; Fax; 01 45 51 32 79; Email: PatrickPavillon@aol.com. Rates: €100-130 (double); €135-180 (family triple or quad). Buffet breakfast: €11.*

This pleasant little hotel is tucked away in a courtyard off the main road. It is situated in a lovely residential neighborhood between the Eiffel Tower and Invalides. The welcome is very friendly and homey. The rates are quite reasonable. In warm weather you can have breakfast in the hotel's little garden. The rooms are not luxurious, but they are comfortable and tastefully decorated. Two of them are large enough for a family of four.

LES JARDINS DE VARENNE CAFÉ, *in the Rodin Museum, 77, Rue de Varenne, 75007 Paris; Metro: Varenne; Closed Mondays and from January through March.*

This is a lovely place to have lunch, even if you are not planning to visit the Rodin Museum. You can enjoy the gardens, filled with famous sculptures by Rodin, for €1 per adult (kids are free). The café proposes a large assortment of salads and sandwiches (€6-7). There is also a daily hot plate special. For dessert there is a nice assortment of tarts and ice cream. When you are done with your food, the kids can frolic among the sculptures.

Les Halles

AU TONNEAU DES HALLES, *28, Rue Montorgueil, 75001 Paris. Metro: Les Halles. Tel. 01 42 33 36 19. Open non-stop 7am-11pm. Closed Sun.*

This restaurant is an old Les Halles institution. It was around in the days when the wholesale food workers in Les Halles would stop in for an onion soup, piece of wild boar, and glass of Beaujolais wine. You can still get good, traditional French food here. Count on €20-40 for a meal. In the summer you can eat on the terrace situated along the lively pedestrian street market of the Rue Montorgueil.

CHEZ CLOVIS, *33, Rue Berger (corner Rue des Prouvaires), 75001 Paris. Metro: Les Halles (west of the Forum des Halles); Tel. 01 42 33 97 07; Open for lunch and dinner. Closed Sunday.*

Another Les Halles institution, this restaurant serves good, traditional French food at reasonable prices. There are traces of the former Les Halles meat markets in the old photographs on the walls. You can also get a feel for them in some of the dishes such as andouillette sausages, beef stew, pheasant terrine, and salad with warm chicken livers. There is also lighter fare with choices of soups and salads. The lunch menu is 18. Dinner runs around €30-60.

Light Fare

NILS', *36, Rue Montorgueil, 75001 Paris; Metro: Les Halles or Etienne Marcel; Open daily for lunch and dinner.*

You can eat in or buy take-out food in this pleasant Scandinavian restaurant. Located in the jolly, Rue Montorgueil market street, Nils' offers interesting sandwiches, salads, meatballs, and hotdogs. It's good kid food — and not bad for adults. The price is right, too. A sandwich, drink, and dessert will set you back less than €10. Kids can get a meatball sandwich, dessert muffin, and drink for €5.

STÖHRER, *51, Rue Montorgueil, 75002 Paris; Metro: Etienne Marcel or Les Halles. Open daily 7:30 am-8:30 pm. Closed last two weeks in August.* The original Mr. Stöhrer was a royal baker who came from Austria to accompany Queen Marie Antoinette in the late 1700s. His pastries were a huge hit, and the shop continues to faithfully produce the same quality that was fit for a queen. You can also get nice sandwiches, quiches, and salads.

Louvre

HÔTEL MOLIÈRE***, *21, Rue Molière, 75001 Paris; Metro: Pyramides or Palais Royal; Tel. 01 42 96 22 01; Fax 01 42 60 48 68; Email: moliere@worldnet.fr; www.hotels-exclusive.com/hotels/moliere/; Rates: €165-190 (double); €195-200 (triple); €300 (4-person suite). Extra bed: €18. Buffet breakfast or continental room service breakfast: €14.*

This pretty hotel is located in a side street between the Palais Royal gardens and Avenue de l'Opéra. It is named for one of France's greatest playwrights, who died on stage at the nearby *Comédie Française* after a performance of his show, The Imaginary Invalid. The hotel's rooms are all air-conditioned, comfortable, and tastefully decorated. The 2-room suite can comfortably sleep four people. The staff is friendly and helpful. The location is very central and convenient to many of the major sights of Paris. You are just a block from the Palais Royal gardens where little ones can unwind.

HÔTEL LONDRES SAINT-HONORÉ**, *13, Rue Saint Roch, 75001 Paris; Tel. 01 42 60 15 62; Fax 01 42 60 16 00; Email: hôtel.londres.st.honoré@gofornet.com; Metro: Pyramides or Tuileries. Rates: €105-140 (double); €160 (triple); €180 (quadruple); €300 (suite) Continental breakfast: €9.*

This hotel offers very friendly service, in a central location, at a good price. They even allow dogs. It's near the Tuileries Gardens, Louvre, and Palais Royal Gardens. The rooms are small, but have modern bathrooms, TVs, a hair dryer, and a minibar. Some of them are air-conditioned.

TOUPARY, *5th floor and rooftop terrace, Samaritaine Department Store 2, Quai du Louvre, 75001 Paris; Metro: Pont Neuf; Tel. 01 40 41 29 29; Lunch: Noon-3pm; Tea Room: 3:30pm-6pm; Dinner: 7:30pm-11:30pm. Closed Sunday.* This restaurant is famous for its wonderful views of the city. You are right on the Seine, overlooking the Pont Neuf, with Nôtre Dame Cathedral to your left and the Eiffel Tower on your right. It's pretty spectacular. What's more, the food is excellent. The lunch menus run €20-30, including a glass of wine. Dinner a la carte will run you about €40-50.

If you are not up for a restaurant meal, you can also enjoy breakfast or lunch in the Samaritaine's café called Les Sands. It is also on the 5th floor, with fine views of the city. Here you can order simple meals, such as salads and sandwiches.

UNIVERSAL RESTAURANT – FOOD COURT, *Located in the underground shopping section of the Louvre complex; 99, rue de Rivoli, 75001 Paris; Metro: Louvre Rivoli or Palais Royal.*

This food court offers a choice of take-out stands from all over the world. American children feel right at home here, and adults appreciate the fact that there is something for everyone. This is where one of our teenage friends decided to start his comparison test of American and French soft drinks. Evidently, a French Coca Cola doesn't taste the same as an American one. Test it out for yourself.

Light Fare

CAFÉ DENON, *On the outdoor terrace of the Denon Wing of the Louvre Museum, Level 1 (around the corner from Géricault's Raft of the Medusa). Metro: Louvre Rivoli or Palais Royal. Open for lunch and tea, 10am-5pm.*

This café offers light sandwiches, hotdogs, and salads. The food is okay, but the main attraction is the location. If the weather is nice, you can sit outside on the terrace, where you can peer through giant statues down onto the Louvre's glass pyramid. The **Café Richelieu** in the opposite wing of the museum also offers light lunch, tea, and great views.

CAFÉS IN THE TUILERIES GARDENS. *Metro: Tuileries. Open daily, noon-11:30 pm.*

There are four different cafés in the gardens. Each has outdoor seating under the chestnut trees, and some have indoor seating, as well. Offerings include sandwiches, salads, hot dogs, and usually a few hot dishes. The location is ideal. Well away from traffic, plenty of room for kids to run around, and a great place to rest weary feet.

CAFÉ DE LA COMÉDIE, *157, Rue Saint Honoré, 75001 Paris (across from Comédie Française Theater and Palais Royal garden entrance); Metro: Palais Royal.*

We like this café for its great location between the Louvre and Palais Royal. It is on a little square, Place Colette, across a funny modern entrance to the Palais Royal metro station. There is the usual café assortment of salads, sandwiches, omelets, hotdogs, pizza, quiche, steak with fries, and more. What's surprising is the freshness of the ingredients and quality of the desserts. When you're fed and rested you can check out the nice bookstore next door; go across the street to the Palais Royal gardens; head up the Avenue de l'Opéra to tour the Opera House; explore the Louvre; or hop into the metro for a ride to the Champs Elysées.

LA FERME, *55, Rue Saint Roch, 75001 Paris; Metro: Pyramides; Closed Sunday.*

This gourmet take-out place features fresh, organic foods. You pick up a basket and choose from a selection of sandwiches, salads, quiches, yogurt, fruit, fresh-squeezed juices, and more. Prices range from 2-5 per item. You can eat there, or enjoy a picnic in the Tuileries or Palais Royal gardens.

ANGELINA'S, *226, Rue de Rivoli, 75001 Paris; Metro: Tuileries.*

This is one of Paris' most classic tearooms, where generations of children have been rewarded for good behavior with a thick cup of hot chocolate and fabulous pastries. The décor is Paris circa 1900. They also offer quiches, salads, and sandwiches. Just make sure you save room for dessert. Note that the lines to get in can become long, but it's worth the wait.

Marais

HÔTEL DU 7IÈME ART★★, *20, Rue Saint Paul, 75004 Paris; Metro: Saint Paul or Sully Morland; Tel. 01 44 54 85 00; Fax 01 42 77 69 10;*

Email: hôtel7art@wanadoo.fr; Rates: €85-145 (double); €135-165 (triple); €185 (quadruple). Continental breakfast: €8. This is a fun hotel, and one of the few family-friendly establishments we could find in the Marais. The owners are very welcoming to their younger guests. The entire place is decorated with old movie posters and paraphernalia (the 7th art = cinema). The top floor room under the rafters is large enough to accommodate up to 4 people. There are also double rooms that can be connected with communicating doors. Guests can use the hotel's laundry room: a real plus! There is a large breakfast room that also serves tea and snacks in the afternoon. The hotel is located in the heart of the Marais. It's a real find, but book your rooms early, because they fill up quickly.

HÔTEL DE LA PLACE DES VOSGES**, *12, Rue de Birague, 75004 Paris; Metro: St. Paul or Bastille. Tel. 01 42 72 60 46; Fax 01 42 72 02 64. Rates: starting at €90 (double or triple); €150 (family room). Baby beds available.*

This hotel is right near the lovely Place des Vosges. In the 1600s the building was a stable. You can still see wooden beams and old stone walls. Today it offers nice clean rooms at a reasonable price, with touches of charm, and a pretty lobby.

MARC ANNIBAL DE COCONNAS, *2 bis, Place des Vôsges, 75004; Tel. 01 42 78 58 16; Open for lunch and dinner. Closed Mondays.*

This restaurant is situated right under the arcades of the Place des Vôsges. The food is excellent and not all that expensive considering the locality (lunch menus are €25 and €32, dinner is about €55). Summer appetizers may include salmon tartar; warm goat cheese on salad; and tomatoes with pesto and mozzarella. The main course offerings include such things as grilled Gambas, leg of lamb, and lobster. Dessert includes such choices as fresh pastry with strawberries, roasted figs, or raspberry crumble. When the weather is nice you can eat outside, where you can watch over the gardens of the Place des Vôsges. The park's playground is just across the street.

RESTAURANT CARUSO, *3, Rue de Turenne, 75004 Paris; Metro: Saint Paul or Filles du Calvaire; Tel. 01 48 87 47 74. Open daily for lunch and dinner.*

This Italian restaurant is a favorite among the neighborhood locals. Kids like the nice selection of pizzas, fresh pasta, and risotto dishes (€12-14). Adults can enjoy antipasti, and exotic dishes such as pasta cooked in black, squid ink. Daily specials are about €14. There are also special lunch and dinner menus that vary with the season.

Light Fare

DAME TARTINE, *2, Rue Brisemiche (across from the Stravinsky Fountain by the Pompidou Center), 75004 Paris; Metro: Hôtel de Ville or Rambuteau.*

This restaurant offers interesting salads and sandwiches made on wonderful Poilane bread. The prices are very reasonable (€10- €15) and the location is excellent. You are on a pedestrian square, next to the Pompidou Center and across from the delightful Stravinsky Fountain. It's a great spot to keep kids entertained. The fountain will keep your children amused for quite a while. To your left is the Saint Merri Church with its wonderful gargoyles, just ready to spit water towards you if it rains.

LE LOIR DANS LA THÉIÈRE, *3, Rue des Rosiers, 75004 Paris; 01 42 72 90 61; Open daily.*

Famous for its cushy chairs, light fare, and weekend brunches, you can choose from a selection of salads, pasta dishes, quiches, and omelets. There also are yummy cakes and pastries. It's friendly, affordable and offers a calm haven in the bustling center of the Marais neighborhood.

SACHA FINKELSZTAJN, *27, Rue des Rosiers, 75004 Paris; Metro: Saint Paul or Pont Marie; Closed Tuesday.*

This store has been in the Finkelsztajn family for three generations. It was originally just a bakery, but over the years they have added more and more deli items, too. You can stay for a bite or buy take out food. We always seem to end up here for dessert or a snack. There are plenty of delicious treats featuring apples and raisins. You can also try different types of cheesecakes. They are not like the typical New York variety we generally see in the US, but are well worth tasting.

MI-VA-MI, *23, Rue des Rosiers, 75004 Paris; Metro: Saint Paul or Pont Marie. Closed Sat.*

In the 1950s and 1960s there was an influx of Jewish immigrants to Paris from North Africa. As a result, you can get excellent kosher food in this traditionally Jewish neighborhood. This shop offers delicious falafel and pita sandwiches of various types. You can sit inside at the few tables or order take-out.

JADIS ET GOURMANDE, *39, Rue des Archives, 75004, Metro: Rambuteau.*

This shop is filled with chocolates that not only taste wonderful but also look beautiful. There are chocolate pianos, chocolate coins, and chocolate letters that you can pick to spell out the names of your loved ones. There are also creatively attractive gift boxes.

Bastille

BRASSERIE BOFINGER, *5 and 7 Rue de la Bastille, 75004 Paris; Metro: Bastille; Tel. 01 42 72 87 82; Fax 01 42 72 97 68; Open daily, 12pm-3pm, 6:30pm-1am (non-stop on weekends).*

This is a beautiful restaurant, a Paris classic, and a fun place to take kids who can enjoy a fancy meal. As with several other classic Parisian bistrots, this one is now managed by the Flo Restaurant chain. The food is no longer as spectacular as it once was but it is good and reliable. Make sure you show your children the beautiful Tiffany style sky-

light in one of the dining rooms. Upstairs there are paintings by Hansi, a famous Alsatian artist, depicting scenes of village life in Alsace. There is a special kids menu.

If you or your children are not quite up for the full Bofinger experience, you might want to try the **Petit Bofinger Restaurant** across the street. This bîstrot offers a 1950s decor, and plenty of excellent food at slightly more moderate prices.

RESTAURANT DE PÂTES LUSTUCRU, *3, Rue du Faubourg Saint Antoine, 75011 Paris; Metro: Bastille. Tel. 01 44 67 44 67. Open daily.*

How kid-friendly can you get? Here is a whole 2-story restaurant devoted to pasta. Lustucru is a popular brand of pasta in French supermarkets, and now they've branched out into the restaurant business. It clearly targets the family market with lots of high chairs and lamps that look like eggs. There are plenty of pasta offerings – you can even order chocolate or banana ravioli for dessert. Prices are very reasonable – €12- €16 for various combinations of appetizers, main course, and dessert.

DALLOYAU, *5, Boulevard Beaumarchais, 75004 Paris, Metro: Bastille. Closed Mon, and August.*

Although you can get wonderful pastries all over Paris, this remains one of the city's best known addresses for fine pastry. Judge for yourself. The tearoom is upstairs.

RAIMO, *59-61, Boulevard de Reuilly, near the Jardin de Reuilly, 75012 Paris; Metro: Daumesnil.*
This is a great stop if you are strolling along the *Promenade Plantée.* There are over 50 flavors of ice cream and sorbet to choose from (and you thought Baskin Robbins was tough with 31). Some are very exotic, such as cinnamon, maple syrup, tea, or chestnut.

Champs Elysées

HÔTEL DU COLISÉE (Best Western)***, *6, Rue du Colisée, 75008 Paris; Metro: Franklin Roosevelt; Tel. 01 56 88 26 26; Fax 01 56 88 26 00; Email: info@bw-colisée.com; Rates: €220-267 (double); €287 (triple). Buffet breakfast: €15.*
This hotel is conveniently located near the Champs Elysées, Arc de Triomphe, Place de la Concorde, and Tuileries Gardens. The rooms are tastefully decorated and are all air-conditioned. They are all doubles, but you can ask for an extra bed, or two rooms next to each other. Some are reserved for non-smokers.

SPICY, *8, Avenue Franklin Roosevelt, 75008 Paris, Metro: Franklin Roosevelt. Tel. 01 56 59 62 59.*
This is a good address for fresh and interesting fare. It is close to the Champs Elysées, but somewhat removed from the heavy tourist scene of the avenue. The décor is hip and modern. You get a nice assortment of appetizers and main courses, such as pasta with olive tapenade sauce, roasted chicken with chutney, or catch of the day with baby vegetables. The €36 menu includes appetizer, main course, dessert (chocolate muffins, for example), and coffee. There is a kid's menu for €15 and a Sunday brunch for €36 with family-friendly entertainment.

THE CHICAGO PIZZA FACTORY, *5, Rue de Berri, 75008 Paris; Metro: George V; Tel. 01 45 62 50 23; Fax 01 45 63 87 56.*
Okay, it's not very French, but this restaurant is a good alternative to the over-priced fast food joints along the Avenue des Champs Elysées. American kids will feel right at home with the decor and menu offerings. It's very kid-friendly and the price is right: €11 and €17 for pizzas, with various menu options, as well.

FLAM'S, *16, Rue du Colisée, 75008; Tel. 01 45 62 84 82; Metro: Franklin Roosevelt.*
This restaurant is part of a chain that features Alsacian-style food. The main offering is Flammenkeuche - a sort of white pizza with bacon, cheese,

and onions. There are also salads and sandwiches. The food is decent and prices very attractive.

PAUL, *51, Avenue Franklin Roosevelt (corner Rue de Pontheiu), 75008; Metro: Franklin Roosevelt. Open daily.*

This large, bright bakery is just off the Rond Point des Champs Elysées. It features very nice pizzas, quiches, fresh fruit juice, and other delicious snacks. It is a great place to stop if you want breakfast, a light meal, or a snack as an alternative to the fast food chains along the Avenue des Champs Elysées. If the weather is good, you can take your food and enjoy a picnic in the gardens between the Rond Point and Place de la Concorde.

Opéra/Grands Boulevards

HÔTEL CHOPIN**, *10, Boulevard Montmartre (in the Passage Jouffroy), 75009 Paris; Metro: Grands Boulevards; Tel. 01 47 70 58 10; Fax 01 42 47 00 70; Rates: €88-102 (double); €120 (triple). Extra bed: free. Buffet breakfast: €7.*

This hotel is utterly charming and located in a wonderful spot. You actually go into one of Paris' pretty 19th century shopping galleries to get to the hotel entrance. Called the Passage Jouffroy, it features wonderful shops and tearooms to delight you and your kids. The gallery also contains Paris' wax museum, the Musée Grévin. The hotel has lovely rooms, especially on the top floor. Some are surprisingly spacious considering the price and class of hotel. You get views over the rooftops and skylights of the Passage Jouffroy. It's an experience unique to Paris that you will neither regret nor forget. Book in advance, however, because the rooms fill up quickly.

TERRACE CAFÉ, GALÉRIES LAFAYETTE DEPARTMENT STORE, *Rooftop Terrace; 40, Boulevard Haussman, 75009 Paris; Metro: Chaussée d'Antin. Open May-Sept, Mon-Sat, for late breakfast, lunch, and afternoon snack.*

This café offers nice pizzas, salads, sandwiches, pasta, and other light fare. The food is pretty good, but what you really come here for is the view. What a panorama it is! You can see most of the city, including a close-up view of the Palais Garnier Opera House roof and straight shot of Sacré Coeur Basilica on top of Montmartre.

TOP FLOOR CAFÉTERIA, LE PRINTEMPS DEPARTMENT STORE, *64, Boulevard Haussman, 75009 Paris; Metro: Havre Caumartin. Open Mon-Sat.*

If it is the wrong time of year or if the weather is too bad to eat at the Terrace Café in the Galéries Lafayette, head on over to this cafeteria. There is a wide selection of hot and cold platters, including a big salad bar. The dining room has big windows overlooking the Paris Opera and rooftops of the city. It's not as spectacular as the Galéries Lafayette terrace, but it's a close second.

LA PETITE RIPAILLE, *6, Passage des Panoramas, 75002 Paris; Tel. 01 53 40 83 15; Metro: Grands-Boulevards; Closed Sunday and Monday.*

This restaurant, located in one of Paris' wonderful XIXth century shopping galleries, offers good French fare at very reasonable prices. There are nice quiches and savory tortes. The €18 menu features an appetizer, main course, and glass of house wine.

Light Fare
BUFFET DE LA COMTESSE, *13, Rue Taitbout, 75009 Paris; Metro: Chaussée d'Antin or Richelieu Drouot; Tel. 01 44 83 03 03. Open Mon-Fri.*

The original Comtesse du Barry shops were known for their foie gras and fancy bon bons. Here, you can sample the gourmet treats and eat in. It's very refined: for example, foie gras on thin slices of toast accompanied with fine green beans and artichoke hearts. The desserts are pretty yummy, too. And because the French see babies as gourmets-in-training, this place is also very kid-friendly. They actually provide high chairs.

LE VALENTIN, *30-32, Passage Jouffroy, 75009 Paris; Metro: Grands Boulevards; Tel. 01 47 70 88 50. Open daily.*

This charming tearoom sells delicious pastries and light meals inside one of Paris' wonderful 19th century shopping galleries. There are salads and sandwiches, as well as a daily hot-plate special. Kids can chose between ham and grilled chicken with mashed potatoes as part of their special menu.

A LA MÈRE DE FAMILLE, *35, Rue Du Faubourg Montmartre, 75009, Metro: Grands Boulevards, Open Tues-Sat, 8:30am-1:30pm, 3pm-7pm.*

This is one of Paris' oldest candy shops. It features not only mouth-watering chocolates, but also many candy special-ties from all over France. Pick some up as gifts to bring back home – if you can resist eating them all up yourselves.

Trocadéro & Passy

HÔTEL PASSY EIFFEL***, *10, Rue de Passy, 75016 Paris; Metro: Passy; Tel. 01 45 25 55 66; Fax 01 42 88 89 88; Email: passyeiffel@wanadoo.fr; Website: www.passyeiffel.com/index-gb.htm Rates: €185 (double); €230 (triple); €250 (4-person suite). Extra bed or crib provided free of charge. Buffet breakfast: €11.*

This hotel offers a very warm welcome to families. There are several, lovely family-sized suites. When those are booked, they will offer to put families in 2 adjoining doubles (with communicating doors) for the price of a suite. All of the rooms have air-conditioning and some have a view of the Eiffel Tower. The hotel is located in the lively Rue de Passy, filled with fun shopping, nice cafés, and an open-air market. You are a stone's throw from the Trocadéro Museums, and within easy access to the Eiffel Tower, Ranelagh Gardens, and Musée Marmottan with its collection of Monet paintings.

BÎSTROT DES VIGNES, *1, Rue Jean de Boulogne (between Rue de Passy and Rue de l'Annonciation); Metro: Passy; Closed on Sundays and in August.*

This restaurant offers delicious, traditional French fare at reasonable prices. Appetizers include choices such as shrimp and grapefruit salad; poached egg with sorrel and smoked salmon; zucchini and eggplant casserole with goat cheese. Main courses feature grilled fish on a bed of fennel; rabbit in mustard sauce; roasted chicken and potatoes; pasta with pesto. Top it all off with a fruit sorbet, chocolate mousse, fresh fruit tart, or cooked pear with ice cream and chocolate sauce. The menus range from €15-€22.

RESTAURANT IN THE MUSÉE D'ART MODERNE DE LA VILLE DE PARIS, *11, Avenue du Président Wilson, 75016 Paris; Metro: Iéna; Open 10am-6pm. Closed Mon.*

When the weather is nice, you can eat on the big terrace next to the museum with a splendid view of the Seine River. You can choose from an assortment of fresh salads, sandwiches, quiches, and cold meat plates.

COFFEE PARISIEN, *7, Rue Gustave Courbet, 75016 Paris; Tel. 01 45 53 17 17; Metro: Trocadéro; Open daily, noon-midnight.*

This is a French version of an American-style diner. The décor and menu look American, but there is also a French twist. You can get American staples, such as chicken wings, nachos, hot club sandwiches, and tuna salad. Then there's salmon tartar, avocado and grapefruit salad, and tarte tatin (French version of apple pie). It's a good Franco-American combination in a nice, relaxed atmosphere. Count on €10-€16 for main courses.

TARTE JULIE, *14, Rue de l'Annonciation, 75016 Paris; Metro: Passy.*

This little restaurant/take out place offers a wide array of yummy quiches (lorraine, zucchini, spinach, feta and basil, salmon, etc). There are also salads, gratinées, and fruit pies. A kid's menu proposes a quiche, drink, and ice cream for €8. Adults can have a slice of quiche, drink, and coffee for €7. Add a dessert, and it's €9. A combination salad, drink, and dessert will cost you €10.

Montmartre

HÔTEL UTRILLO**, *7, Rue Aristide Bruant, 75018 Paris (Metro: Abbesses or Blanche); Tel. 01 42 58 13 44; Fax 01 42 23 93 88; Email: adel.utrillo@wanadoo.fr; Website: www.hotel-paris-utrillo.com/; Rates: €90-95 (double); €110 (triple); Extra bed: €12; Buffet Breakfast: €7. Preferential rates offered on-line.*

This cheerful hotel is comfortably nestled towards the bottom of the Montmartre hill. The rooms are tastefully decorated in bright colors to celebrate the hotel's name (Maurice Utrillo was a Montmartre painter) and artistic history of the neighborhood. There's a warm welcome and even a sauna.

RELAIS DE LA BUTTE, *Corner of Rue des Trois Frères and Rue Ravignan, on the Place Emile Godeau; 75018 Paris; Metro: Abbesses.*

This is a fun restaurant, especially in the summer when you can eat outside on the pretty terrace. It is just off a quiet square where children can run between courses. On the upper half of the square is the historic Bateau Lavoir building where Picasso, Modigliani, Juan Gris, and many other artists and poets lived for next to nothing. The original building was destroyed in a fire in 1970, but was rebuilt according to the original plans. It still houses starving artists. The restaurant serves up fresh salads, pasta dishes, daily specials, and Italian-style desserts at very reasonable prices. The daily menu runs about 16: main courses €12-€15.

RESTO ZÈBRE, *38, rue Lepic, 75018 Paris; Metro: Blanche or Abbesses. Open Mon-Sat.*

This lively little place is tucked along the jolly Rue Lepic. It attracts lots of locals who come to enjoy a light salad, pasta dish, or daily specials such as grilled tuna and onglet de boeuf. Prices are very reasonable.

LA BUTTE GLACÉE. *14, Rue Norvins, 75018 Paris (near Place du Tèrtre); Metro: Abesses.*

A great place to stop for ice cream or sorbet, with all sorts of tantalizing fruit flavors.

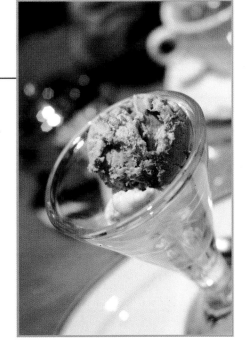

PART TWO: PLANNING YOUR TRIP

Traveling with kids, especially very small children, can involve a lot of stuff. I used to pride myself on traveling with bags that were so compact I could carry them long distances and never had to check my luggage. That ended when we took our first-born son to Paris as a 7-month old. Suddenly we had a stroller, car seat, porta-crib, diaper bag, favorite teddy bear, toys, baby snacks, and full supply of pint-size clothes. Thankfully, as our boys got bigger, the amount of stuff they needed got smaller. They also started pulling their own roller-board suitcases. From ages 3-6 they used kid-size suitcases. Now if we have a trip lasting 1-2 weeks, we all use the size that can fit in the overhead compartment of a plane (12" X 20").

Most children like to pack or help pack their own bags. It is exciting and empowering. Just make sure that you maintain supervision authority (and if needed, veto power). Once they are done, go through a checklist together to ensure they haven't forgotten anything important.

When packing, try to remember that **less is better**. No matter how many times you expect to find an elevator or luggage cart, there will those when you are the one who has to lift or carry your suitcases. You will have a hard time finding a cab if you have lots of gear, and big bags will take up a lot of space in your hotel or apartment room (generally small anyway by American standards).

If your trip includes airplane travel, be sure to bring enough toiletries, medicine, clothing (such as a fresh shirt and set of socks and underwear), and necessities in your carry-on luggage to last you an extra day. This will see you through if your plane or suitcases are delayed. If you are traveling with a baby or small children pack several sets of clothes, a blanket, snacks, small toys and other entertainment, and a 2-day supply of diapers and wipes in your carry-on luggage to get through the flight and first day.

Note that other than special medications, most things you will need are readily available in Paris.

Parent Tip: Small toys and activities will help make the plane trip and down time more fun. Some suggestions:

- Teenie-beenies and other small stuffed animals
- Micro-machines, Polly Pocket, Legos, beads, and other small toys. Carry them in Ziploc bags.
- Small pads of paper, art supplies, stickers, activity books
- Travel versions of chess, checkers, or other games
- Books on tape or CD and favorite music with a walkman, CD player, iPod
- Lightweight, paperback books. You may want to use this trip as an opportunity to introduce your kids to classic chapter books, such a *Charlotte's Web, From the Mixed Up Files of Mrs. Basil E. Frankweiller*, Harry Potter, the Chronicles of Narnia, or *A Series of Unfortunate Events*. �֍

Other useful items include:

Binoculars: Bring some for yourself and for your kids. They are very useful for looking at gargoyles and other faraway features.

Cameras: You will want pictures to remember your trip, so don't forget to bring along your camera or video recorder. Consider bringing cameras for your children, too. It's a great way to keep them engaged and looking at the sights around them.

When the trip is over, encourage your children to create an album using their favorite photos, post cards, ticket stubs, and other flat souvenirs. It makes a great keepsake, especially if they add notes or comments in the margins.

Art supplies: It's amazing how something as simple as a pad of paper and box of colored pencils, markers, or crayons can help while away the hours on a plane ride or waiting for the next course in a restaurant. If your children are budding artists they will find ample inspiration in Paris. They may want to copy something they see in a museum. Or like many painters before them, they can try their hand at drawing the Eiffel Tower, a view from the Pont des Arts, a pony from a carrousel, flowers in Monet's garden at Giverny, the list is endless...

If your children balk at the sight of a blank piece of paper you may want to bring such items as coloring books, fun pads, activity books, mazes and puzzles. You can also purchase nice examples of these in most of the major museum gift shops in Paris. They are useful for keeping growing minds busy anytime you want a breather or face a wait.

Travel diaries: Travel diaries are a great way for both parents and kids to record souvenirs and impressions of their trip. They don't need to be fancy, a small spiral notebook works well. You can also purchase special kids' diaries, travel diaries, or even kids' travel diaries at any major bookstore.

What to Know Before You Go

Passports: Each member of your family must have a valid passport to enter France. No visa is necessary for stays of less than three months. If you need to obtain or renew a passport for any member of your family, do not put it off until the last minute! It can take as many as 90 days or more to process – even longer if you need to obtain a copy of your birth certificate or other required proofs of citizenship or identity. Passport application forms and instructions are available at your local Passport Agency Office, county courthouse, some post offices, and some travel agencies. They are also accessible online at: *http://travel.state.gov/*, or you can get them via mail by calling the National Passport Information Center: Tel. 900/225-5674.

Remember that adult passports are valid for 10 years – **but children's passports are only valid for 5 years.**

Be sure to check the latest rules for children's passports, as they are subject to change.Information is available at: travel.state.gov/passport/geet/minors/minors_834.html.

• Any child under the age of 14 must have an application signed and presented by BOTH parents (or by one parent with a form and notarized signature from the other).

• Single parents or guardians must submit proof that a sole parent has custody or guardianship of that child.

• Even if you are renewing a child's passport and have the previous one with you, you also will be asked to present the child's birth certificate.

• Children's passport forms must be submitted in person at a designated post office or Passport Agency Office. Your child also must be present.

• Note that in some busy cities, you must call in advance for an appointment and may not get one for 2-3 weeks.

Climate: Although Paris is roughly on the same latitude as Fargo, North Dakota, the climate is much milder. Days are short in the winter, but gloriously long in the summer (in June the sun doesn't set until 10 pm). Winters are chilly, but temperatures do not dip much below freezing. The late fall and early spring can be quite rainy. Early fall and late spring are often sunny and pleasant. Summers are generally warm with occasional showers. Very hot weather is uncommon, which is lucky because it makes the city muggy and uncomfortable, and it raises pollution levels.

Customs & Fashion: French society tends be more formal than American. You will win major points by greeting people with a *Bonjour Monsieur* or *Bonjour Madame*, even if they are the only words of French you ever learn. If you do speak some rudiments of French, be sure to use the formal form "vous" rather than the informal "tu" with anyone other than close friends or children. If you are invited for dinner to someone's home, try not to arrive empty handed. A bouquet of flowers or box of chocolate is appropriate. If you know before you go that you will be visiting French people during your stay, you may want to bring something representing where you live. Examples could include a bottle of the local BBQ sauce, sports memorabilia from your local team, or a book of photographs featuring your hometown or state.

Clothing standards also tend to be a bit more formal in Paris. After all, it's one of the world's fashion capitals. As an adult you won't actually get kicked out of most places for wearing jeans, a t-shirt, and a baseball hat, but you will stand out (and do remember to remove your hat anytime you are indoors). Somehow, even when Parisians dress that way, they seem to look more put together. Maybe it's because they iron everything. If you want to blend in more, simply dress as people do for casual Fridays at work. Standards for children are pretty lenient, although you may want to avoid t-shirts with loud logos. If you want nice clothes for your kids, Paris is a great place to buy them. See below for a list of kids' clothing stores.

Regardless of the time of year you visit Paris, it is always a good idea to dress in layers. Even in the summer, the weather can switch from cool to warm and back again. Winters can be damp, and you will glad you packed that extra sweater or layer of fleece to ward off the cold. Be sure to bring a folding umbrella and rain gear for the kids.

Tipping: A 15% tip is usually included (*service compris*) with your bill in a restaurant or café. If the bill says *service non compris*, then you should leave a 15% tip. The customary tip for taxi rides is 10% as is the usual tip for hairdressers. A small tip of €0.50-1 is customary for washroom or cloakroom attendants. For hotel porters and room service €1.50 is the norm. A €1-2 tip is customary for tour guides and tour bus drivers.

Health insurance: Before you leave home, contact your health insurance company to see if it covers medical expenses abroad. If so, don't forget to bring along your membership card. If not, you may want to purchase supplemental health insurance for travelers.

The US Department of State maintains an extensive list of US-based companies that offer travel health insurance and emergency evacuation services (http://travel.state.gov/travel/tips/health/health_1185.html). The website www.insuremytrip.com allows you to compare travel insurance plans.

Another option for children and students ages 12 to 26 years; adults who are teachers or faculty members; and university students is coverage through the international student, youth, or teacher's ID available for $25. This card offers advantageous rates for insurance to cover medical expenses and evacuation fees. It also offers many discounts to museums and other attractions. For more information visit www.isecard.com/index.html.

Safety: Paris is a relatively safe city, particularly compared to American ones. You can walk comfortably in nearly any neighborhood, especially the popular tourist and residential areas. As always, you do need to exercise common street sense and be careful of traffic.

Visitors to Paris do need to be mindful of pickpockets, however, particularly in crowded tourist areas or on public transportation. Stay alert as to the whereabouts of your wallet and valuables.

Our greatest fear as parents has always been of losing track of our children in unfamiliar places. Here are some tips to lesson the risk and anxiety of a lost child:
• If your children are old enough, have them learn the name of your hotel, hosts, or street and address where you are staying. Show them where it is on a map. Point out nearby landmarks. Pick up several of your hotel's business cards at the front desk and distribute one to each member of your group.
• If your children are small, secure a label to their clothes, such as the paper luggage labels you get at the airport. Include the child's name, your name, and your address and phone information in Paris. Make sure to show you kids what you are doing and explain why, with words such as, "If you are ever lost, this tag will show a grownup your name and where we are staying, so we can find you."

- When visiting a large museum or sight, be sure first to establish an easy-to-find meeting place in case you become separated. We learned this lesson one day when our older son got ahead of us in the Louvre (the world's largest museum) without a rendez-vous plan. When I caught up with him, I asked what he would have done if he had become lost. He answered with perfect 9-year old confidence, "I would have waited for you under the glass pyramid, of course." It was a great plan, except that the rest of us had not been clued in to it.
- Be sure to teach your children the age-old rule of staying in one place if they do get lost. You are more likely to find them if they are not a moving target. We also tell our kids to use the same advice we give at home. If you are lost, tell an official helper (like a police officer or museum guard) or look for another family with children and ask them to help.
- Don't forget to keep track of your adult companions, too. While my husband and I have yet to lose a child in a foreign place, we have lost track of each other. Be sure to have a meeting plan if you are off on separate missions, and throw in a back-up plan just in case.
- Equip everyone with a walky talky. Modern ones are lightweight, easy to use, and have a range of 2 miles or more. They come in sets of two, but you can buy more and set them all to the same frequency. Not only can you use them to keep track of each other, they are also handy when you need to stand in a long line. You can leave one adult in line, while the rest of the group looks at souvenirs, gets a snack, or runs around until it is nearly your turn.

Books, Videos & Websites on Paris

Fiction for Younger Children

Anatole over Paris, and other Anatole adventures by Eve Titus. Whittlesey House Weekly Reader Children's Book Club,1961. These stories describe the adventures of Anatole, a clever mouse who lives in Paris.

Eloise in Paris, by Kay Thompson, 1957, Six-year old Eloise, who normally lives at the Plaza Hotel in New York, visits Paris with her usual pluck and humor. Although the pictures were drawn in the 1950s, they still give an excellent view of Paris today.

Linnea in Monet's Garden, by Christina Bjork and Lena Anderson, Stockholm, Rabén and Sjögren Publishers, 1985. Young Linnea and her friend Mr. Bloom visit Monet's paintings in Paris and his house and gardens at Giverny. A lovely introduction to Impressionist art.

Madeleine, Madeleine and the Gypsies, Madeleine and the Bad Hat, and other Madeleine stories by Ludwig Bemelmans. The classic adventures of a little girl who lives in a boarding school located "in an old house in Paris". Lovely illustrations feature major city sights.

Metro Cat, by Marsha D. Arnold, Golden Books Pub. Co. Inc., 2001. Sophie is a pampered cat who accidentally finds herself in the subway one day where she discovers a new life of adventures.

The Red Balloon, (adapted from the movie) by Albert Lamorisse, New York, Doubleday & Company Inc, 1956. The adventures of a lonely boy and the balloon that brightens his life in the Belleville neighborhood of Paris.

Non-fiction for Younger Kids

Daily Life in Ancient and Modern Paris (Cities Through Time Series), by Sarah Hoban and Bob Moulder, Lerner Publications Company, 2000. This book brings together glimpses of Paris' history and everyday life.

The Inside-Outside Book of Paris, by Roxie Munro, E.P. Dutton, 1992. This books looks both inside and outside great Parisian sights, such as the Eiffel Tower and Pompidou Center, as well as more mundane places such as a pastry shop or booksellers along the Seine. An interesting and kid-friendly introduction to the city.

Let's Visit the Louvre Museum, by Claude Delafosse, Gallimard Jeunesse, (English edition, Moonlight Publishing, London, 1995. A handsome introduction to some of the greatest treasures of the Louvre Museum highlighted with transparent pages that let you see inside the glass pyramid or Egyptian mummy case.

Look What Came from France, Harvey Miles, New York, Franklin Watts, a division of Grolier Publishing, 1999. From scuba gear to April Fools' Day jokes, a nicely illustrated book outlining common products and customs that have come to us from France.

Monuments That Tell the Story of Paris, by Jean Daly, Editions Parigramme, Paris, 2001. A chronological introduction to some of the great monuments of Paris: from the Roman Arena and Baths, through Medieval and Renaissance splendors, to modern constructions such as the Pompidou Center, Grand Arche de la Défense, and La Villette Science Museum.

Paris (Cities of the World Series), by Conrad R. Stein, Children's Press, A Division of Grolier Publishing Co, Inc. New York, NY. 1996. This is an excellent introduction to the history and culture of Paris, described in broad strokes and illustrated with big, attractive photos.

Paris 1789: A Guide to Paris on the Eve of the Revolution, by Wright, Larousse Kingfisher Chambers, 1999. This book is written as a real travel guide to the Paris of 1789. It is a witty and clever introduction to Paris and the French Revolution.

This is Paris, by Miroslav Sasek, The Macmillan Company, 1959. With 1950s graphics and simple text, this remains one of the most delightful books on Paris for children. Look for it at your public library.

Books for Children About French Artists

Suzette and the Puppy: A Story About Mary Cassatt, by Joan Sweeny and Jennifer Heyd Wharton, Barron's Juveniles, 2000. This is a fictionalized tale about a little girl and a dog based on a painting by Mary Cassatt. It evokes life in Paris in the 1870s among the Impressionists.

Picasso and the Girl with a Ponytail: A Story About Pablo Picasso. By Laurence Anholt, Barron's Educational Series, Inc. 1998. Based on a true story of Picasso and a young girl named Sylvette whose profile and ponytale inspired many of his paintings.

Smart About Art Series, Grosset and Dunlap. This series features fictionalized stories about famous artists. Titles include:

Edgar Degas: Paintings that Dance by Maryann Cocca-Leffler; *Henri Matisse: Drawing with Scissors* by Jane O'Connor; *Claude Monet: Sunshine and Waterlilies* by True Kelley; *Pablo Picasso: Breaking All the Rules* by True Kelley; and *Vincent van Gogh: Sunflowers and Swirly Stars* by Joan Holub.

Katie Meets the Impressionists; *Katie and the Mona Lisa*; and *Katie and the Sunflowers,* by James Mayhew, Orchard Books. A little girl goes on adventures when she steps into famous paintings and gets to know some of the artists, their subjects, and styles.

Getting to Know the World's Greatest Artists Series by Mike Venezia, Grolier Publishing, Children's Press, New York. These books are wonderfully written for children with copies of the artists' works juxtaposed with those of their contemporaries. There are also funny cartoon illustrations by the author to help put each artist's story into a context that kids can understand. Some of the featured artists include: Mary Cassat, Paul Cezanne, Leonardo Da Vinci, Paul Gauguin, Henri Matisse, Claude Monet, Pablo Picasso, Pierre Auguste Renoir, Henri de Toulouse-Lautrec, Vincent Van Gogh.

Fiction for Preteens

The Adventures of Asterix the Gaul, and other Asterix comic books by Albert Uderzo and René Goscinny. These delightfully witty comic books feature the Gaul warrior Asterix and his pal Obelix living in 50 BC, who help their little Breton village resist the Roman occupation. Although they to not take place in Paris per se, they are a wonderful introduction to French history and culture.

A Chapel of Thieves, by Bruce Clements, Farrar Straus & Giroux (Juv), 2002. A teen boy adventure story set in 19th century Paris.

The Family Under the Bridge, by Natalie Savage Carlson, Harper Collins Children's Books, 1958. The story of a beggar and a poor family who meet as they live under a bridge in post-WWII Paris.

Mystery of the Metro (My Name Is Paris, Book 1), by Elizabeth Howard, Random House, 1987. This is a teen girl mystery adventure set in Paris at the turn of the 20th century.

Rosemary in Paris by Barbara Robertson, Hourglass Adventures #2, Winslow Press, 2001. A 10-year old girl's adventure at the 1889 Paris International Exhibition.

Books for Teenagers

The DaVinci Code, by Dan Brown. This mystery/adventure story has become a best-seller and Hollywood movie. It involves great escapes from the Louvre and other Paris spots. True fans can go on entire DaVinci Code tours of Paris, but most teens will enjoy looking for clues from the book in the St. Sulpice Church and Louvre Museum.

The Hunchback of Nôtre Dame, by Victor Hugo. Set in Medieval Paris, this is the tale of the deformed hunchback Quasimodo, his love for the Gypsy girl, Esmeralda, and the public intolerance that leads them both to tragic fates.

Les Miserables, by Victor Hugo. The saga of Jean Valjean, an escaped convict trying to make good but dogged by the relentless police agent, Javert. His tale criss-crosses those of other characters forced into desperate situations by the trials of war, poverty, and revolution in 19th century Paris.

An Immovable Feast, by Ernest Hemingway. This largely autobiographical account describes Hemingway's life in Paris as a starving young writer.

Is Paris Burning? by Larry Collins and Dominique Lapierre. A factual account of the Liberation of Paris during WWII, including how close Hitler came to destroying every major monument and bridge in the city.

The Man in the Iron Mask, by Alexandre Dumas. Set during the reign of King Louis XIV, a man is mysteriously imprisoned with his identity hidden behind an iron mask.

Père Goriot, by Honore de Balzac. This 19th century novel contrasts the lives of Pere Goriot whose love for his daughters leads to his ruin, with that of Rastignac, an upstart from the country bent on climbing the ladder of fortune and social ambition in Paris.

A Tale of Two Cities, by Charles Dickens. A Dickens classic set in Paris during the French Revolution.

The Three Musketeers, by Alexandre Dumas. This heroic adventures of Athos, Porthos, Aramis, and d'Artagnan, Royal Musketeers in the service of King Louis XIII.

The Bald Soprano, by Eugene Ionesco. A delightful example of French Modern Theater of the Absurd. It has played non-stop at the Théâtre de la Huchette in Paris since its first opening in the 1950s.

DVDs

The Aristocats. A Walt Disney classic featuring a great jazz party among the rooftops of Paris.

Everafter. A charming version of the Cinderella story, set during the reign of France's king Francois 1st. Though it does not take place in Paris, it gives a nice glimpse of Renaissance France, including a Jeu de Paume match and Leonardo da Vinci, whose masterpieces such as the Mona Lisa still hang in the Louvre.

Madeleine. A delightful romp through Paris based on the books by Ludwig Bemelmans.

The Man in the Iron Mask. A French classic by Alexandre Dumas set during the reign of Louis XIV and filmed at the Vaux le Vicomte Palace outside of Paris.

The Red Balloon. A French classic about a lonely boy named Pascal whose life is brightened by a magical red balloon that follows him everywhere. It is set in the Belleville neighborhood of Paris during the 1950s.

Note: Avoid the Mary Kate and Ashley Olsen movie on Paris. The twins provide poor role models for making good travelers out of your kids.

Internet Sites

- France for Kids, from the Embassy of France, *www.info-france-usa.org/kids/*
- Official Site of the Eiffel Tower, *www.tour-eiffel.fr/teiffel/uk/*
- Webmuseum, Paris, *www.ibiblio.org/wm/*
- Cluny Museum, kids page (in French), *www.culture.fr/cluny/intro.htm*
- Louvre Museum (in French), with virtual visit, *www.louvre.fr/*

- Musée d'Orsay, *http://www.musee-orsay.fr/ORSAY/orsaygb/HTML.NSF/ By+Filename/mosimple+index?OpenDocument*
- Versailles Palace, *www.chateauversailles.fr/*
- French Government Tourist Office, *www.francetourism.com*

Flying to Paris

Generally speaking, you will save money on airfares if you book your tickets 4-6 months in advance, especially for travel during the high-seasons

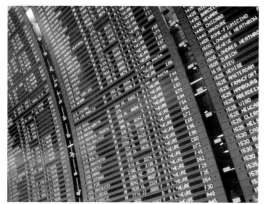

(June-August, December 15-January 5). However, discounts and charter tickets vary greatly from year to year, so there is no hard, fast rule. Keep your eye out for special fares advertised in the travel section of major newspapers. Remember to ask about reduced fares for children. If you have a trusted travel agent, this is a good place to start looking for bargain airfares. You can also let your fingers do the walking online. **Expedia** *(*www.expedia.com); **Travelocity** (www.travelocity.com); and **Orbitz** (www.orbitz.com) allow you to compare flights and rates on several major airlines.

If you go directly to different airline sites to book tickets, you will often get a lower rate than over the phone. You can also surf the web for travel consolidators with names such as cheaptickets.com or budgettravel.com that can easily save you 25% on flights and car rentals. Several car rental consolidators such as **AutoEurope**, Tel. 888/223-5555; www.autoeurope.com, and **Kemwel**, Tel. 877/820-0668; www.kemwel.com, also sell discounted flights.

Note that rules vary from airline to airline regarding children's discounts, how to seat babies, and regulations about traveling with young children. Check for specifics with your travel agent or directly with the airline.

Here are some tips for planning your plane trip:

- If you are flying to Paris directly from the US, try to book the overnight, trans-Atlantic flight as late in the evening as possible. The later you leave, the more likely you (and your kids) will get some sleep. The later you arrive in Paris, the more likely your body clock will be ready to face a new day.
- The return flight from France to the US is always a daytime trip. Be sure to bring plenty of snacks, (diapers, if needed), small toys, books, activities, and entertainment.
- Take advantage of stopovers and connections. Let kids stretch their legs, get some food, and watch other planes take off and land.
- Bring food (though you will have to purchase liquids after you've passed through security). Waiting for meals on an airplane can be long and disappointing, especially for fussy eaters. Bring your own to play it safe.

Some of the major carriers offering flights from the US to Paris include:
- **Air France** – Tel. 800/237-2747; www.airfrance.com
- **American Airlines** – Tel. 800/433-7300; www.aa.com
- **British Airlines** (connections through London) – Tel. 800/247-9297; www.britishairways.com
- **Continental Airlines** – Tel. 800/231-0856; www.continental.com
- **Delta Airlines** – Tel. 800/241-4141; www.delta.com
- **Northwest Airlines** – Tel. 800/447-4747; www.nwa.com
- **United Airlines** – Tel. 800/241-6522; www.united.com
- **USAir** – Tel. 800/622-1015; www.ual.com

Getting To & From Charles de Gaulle/Roissy Airport

The **Charles de Gaulle/Roissy Airport** is where all transatlantic flights arrive. It is located 30 kilometers (19 miles) northeast of Paris. It is well linked to the city via public transportation and taxis.

Taxi
This is the easiest option with suitcases and small children, and is not that much more expensive than public transportation if you are traveling as a family. If there are more than four of you, you may have to wait a bit for a minivan taxi, but it is very doable. Count on €50 or more for fare into the city, plus a charge for luggage and a tip.

Train

The **Roissy-Rail Suburban B Line** (RER B) connects the Charles de Gaulle Airport train station to the Gare du Nord train station and several other major subway stations in Paris, including Châtelet/Les Halles (a major subway hub), Saint Michel-Nôtre Dame; Luxembourg; Port Royal; Denfert Rochereau; and Cité Universitaire. From the airport you can follow the signs marked Paris par Train or take the free airport shuttle to the RER B Station. Trains run from 5 am to midnight approximately every 15 minutes (more often during rush hour). The fare varies depending on where you stop in the city. Count on €10-14 for adults. Kids ages 4-10 are half price. Kids under 4 are free. Tickets are sold at electronic kiosks that take credit cards and coins.

This is the quickest mode of public transportation into the city, but it requires taking the airport shuttle or walking and negotiating escalators at the train station. There are no elevators. It's fairly easy provided you are not loaded down with lots of luggage.

Roissy Bus

The Roissy Bus connects the Charles de Gaulle/Roissy terminals to the Place de l'Opéra in central Paris. Fare: €8.40.

Air France Bus

There are two Air France buses that will take you from the terminals into the city. One will take you to the Arc de Triomphe (Charles de Gaulle/ Etoile metro stop) then to the Porte Maillot metro.and stops. The other will take you to the Gare de Lyon and Gare Montparnasse train stations. Fare is €12 for adults and €6 for kids ages 2-11. Kids under 2 are free.

Getting To & From Orly Airport

The **Orly Airport** is located 18 kilometers (11 miles) south of the city. It is also well served by public transportation and taxis.

Taxi

This is the easiest option with suitcases and small children, although you may have to wait for a minivan taxi if you are traveling with more than 4 people. Count on €30-40 for fare into the city, plus a charge for luggage and a tip.

Train (option 1)

You can catch an airport shuttle bus to the Suburban C Line train station called Pont de Rungis. This train line connects Orly to several subway stops in the city including the Gare d'Austerlitz train station; St Michel Nôtre dame, Musée d'Orsay; Invalides, Pont de l'Alma; and Champ de Mars/Tour Eiffel. The fare varies depending which stop you go to in the city. Count on €8-12 for adults. Kids ages 4-10 are half price. Kids under 4 are free.

Train (option 2)

You can catch a shuttle bus to the Suburban B line train station at Antony. This train will take you to numerous major subway stations in the city including Denfert Rochereau; Port Royal; Luxembourg; St Michel Nôtre dame; Châtelet Les Halles (a major subway hub); and the Gare du Nord train station. The fare varies depending which stop you go to in the city. Count on €8-12 for adults. Kids ages 4-10 are half price. Kids under 4 are free.

Orly Bus

The Orly Bus connects the Orly terminals to the Place Denfert Rochereau in Paris. Fare: €5.80.

Air France Bus

You can catch an Air France bus from the Orly terminals to the Invalides or the Montparnasse train station in Paris. Fare: €10.

Arriving By Train

If you are traveling to Paris by train you will arrive in one of Paris' six main train stations. Each of these stations is well connected to the rest of the city by subway and public buses.

Trains from northern France, England (via the Chunnel), Belgium, Luxembourg, Holland, and northern Europe arrive at the **Gare du Nord**.

The **Gare de l'Est** serves cities in eastern France, Germany, Switzerland, and Austria.

If you are arriving from southern France or Italy you will come into the **Gare de Lyon**.

The **Gare Montparnasse** serves Brittany and western France.

The **Gare d'Austerlitz** is where you will arrive from Spain and southwestern France.

If you are coming from Normandy or have taken a ferry across the English Channel you will arrive at the **Gare Saint Lazare**.

Tourist Offices in Paris

- **Central Tourist Office**, 25 rue des Pyramides, 75001; Tel. 08 92 68 31 12 / 08 92 68 3000; website: www.parisinfo.com. Open Mon-Sat 10am-7pm; Sun and holidays 11-7. Gare du Nord Train station; 01 45 26 94 82; Open daily.
- **Gare de Lyon Train station**; Tel. 01 43 43 33 24; Open Mon-Sat.
- **Eiffel Tower Tourist Office**; Tel. 01 45 51 22 15; Open daily, May-Sept.
- **Carrousel du Louvre Shopping Center Visitor Center**; Tel. 01 44 50 19 98; Open daily except Tues.

Getting Around Paris

Paris is an easy city to navigate. Most hotels and major department stores offer free street maps. You can also obtain a free bus and subway map in any subway station.

Walking

Much of Paris' charm is best discovered on foot, so you will want to have comfortable walking shoes. This is an excellent way to explore the parks, shops, museums, markets, and cobbled streets of the city. When you need a rest, there is always a handy café or park bench where you can take a break. When our boys were little we relied on baby backpacks and sturdy but lightweight umbrella strollers to get around as a family. We found that these were best for negotiating narrow sidewalks, handling cobble-stoned streets, going into shops or museums, descending subway stairs, or climbing on and off of buses. As our children have grown older, they have become good walkers themselves, especially with the promise of an interesting activity and occasional bribe of ice cream or other treats.

Public Transportation

When you need to cover more distance, you can use Paris' very reliable and user-friendly public transportation system, the RATP.

Subway tickets (*tickets de métro*) are good on all buses and subways within the city limit. You can purchase them in any subway station and in many *Tabac* stores. Individual tickets can also be purchased on a bus, but you will need exact change. You can buy tickets one at a time (€1.40), but it is easier and cheaper to buy a *carnet* of 10 tickets (€10.70). For children ages 6 to 10 you can purchase half-price *carnets*, called *demi-tarif* (€5.35). Children 5 and under ride for free.

There are also one-day or multi-day **passes** that are good on subways, public buses, the RER, the Montmartrobus and Montmartre Funiculaire. These can be purchased in any subway station. The *Mobilis* pass is good for unlimited travel for one day at a cost of €5. The *Paris Visite* pass allows unlimited travel for 1, 2, 3, or 5-days and includes free trips on the RER to Disneyland Paris or to the Paris Airports. It is easy and worthwhile if you will be taking numerous bus or subway trips each day. Rates for kids/adults are: €4.55/8.35 for a 1-day pass; €6.85/13.70 for a 2-day pass; €9.15/18.25 for a 3-day pass; and €13.70/26.65 for a 5-day pass.

If you are going to be staying in Paris more than a week and using public transportation, the best bargain for adults is the **Carte Orange** pass. A 1-week pass for unlimited travel costs €15.70 and a 1-month pass costs €51.50. You will need to supply a small ID photo when you apply for the card.

The public transit system also sells a card called **Musée et Monuments** for €18 per day. This card gives you free and priority access to 70 museums and monuments across the city. It may be an advantage for adults in your group. Children already benefit from reduced fares or free access to most of these sites.

Métro

Paris has an extensive subway system called the *métro*. There are over 370 metro stations and 15 lines. Trains run daily from approximately 5:30 am to 1 am. The train lines are identified by the name of the last station at each end. An overhead sign on the train platform indi-
cates which direc-
tion the train is heading. Transfers are also well indi-
cated on orange and white overhead signs. The one downside to using the metro with small

children is that it involves lots of stairs, which can be tricky with toddlers and strollers. On the other hand, older kids love riding the metro, especially if you let them figure out your route on the map.

RER

Some of the stations within the city will connect you to the suburban train system known as the RER or to the new Meteor trains which run automatically without a conductor. If you take the RER beyond the city limits, you will need to purchase a higher priced ticket from a station ticket agent or automatic machine. Hang on to your ticket for the whole ride. You may need it to exit the train station or be asked to present it during a random ticket control. Be aware that once the RER trains leave the city limits they don't necessarily stop at all the stations along the line. Check the lighted display board on the train platform. Make certain that the light next to the name of your destination is lit. If not, wait for another train.

Buses

Public buses are a great option, because they allow you to see more of the city. They are also easier than the metro to navigate with a stroller or small children because they don't involve stairs. Bus maps are available free of charge in any subway station. The bus stops are well marked by either a shelter with glass walls and a big bus map or a pole featuring a yellow and red bus symbol with the name of the stop. Many major streets and avenues have special lanes reserved for buses and taxis, so it is often faster to ride a bus than to try to drive through the city. You can ride on any bus within the city limits for one ticket, but if you transfer from one bus to another you will need to use a new ticket. You use the same tickets as for the metro and can purchase them in any metro station and many Tabac stores. Buses run Mon-Sat from 6:30 am to 8:30 pm. Special routes run until midnight and on Sundays and holidays. These are indicated at the stops. The *Noctambus* runs during the night.

Bâtobus

This is a system of boats that crisscross the Seine River serving 7 stops between the Jardin des Plantes and the Eiffel Tower, including Hôtel de Ville, Nôtre Dame, Saint Germain, Louvre, Musée d'Orsay, and Champs Elysées.

The price of each ticket is calculated according to how far you want to go along the route. The first stop is €3.50 and each additional stop is an extra €2 per person. The Bâtobus is more expensive than other forms of public transportation, but it's fun. The best deal is a one-day or two-day pass that lets you come and go all day. A one-day pass is €10 for adults and €5.50 for kids. A two-day pass is €12.50 for adults and €6.50 for kids. The service runs approximately every 15-25 minutes from 10 am to 11 pm, April through October.

Open-Tour Bus

If you have never ridden on a double-decker bus, you may want to explore Paris on the light green *Open Tour* tourist buses. This is a service that is jointly run by the public transportation system and two private tour companies. There are three routes: Grand Tour; Bastille-Bercy; and Montmartre. You buy a pass for one route that is good for one or several days and can climb on and off the bus as much as you like. Buses run daily. The three routes go past major tourist sights and stop at clearly marked bus stops. Each rider gets a pair of headsets that you can plug in to each bus for a commentary in English or French. The lower deck is like a normal bus and the upper deck is open-air.

This is a great way to see major city sights in a short period of time. Kids love it. It is also a good option if you are jet-lagged and want to get a view of the city without having to expend a lot of energy – although you will have to spend some cash, because the tickets are pricey. You can buy your passes from the bus conductor or at Open Tour; 13, Rue Auber, 75009, Metro: Auber. Rates are: 1 day Adult Pass = €25, 2 day Adult pass = €28; Kids 4-11years = €12 for a 1 or 2 day pass; Kids under 4 are free.

Taking a Cab

Taxis are readily available at airports and train stations. There are also many taxi stands scattered throughout the city where you can generally find a cab quickly. It is difficult to hail a cab on the street, since they are generally full. However, they respond quickly to phone requests. You also can reserve a taxi in advance, especially if you need an early morning ride or a car that can fit more than 3 people. The front desk person at your hotel should be able to help. Here are some services you can call: **Alpha-Taxi**: Tel. 01 45 85 85 85. **Taxi-Bleu**: Tel. 01 49 36 10 10. **Taxi-Etoile**: Tel. 01 42 70 41 41. **Taxi-G7**: Tel. 01 47 39 47 39. The fare is displayed on a meter. Add a 15% tip.

Driving

Driving in Paris is **not recommended** since traffic is very congested and parking is both difficult and expensive. Having said this, we often end up in Paris with a rental car to use for day trips and for traveling to other parts of France. One advantage of the traffic congestion is that it gives you

time to figure out where you are and need to go. Fortunately, the streets and access to highways are generally well marked. Make sure to stay out of the bus/taxi lanes – generally the one furthest on the right.

Parking in Paris is a headache. Street parking is limited to two hours between 7 am and 7pm, and it's expensive. You will not find an American-style parking meter. Instead there are parking payment machines located along the street. Most of these no longer accept coins. Instead you must purchase a prepaid payment card from a Tabac store. As you insert your card, the clock on the parking payment machine will advance for up to 2 hours. When you've reached the time you need, push the green button. A printed ticket will appear that you must put on the dashboard of your car. Note: in most residential neighborhoods, parking is free on Saturday and Sunday, from 7 pm to 7 am, and during the month of August, but you should verify this on the parking machine. If you cannot feed the parking machine every two hours, you are better off putting your car in a parking garage. These are indicated by blue signs with a white letter "P." Most garages offer hourly, daily, and weekly rates.

If you get a parking ticket, you can buy a payment card at any Tabac store. Mail it in with the ticket.

Renting a Car

To drive in France you must be at least 18 years old and have a valid driver's license. If you want to rent a car, you will save money by reserving it in advance through an American consolidator or car rental company. Try:

- **AutoEurope**: Tel. 888/223-5555; www.autoeurope.com
- **Kemwel**: Tel. 877/820-0668; www.kemwel.com
- **Hertz**: Tel. 800/654-3001; www.hertz.com
- **Avis**: Tel. 800/331-1084; www.avis.com

Basic Information

Holidays & Business Hours

Most stores, museums, and public buildings are closed on holidays. Hospitals and police stations remain open, and there are always a few pharmacies on call. Holidays include:

January 1: New Year's Day
March or April (date varies): Easter and the Monday after Easter
May 1: Labor Day
May 8: Armistice Day (celebrating the end of World War II)
May (date varies): Ascension
May (date varies): Pentecost
July 14: Bastille Day (celebrating the French Revolution)
August 15: Assumption
November 1: All Saints' Day
November 11: Armistice Day (celebrating the end of World War I)
December 25: Christmas

Business hours vary. Most museums are open 9am-5pm (possibly later one night a week). National museums are closed on Tuesdays. City museums are closed on Mondays. Banks are generally open 9am-4pm, Monday-Friday. Some close for an hour at lunchtime. Post offices are open 8am-7pm, Monday-Friday, and Saturday 8am-12pm. Many food shops are open 9am-7pm, with a several hour break in the afternoon. Open-air markets are generally open 5am-1pm. Restaurants usually serve lunch between 12pm and 2pm, and dinner from 7pm-11pm. Many stores are closed on Sundays, including large department stores.

Money

Paris is well equipped with automatic teller machines that accept most American bank and credit cards (with a PIN). We have found that this is not only the most convenient way to get cash but also the one that offers the best exchange rate and lowest service charges. You can also change cash or travelers checks at an exchange office, most banks, and fancy hotels – but the fees and exchange rates are less advantageous. The **Euro** is the standard currency in France, Austria, Belgium, Finland, Germany, Greece, Holland, Ireland, Italy, Luxembourg, Portugal, and Spain. **Its value as of press time is approximately equal to $1.30.**

You may want to obtain 100 Euros before you leave home, especially if you are arriving in Paris by plane. This avoids the hassle of locating the airport ATM or exchange office and waiting in a long line when you are already dealing with jetlag, luggage, and tired children.

Credit cards, especially VISA, are widely accepted in France, everywhere from restaurants, hotels, and grocery stores to highway toll booths.

Note: Once in a while, credit cards or ATM machines just won't work. This is generally because the electronic lines connecting your transaction to the rest of the world are busy or down. You may have to try several ATMs or wait a few hours to obtain cash. Similarly, if your VISA card is not approved when you are making a store purchase, ask the merchant to try again once or twice. Sometimes, the third try is a charm.

Electricity

Electricity in France runs on **220 volts**, compared to only 110 volts in the US. If you want to use American appliances in France safely you will need a converter and an adapter. These can be purchased at travel and major hardware stores in the U.S or in Paris at FNAC and Darty stores, or in the basement of the BHV department store.

Electricity is much more expensive in France than in the US. If you are a guest in someone's home, it is best to be mindful of this fact in your use of heating, hot water, lights, and electrical appliances. Note, too, that garbage disposals are nonexistent in France. Toss food remains into the trash, not down the sink.

TV Formats

French televisions are set to a different standard of lines per frame, called SECAM, than are American ones which function on the NTSC standard. As a result, you cannot use American-made videos in a French machine or vice versa. Similarly, DVDs are set to different standards.

Laundry

While laundry can be just a menial chore at home, it can become a real challenge when traveling, especially with messy kids. We've encountered a variety of strategies for dealing with this issue:

- One family we know simply didn't do laundry during their 3-week trip to Europe. They packed cheap socks and underwear and just threw them away after each use. For the rest, they packed enough to wear for three weeks. This works, of course, but means that you will be carrying a lot of dirty clothes around.
- Our New York City friends were accustomed to taking their family's dirty clothes to the bulk laundry service at home. In Paris, they used the same method, dropping off bulk laundry at the local "*Pressing*," which also does dry-cleaning.
- You can always rinse out your clothes in the hotel sink. Many hotels frown on this, especially if you start stringing drippy clothes all over the room. However, they generally won't balk if you just rinse out a few items and dangle them carefully over the bathtub.
- Some hotels offer laundry and dry-cleaning services.
- One of the advantages of renting an apartment is that it is more likely to have a washing machine. However, few, if any will, have a dryer.
- The other solution is to take an hour out of your day and head to the local Laundromat (*Laverie*). Ask your hotel to recommend the nearest one. We suggest going first thing in the morning, when it is less crowded. You can always nibble on a breakfast pastry, plan out the day's activities, and write some post cards while you wait. Some Laundromats have detergent dispensers, or you can buy your own at the local supermarket, Monoprix or Prisunic, or corner grocer's. Increasingly, French Laundromats do not have coin-operated machines. Instead you go to a wall-mounted device, indicate which machine you want to use, and insert the money there.

Health & Medical Tips

- Be sure to fill out the emergency contact information page in the passport of each family member.
- If you or any member of your family uses a prescription medication, bring enough to cover your trip. Ask your health care provider to give you a prescription with the generic name in case you need a refill.
- Know your child's weight in pounds and divide it by 2.2 to convert it to kilos. You may need to know this to find the proper dosage for French medications.

• Bring your own fever thermometer. French ones calculate temperature in Celsius not Fahrenheit.

• Stock your dop kit with fever-reducing medication (kid and adult varieties), a liquid antihistamine/decongestant such as Benadryl, anti-itch cream, antibiotic cream, Band-Aids, a fever thermometer, tablets for indigestion, Bandaids, and eye drops.

Emergency Contacts
• **SOS Help English-Speaking hotline** (open daily 3 pm-11 pm): Tel. 01 47 23 80 80
• **US Embassy:** Tel. 01 43 12 22 22
• **Ambulance:** Tel. 15 or 01 43 78 26 26
• **Police:** Tel. 17
• **Fire Department:** Tel. 18
• **Anti-Poison Center:** Tel. 01 40 37 04 04
• **Blood Transfusion Center:** Tel. 08 00 10 01 09
• **Burn Center:** Tel. 01 42 34 17 58

Doctors & Dentists
The US Embassy in Paris maintains a list of doctors, medical specialists, and dentists who speak English. It is available on their web site at (www.amb-usa.fr/consul/acs/guide/default.htm) or at the Embassy's **American Citizen Services**, open Monday-Friday, located at 2, Rue Saint Florentin by the Place de la Concorde (Metro: Concorde). The Embassy phone number is: Tel. 01 43 12 22 22. For Emergencies during weekends and holidays, call that number and ask for the Embassy Duty Officer.

If you just want to find the nearest doctor, go to your neighborhood pharmacy. Each pharmacy maintains a list of local doctors, dentists, and specialists, including which ones who are open during holidays and weekends.

English-Speaking or Bilingual Hospitals
• **American Hospital of Paris** (medical and dental care), 63, Boulevard Victor Hugo, between the Boulevard Victor Hugo, Rue Chauveau, Boulevard du Château, and Boulevard de la Saussaye in the western suburb of Neuilly. It is two blocks from the Seine (Metro: Pont de Levallois – a good 6 blocks away). Tel. 01 46 41 25 25.
• **Children's Hospital Emergency Care: Hopital Necker,** 146-151, Rue de Sevres, in Paris at the intersection of the Rue de Sevres and the Boulevard Montparnasse, and Rue de Vaugirard (Metro: Duroc or Falguière). Tel. 01 44 49 40 00.

- **Hertford British Hospital**, 3, Rue Barbis, between the Rue de Villiers, Rue Chaptal, and Rue Voltaire in the northwestern suburb of Levallois-Perret, (Metro: Anatole France). Tel. 01 46 39 22 22.
- **Hopital Foch** (many English-speaking staff members), 40, Rue Worth, 92150 (western suburb) Suresnes. Tel. 01 46 25 20 00.

Late-night House Calls
- **S.O.S. Médecins** provides after-hours house calls throughout the night. Tel. 01 47 07 77 77.
- **S.O.S. Dentistes** will send a dentist to you in the middle of the night if it's urgent. Tel. 01 43 37 51 00.

Pharmacies
French pharmacists go through 6 years of specialized university training. They are well qualified to give advice about medications and will administer first aid. Pharmacists also maintain a list of local doctors, dentists, and other health care providers, including those that remain on call during weekends and holidays.

You can recognize a French pharmacy by its green cross symbol. English-speaking pharmacies in Paris include:
- **Anglo-American Pharmacy**, 6, Rue de Castiglione, Metro: Tuileries, Tel. 01 42 60 72 96.
- **British and American Pharmacy**, 1, Rue Auber, Metro: Opéra, Tel. 01 47 42 49 40.
- **British Pharmacy**, 62, Avenue des Champs-Elysées, Metro:Franklin Roosevelt, Tel. 01 43 59 22 52.
- **Anglo-American Pharmacy**, 37, Avenue Marceau, Metro: George V or Alma Marceau, Tel. 01 47 20 57 37.

Late-night or all-night pharmacies in Paris:
- **Pharma Presto**. Provides 24-hour prescription delivery service. Tel. 01 42 42 42 50.
- **Pharmacie des Halles**. Open until midnight Monday-Saturday and until 10 pm on Sunday. 10, Boulevard de Sébastopol, Metro: Châtelet, Tel. 01 42 72 03 23.
- **Dérhy/Pharmacie des Champs**. Open 24 hours/day. 84, Avenue des Champs-Elysées, Metro: George V, Tel. 01 45 62 02 41.
- **Matignon**. Near the Champs Elysees, Open until 2 am, daily. 2, Rue Jean-Mermoz, Metro: Franklin Roosevelt, Tel. 01 43 59 86 55.
- **Pharmacie Européenne de la Place de Clichy**. Open 24 hours/day. 6, Place de Clichy, Metro: Place de Clichy, Tel. 01 48 74 65 18.

• **Pharmacie de la Place de la Nation**. Open until midnight, daily. 13, Place de la Nation, Metro: Nation, Tel. 01 43 73 24 03.
• **Pharmacie d'Italie**. Open until midnight daily. 61, Avenue d'Italie, Metro: Tolbiac, Tel. 01 44 24 19 72.

Air Quality
Paris can become quite polluted due to the high volume of vehicle traffic, especially if the weather is hot and muggy. The AirParis phone service gives updated air quality information (in French) from 9 am to 5:30 pm daily. Tel. 01 44 59 47 64.

Public Restrooms
Always take advantage of rest rooms (toilettes) in public monuments, museums, department stores, cafés, and restaurants. They are generally clean and easy to find, although occasionally you will still stumble across an old squat-type hole-in-the-ground toilet. These are relics of a bygone era and pretty unappealing if you or your kids are not hardened globe trotters. Most large parks also have public rest rooms. Men's rooms may be labeled as Messieurs, Hommes, or a picture of a man. Ladies' rooms may be labeled as Mesdames, Dames, or a picture of a woman. Some public toilets require a small payment to an attendant or in the door handle.

Water Fountains
We have only ever found one American-style drinking fountain in Paris. It is in the Louvre Museum's Egyptian galleries by the red granite Sphinx statue from Tanis. Instead you will find plenty of outdoor fountains with clean, drinkable tap water. The most common and attractive of these are called *Fontaines Wallace* after the benefactor who installed them on Paris streets in the 1870s. They are dark green, and feature four female statues holding up a dome that is decorated with dolphins. A steady stream of water flows from under the dome. These are very handy for refilling water bottles as you explore the city.
Many public parks and squares feature another type of public water fountain that is dark green, squat, and sort of resembles a square fire hydrant. Some have a handle on the top that you rotate to get the water flowing. Others have a small spout with a button that you push to get water. There is one near the Arch du Carrousel in the Tuileries Gardens that draws long lines on hot days.
Do not drink from decorative fountains or from a park's garden hose. Their water comes from the Paris canals and is not clean. If you see a sign

that says "eau non potable," do not drink the water. "Eau potable" means that it is safe to drink. Many French people prefer the taste of bottled mineral water to tap water. There are at least 50 brands of mineral water available in France. The French drink an average of 100 liters of bottled water per person each year. That's twice as much as their annual wine consumption. Maybe it's the reason they outlive Americans.

Smoking

Smoking remains far more prevalent in Paris (and throughout Europe) than in the US, though the European Union is increasingly passing laws to limit exposure to second-hand smoke. Restaurants are supposed to be non-smoking though outdoor terraces are not. Smoking is not allowed on public transportation nor at the airport. Some hotels have floors reserved for non-smokers.

Newspapers & Magazines

The *International Herald Tribune*, published in Paris, will keep you up to date on American news, sports, comics, and crossword puzzles. It is available, as are many other foreign papers, at most newsstands and newspaper shops (Magasins de Presse).

You can find foreign editions of major American and English-language magazines at large newsstands, in *Magasins de Presse*, and in large English-language bookshops. The most popular French weeklies are the left-wing *Le Nouvel Observateur* and *L'Evenement du Jeudi*, the centrist *L'Express*, and right-wing *Le Point* or *Figaro Magazine*.

If you want information on the week's artistic, cinematic, and cultural happenings, pick up a *Pariscope* (which includes a short section in English) or *Officiel des Spectacles*. They come out each Wednesday.

English-language bookshops
- **WH Smith**, 248, Rue de Rivoli, across from the Tuileries Gardens (Metro: Tuileries). Closed Sun. This is a big bookstore, with a large children's section upstairs.
- **Galigliani Bookseller**, 224, rue de Rivoli, across from the Louvre (Metro: Palais Royal/ Musée du Louvre). Closed Sun. France's oldest English-language bookshop, this store offers an excellent selection of English-language books for both children and adults.
- **Librairie du Musée du Louvre**, near the glass pyramid entrance of the Louvre. Open daily. You will find some books in English in both the children's and adult sections of this museum bookstore/gift shop.

- **Bouquinistes along the Seine**, especially on the Quai Montebello and Quai Saint Michel. (Metro: Saint Michel). Closed Mon. These are fun to browse and a great place to pick up small souvenirs. If you're lucky, you can find titles in English.
- **Brentano's**, 37, Avenue de l'Opéra (Metro: Opéra or Pyramides). Closed Sun. This store has been around for over 100 years. It offers a huge selection of English-language books on two floors. It also hosts a children's book club.
- **Librairie Cultaire-Mona Lisait**, 17, bis Rue Pavée (Metro: St. Paul). Closed Sat. Although many of the books offered in this stores 3 floors are in French, there is a selection of English-language books in the back of the top floor. Many are at bargain prices.
- **The Red Wheelbarrow**, 13, Rue Charles V (Metro: St. Paul). Closed Sun. This shop is small but filled with books in English.
- **Shakespeare and Company**, 37, Rue de la Bucherie, across the river from Nôtre Dame Cathedral (Metro: St. Michel-Nôtre dame). Open daily. This famous hangout for English and American expatriate writers sells new and used books in English, and still retains its dusty charm and warm atmosphere. The kids' section is upstairs and discounted paperbacks are in racks and boxes outside.
- **Joseph Gibert**, 26-30, Boulevard Saint Michel (Metro: Saint Michel). Closed Sun. Part of the 100+ year old Gibert bookstore chain, this shop offers new and used books in English both in the sidewalk racks and upstairs.
- **The Abbey Bookshop**, 29, Rue de la Parcheminerie (Metro: Saint Michel or Cluny - La Sorbonne). Closed Sun. This store offers new and used English, Canadian, and American books.
- **Nouveau Quartier Latin**, 78, Boulevard Saint Michel (Metro: Luxembourg). Closed Sun. This international bookshop offers books and videos in many languages, including English.
- **Tea And Tattered Pages**, 24, Rue Mayet (Metro: Duroc). Open every afternoon. This shop offers both used books and a tearoom for a comfortable book browsing and buying experience.

- **San Francisco Book Co.**, 17, Rue Monsieur le Prince (Metro: Odeon). Open every afternoon. This store is chock full of bargain books in English, starting with the outdoor racks and continuing inside.
- **The Village Voice**, 6, Rue Princesse (Metro: Mabillon). Closed Sun. This shop offers English language books, as well as poetry readings, book signings, and other presentations.

Telephones & Internet

Making a phone call in Paris can be somewhat confusing. All French phone numbers include 10 digits. The first two are the equivalent of an area code and must be dialed every time whether you are making a local call or phoning another region in France. The codes work as follows:

- 01: Paris and its suburbs
- 02: Northwestern France
- 03: Northeastern France
- 04: Southeastern France
- 05: Southwestern France
- 06: Cell phones
- 08: toll-free calls

If you are calling from Paris to another town in France: Dial the full ten-digit number. There is no special access code.

If you want to make an international call from France: Dial 00 + country code + area or town code + number.

Country codes are listed in phone booths and phone directories. The US and Canada are 1, except for Hawaii (1808) and Puerto Rico (1809). The UK is 44.

If you are trying to call France from the US: Dial 011 + 33 (Code for France) + drop the "0" and dial only the remaining 9 digits. For example to call the number 01 43 45 46 47 in Paris: Dial 011+33+1+43 45 46 47.

If you want to use a pay phone: Almost all the public phone booths in France now accept a *télécarte* rather than coins. These look like a credit card with a small memory chip on one end that slides into the pay phone. They can be purchased in increments of 50 or 120 units at any *Tabac* store, tourist office, post office, and even some newsstands. You can also buy phone cards similar to American ones, with a scratch-off code number that you dial from any telephone.

Many cafés have pay phones, generally next to the restrooms. Some accept coins, others require you to purchase a token from the cashier.

If you want to use a cell phone while you are in Paris: If your American cell phone functions on the GSM (Global System for Mobile communications) standard, you can contact your service provider and ask them to allow you access to international service. Count on spending $1-2/minute for local and long-distance calls. You can get cheaper service for calls within France by purchasing and installing a special phone chip, called a SIM card, available at large FNAC stores in Paris.

You can rent a cell phone to use in Europe from American companies such as **Europecar** (Tel. 888/223-5555; www.autoeurope.com) and **Kemwel** (Tel. 877/820-0668; www.kemwel.com). Plan on spending $25-50/week for the phone rental, plus a shipping charge in some cases. Local and long-distance calls will run you $1-2/minute.

A cheaper option is to rent a cell phone in Paris from **Call Phone**, located at both Roissy/Charles de Gaulle and Orly Airports. There is also an office in the city at 2, Avenue de la Porte de Saint Cloud, 75016 Paris, Metro: St. Cloud (Tel. 01 40 71 72 54; www.callphone.com). The phone rental and delivery are free. Calls cost $0.80/minute for within France and $1.50/minute for international calls.

Internet Access: Many hotels offer wi-fi or you can go to an Internet Café. Here are some addresses:

• **Cyberport Forum des Images**, in the Forum des Halles, Porte Sainte-Eustache, 75001 Paris; Metro : Châtelet-Les Halles; Tel. 01 44 76 63 44.

• **Voyageur du Monde**, 53 Rue Sainte Anne, 75002 Paris, Metro: Pyramides; Tel. 01 42 86 16 00; www.vdm.com.fr.

• **Le Shop Cybercafé**, 3 Rue d'Argout, 75002 Paris. Metro: Sentier; Email: shop@shop.imaginet.fr.

• **Le Web Bar**, 32, Rue de Picardie, 75003 Paris, Metro: Filles du Calvaire; Tel. 01 42 72 66 55; www.webbar.fr.

• **Cyberia**, in the Pompidou Center, 75004 Paris, Metro: Rambuteau; E-mail: cyberia@easynet.fr.

• **Cyber Café Latino**, 13 Rue de l'Ecole Polytechnique, 75005; Metro: Maubert-Mutualité; Tel. 01 40 51 86 94; www.cybercafelatino.com.

• **Café Orbital**, 13 rue de Medicis, 75006; Metro: Odeon; Tel. 01 43 25 76 77; www.cafeorbital.com.

• **Cybermetropole**, in the Palais de la Découverte Museum, Avenue Franklin Roosevelt, 75008; Metro: Champs Elysées Clemenceau; Tel. 01 40 74 80 00.

• **Espace AOL Vivendi**, 6-8, Rue de Tilsitt, 75008 Paris; Metro: Charles de Gaulle/ Etoile.

• **Cyberzen Café**, 85, Rue Amelot, 75011 Paris; Metro: Chemin-Vert; Tel. 01 53 36 76 13.

- **Apache Cybercafé**, 84, Rue du Faubourg Saint Antoine, 75012 Paris; Metro: Ledru Rollin; Tel. 01 53 46 60 10. Offers special kids' programs.
- **High Tech Café**, in the Tour Montparnasse Shopping Center, (Above C&A Department Store), 75014; Metro: Montparnasse; E-Mail: info@htc.fr.
- **Planet Cybercafé**, 173, Rue de Vaugirard, 75015 Paris; Metro: Pasteur; Tel. 01 45 67 71 14.
- **Travel Café**, 2 Rue d'Alleray, 75015 Paris; Metro: Vaugirard; www.abcvoyage.com/travelcafe.html.

Post Offices

Post Offices are open Mon-Fri, 8am-7pm, and Sat, 8am-12pm. You can purchase stamps (timbres), buy shipping boxes and send packages (colis), and access the Minitel there. You can also purchase stamps in a Tabac store.

You can also send packages through UPS. For toll-free information call: Tel. 08 00 87 78 77. There are two **UPS Express Shop** offices in Paris:
- 107, Rue Réaumur, 75002 Paris, Metro: Sentier
- 34, Boulevard Malesherbes, 75008 Paris, Metro: Saint Augustin or Madeleine

Time

Paris time is 1 hour ahead of London; 6 hours ahead of New York; 7 hours ahead of Chicago; 8 hours ahead of Denver; and 9 hours ahead of San Francisco.

Most schedules and timetables in France are written in military time, using a 24-hour clock. Thus 6 h is 6 am; 11 h is 11 am; 12 h is noon; 14 h is 2 pm; 20 h is 8pm; and 24 h is midnight.

Temperature Conversion Chart

°F	0	23	32	41	50	59
°C	-18	5	0	10	15	20

°F	68	77	86	98.6	100	104
°C	20	25	30	37	38	40

Shopping

Where to Buy Baby Products

Diapers: Known as *couches* (pronounced koosh), they are sold in large supermarkets, some small corner markets, in pharmacies, and at Monoprix and Prisunic stores.

Baby Bottles: You can find both glass and plastic baby bottles (*biberons*) at your local pharmacy. Plastic bottles and sippy cups are also sold at Monoprix or Prisunic stores and in some large supermarkets.

Baby Formula: Look for it in the baby food section of the supermarkets or at your local pharmacy.

Baby Food: Known as *petits pots*, you will find a wide range of baby food, including gourmet varieties, in grocery stores, supermarkets, and pharmacies.

Baby Sunscreen, Lotion, Shampoo, Powders, Teething Rings: These are sold in pharmacies and in Prisunic or Monoprix stores.

Strollers, Snuglis, Baby BackPack Carriers, etc: The best place to look for these are large department stores such as the Samaritaine, Galeries Lafayette, Printemps, and Au Bon Marché. Baby specialty stores, such as Natalys (see below) also carry these items.

Baby & Children's Clothing

• Any **Prisunic** or **Monoprix** store: branches all over the city. These stores offer kids' clothing and gear for all ages at relatively low prices.

• **Du Pareil au Même**: This is a great address for colorful kids' clothing from infancy to age 14. The prices are very reasonable and selection is good, even for boyswear. Branches located at 1, Rue Saint Denis, 75001, Metro: Châtelet; Forum des Halles, Level –2, 75001, Metro: Les Halles; 7, 14, and 34, Rue Saint Placide, 75006, Metro: Saint Placide; 168, Boulevard Saint Germain, 75006, Metro: St. Germain des Pres; 17, Rue Vavin, 75006, Metro: Vavin; 15, 17, and 23, Rue des Mathurins, 75008, Metro: Haver Caumartin; 120-122, Rue du Faubourg Saint Antoine, 75012, Metro: Ledru Rollin; 165, Rue du Chateau des Rentiers, 75013, Metro: Nationale.

• **Dipaki**: Fun colorful clothes at reasonable prices for kids from infancy to age 8. Branches located at 20, Rue du Pont Neuf, 75001, Metro: Pont Neuf; 22, Rue Cler, 75007, Metro: Ecole Militaire; 18, Rue Vignon, 75009, Metro: Madeleine; 98, Rue d'Alésia, 75014, Metro: Alésia.

- **Jacadi:** What the well-groomed, *bon chic bon genre*, Paris child is wearing. Excellent quality cotton and wool clothing. Don't miss the sales in early January and late July. Branches located at 9, Avenue de l'Opéra, 75001; 17, Boulevard Poissonière, 75002; 27, Rue Saint Antoine, 75004; 4, Avenue des Gobelins, 75005; 76, rue d'Assas - Angle 2, rue Vavin, 75006; 73, rue de Sèvres , 75006; 256 Boulevards Saint Germain, 75007; 17, Rue Tronchet, 75008; 54, Boulevard du Temple, 75011; 116, Rue d'Alésia, 75014; 331, Rue de Vaugirard, 75015; 114, Rue Lafontaine, 75016; and 60, Boulevard de Courçelles, 75017.
- **Natalys:** Not as highbrow as Jacadi, but a charming assortment of baby clothes and equipment. Branches located at 74, Rue de Rivoli, 75001, Metro: Châtelet; 74, Rue de Seine, 75006, Metro: Odeon; 47, Rue de Sevres, 75007, Metro: Sevres Babylone; 109 Bis, Rue Saint Dominique, 75007, Metro: Ecole Militaire; 42, Rue Vignon, 75009, Metro: Havre Caumartin; 43, Avenue des Gobelins, 75013, Metro: Gobelins; and 5, Rue Guichard, 75016, Metro: Muette.
- **Petit Bateau:** Good quality cotton clothing for babies and toddlers. Branches located at Forum Des Halles, 75001, Metro: Les Halles; and 323, Rue de Vaugirard, 75015, Metro: Convention.
- **Tartine et Chocolat:** Cute clothes for children from infancy to age 10. Branches located at 24, Rue de la Paix, 75002, Metro: Opéra; 266, Boulevard Saint Germain, 75007, Metro: Solférino; 105, Rue du Faubourg Saint Honoré, 75008, Metro: Metro: Saint Phillipe du Roule; 22, Rue Boissy d'Anglas, 75008, Metro: Concorde; and 60, Avenue Paul Doumer, 75016, Metro: Muette.

Department Stores

If you're the least bit interested in shopping, you'll want to check out one or more of Paris' famous Grands Magasins (Department Stores). They are quite spectacular, which is not surprising since Paris invented the first department store. Launched in 1876 by a man named Aristide Boucicaut, it was called the Bon Marché (Good Bargain) and housed in a grand building designed by Gustave Eiffel (of Eiffel Tower fame).

- **Au Bon Marché**, 24, rue de Sèvres (Metro: Sèvres-Babylone), Open Mon-Sat 9:30 am-7 pm. The world's first department store is still going strong. Don't miss the gourmet delis in the Grande Epicerie and nice children's sections in the basement.
- **Au Printemps**, 64, boulevard Haussmann, Metro: Havre-Caumartin, RER: Auber or Haussmann-Saint Lazare. Open Mon-Sat. 9:30 am-7

pm (Thurs. until 10pm). Other branches of this store exist throughout Paris, but this one is by far the best. The main cafeteria offers terrific views of the back of the Opera.

• **Galeries Lafayette**, 40, boulevard Haussmann, Metro: Chaussée d'Antin. Open Mon-Sat. 9:30 am-6:45 pm, Thurs until 9 pm. You will find other branches of this store in town, but this one is definitely the most spectacular. Don't miss the stained glass skylight. The rooftop café is a must stop in the summer for the great view. There is a big souvenir section, excellent toy section, and free fashion shows.

• **La Samaritaine**, 19, rue de la Monnaie, Metro: Pont Neuf. Open Mon-Sat 9:30 am-7 pm, Thurs until 10 pm. The building is a beautiful example of Art Nouveau architecture. The top floor restaurant and rooftop café offer one of the best views in town.

• **Aux Trois Quartiers**, 17, Boulevard de la Madeleine (Metro: Madeleine), Open Mon-Sat 9:30 am-7 pm. This store houses all kinds of interesting shops and eateries in its Art Deco style building.

• **BHV (Bazar de l'Hôtel de Ville)**, 52-64, rue de Rivoli (Metro: Hôtel de Ville), Open Mon-Sat 9:30 am-7 pm (Wed until 10 pm). This store features everything for the home from furniture to thumb tacks. You'll find converters and adapters for electrical appliances in the basement.

Toy Stores

There are wonderful toy sections in all the major department stores (see above). Other good addresses include:

• **Le Ciel est à Tout le Monde**. Branches located in the Carrousel du Louvre shopping center, 75001, Metro: Palais Royal or Louvre; at 10, Rue Gay Lussac, 75005, near the Luxembourg Gardens, Metro: Luxembourg; and at 7, Avenue Trudaine, 75009, Metro: Anvers. This store has lots of nice wooden toys, models, kites, and sailboats that you can float on the pond.

• **La Ronde des Jouets**, 86, Rue Monge, 75005, Metro: Place Monge. Another good address for good quality wooden toys, games, dolls, and activities.

• **Le Train Bleu**, 55, Rue Saint Placide, 75006, Metro: Saint Placide. True to its name, this shop features lots of trains, as well as electric powered cars, planes, and other toys.

• **Si Tu Veux**, branches at 10, Rue Vavin, 75006, Metro: Vavin or Nôtre Dame des Champs, and 68, Galerie Vivienne, 75001, Metro: Bourse. These are lovely stores with plenty to stimulate your child's imagination including costume and dress-up clothes.

• **L'Oiseau du Paradis**, 211, Boulevard Saint Germain, 75007, Metro: Rue du Bac. A classic toy store with lots of animals and things to play with.

• **Décembre en Mars**, 65, Avenue de la Bourdonnais, 75007, Metro: Ecole Militaire. Lots of games, doll houses, and reproductions of old-fashioned toys.

• **Territoire**, 30, Rue Boissy d'Anglas, 75008, Metro: Madeleine. This is a ritzy store in a ritzy neighborhood with dollhouses and wooden toys.

• **Au Nain Bleu**, 5, Boulevard Malesherbes, 75008 Paris, Metro: Madeleine. An old favorite that features lots of wooden toys and other joys, most of which are made in Europe.

• **La Boite à Joujoux**, 41, Passage Jouffroy, 75009, Metro: Grands Boulevards and La Boite a Doudou, 24, Passage Jouffroy. Both of these stores feature all sorts of toys, t-shirts, and collectables related to favorite cartoon figures such as Tintin, Asterix, and Betty Boop. They are worth a visit if for no other reason than it's a chance to check out Paris' wonderful shopping galleries and passages.

• **Pain d'Epices**, 29, Passage Jouffroy, 75009, Metro: Grands Boulevards. This delightful shop, also located in one of Paris' lovely shopping passages, is filled with miniatures, ranging from soldiers and cartoon figures to everything you could want to outfit the dream dollhouse.

• **Jouet International du Monde**, 28, Rue des Trois Bornes, 75011, Metro: Parmentier. Lots of fun toys from all over the world.

• **La Grande Recré**, in the Galaxie Shopping Mall, 75013, Metro: Place d'Italie. A big toy store with a wide variety, including a large section for preschoolers.

• **Les Cousins d'Alice**, 36, Rue Daguerre, 75014, Metro: Denfert Rochereau. This little shop is full of small, inexpensive treasures as well as books, games, and other toys.

Playgrounds & Sports

Paris is dotted with fine **playgrounds** from the smallest tot lot to large, elaborate ones. Here are some favorites:

The **Tuileries** garden has a small, but pleasant playground, located towards the middle of the gardens, closer to the Rue de Rivoli side, 75001. In July-August and December-January, you can go to the Tuileries Fair and enjoy wild carnival rides and games. Metro: Tuileries. Entrance to the park is free.

The **Jardin des Enfants aux Halles** is a garden/playground that is exclusively reserved for children. It features tunnels, secret dens, rope swings, and pools of plastic balls. There are also organized games, led by friendly counselors. Although games are conducted in French, the rules are pretty universal. Our boys had no trouble joining in. Located in the Les Halles Gardens, at 105, Rue Rambuteau, 75001, Metro: Les Halles. Hours vary during the week and during the year. Call for a schedule (Tel. 01 45 08 07 18) or check the sign on the gate. There is a small entrance fee for a well-supervised, one-hour session.

The **Jardin des Plantes** has a small playground near the labyrinth and a lovely merry-go-round that features endangered and extinct animals. It is located near the Rue Geoffroy Saint Hilaire, and Rue Cuvier sides of the

garden. Metro: Jussieu or Place Monge, 75005. Entrance is free.

The **Parc Floral** (*photo at left*) in the Bois de Vincennes features beautiful playgrounds for children of different ages. There are also fun rides and a delightful mini-golf that features the major monuments of Paris, plus concerts, plays, and a small museum. Located between Avenue des Minimes and Rue de la Pyramide in the Bois. Metro: Château de Vincennes. There is a small fee to enter the park. Rides and minigolf are extra.

The **Arènes de Lutèce** park has a nice playground, plus room to play soccer and other ball games in the old Roman arena. Located off the Rue Monge, Rue des Arènes, and Rue de Navarre, 75005. Metro: Place Monge or Jussieu. Entrance is free.

The **Luxembourg Gardens** feature a magnificent playground, along with a wooden merry-go-round, puppet show, and wonderful old-fashioned double swings. They are located on the western side of the park, towards the Rue d'Assas, 75006. Metro: Nôtre Dame des Champs. There is a small fee to enter the playground.

The **Parc André Citroen** has several small playgrounds and lots of wide open spaces. In the summer, don't miss the dancing fountains. They come right out of the pavement at irregular intervals. Kids love trying to run through them in warm weather. This is also where you can ride in a (tethered) hot air balloon above the rooftops of Paris. Located between Quai Andre Citroen and Rue Balard, 75015. Metro: Lourmel. Entrance is free.

The smaller **Parc Georges Brassens** has several playgrounds, including one for kids with disabilities. There is a fun climbing wall, and in the summer you can rent remote-control boats on the pond. Located in the Rue des Morillons, 75014, Metro: Convention. Entrance is free.

The **Jardin d'Acclimatation** in the Bois de Boulogne has wonderful playgrounds divided by age group and skill level. There are also carnival rides and games. The playgrounds are located on the western side of the Jardin d'Acclimatation. Metro: Les Sablons or take the little train from the Porte Maillot metro station. There is a small fee to enter the park. Rides are extra.

The **Parc de Belleville** has a big climbing castle with several reallylong slides built right into the hillside. Located on the Rue des Courrones and Rue Julien Lacroix side of the park, 75019. Metro: Couronnes. Entrance is free.

The **Parc de la Villette** has terrific playgrounds. Attractions include a giant dragon slide, numerous moon bounces for different ages, foot-powered windmills, and other fun stuff. Located near the Cité des Sciences (Science Museum), 75019, Metro: Porte de la Villette. Entrance is free.

Bicycling
    This is a great way to enjoy some of Paris' major sights as a family. There are more than 150 kilometers of bicycle paths and lanes within the city. You can also bicycle in the Tuileries Gardens, by the Seine River, along the Saint Martin Canal, and under the Eiffel Tower free from motorized

traffic. If you are in Paris on a Sunday, or any day between July 15 and August 15, you can ride on the expressways along the Seine, which are closed to motorized vehicles.

Here are some good addresses for bike tours and rentals. If you need a kid-sized bike or kid carrier, it's a good idea to reserve in advance:
• **Fat Tire's Bike Tours and Rentals.** Store located at 24, Rue Edgar Faure, Metro: Dupleix (3 blocks south and west of the Eiffel Tower), Tel. 01 56 58 10 54. 24, Rue Edgar Faure, Metro: Dupleix (3 blocks south and west of the Eiffel Tower), Email: info@FatTireBikeToursParis.com Website: http://www.fattirebiketoursparis.com/bikes/about-fat-tire/index.shtml. This company organizes bike tours with English-speaking guides. Kids are welcome. Tours last 3-4 hours with plenty of breaks for photos, food, and rest. The groups leave at 11am and 3:30 pm (May-Aug) and 11am (Sept) from under the Eiffle Tower on the south side (look for the company's flag). Note: they also offer Segway tours of the city. Check out details on the Website.
• **Roue Libre-Tours and Rentals.** This group, run by the public transit system, organizes free 2-hour bike tours every last Saturday of the month. Groups meet at 9 am for hot drinks and pastries at the Maison Roue Libre, 95, bis Rue Rambuteau in Les Halles, Metro: Les Halles. The tour leaves at 10 am. Open daily. Tel. 01 53 46 43 77. You can also rent bikes and gear for adults and kids through Roue Libre every weekend, Mar- Oct, 9am-7pm at designated metro stations, including: Porte d'Auteuil; Château de Vincennes; Place Denfert Rochereau; Jaures-Stalingrad; Nationale; and Châtelet (exit Place du Châtelet on Avenue Victoria).

If you are in Paris in late July, don't miss the last leg of the **Tour de France**. This is one of the most famous bicycle races in the world. It takes place in July, lasting 3 weeks. The final stage of the race is traditionally in Paris, with the finish line on the Champs Elysées. The exact route through the city is published in one of the local papers on the morning of the race. If you want to avoid the crowds on the Champs Elysées, you can watch the riders from any other spot along the route.

Roller blading

If you like to roller blade, you'll feel right at home in Paris where it's hugely popular. There are plenty of car-free paths through the Luxembourg Gardens, Metro: Nôtre Dame des Champs or Luxembourg; Parc Monceau, Metro: Monceau; Jardin des Tuileries, Metro: Tuileries; on the

Champs de Mars, Metro: Bir Hakeim or Ecole Militaire; in the Bois de Vincennes, Metro: Chateau de Vincennes, or Porte Doree or Bois de Boulogne, Metro: Porte d'Auteil or Sablons; and along the Promenade Plantée, Metro: Daumesnil, Gare de Lyon, or Bastille. On Sundays, you can also ride along the parkways next to the Seine where they are closed to motorized vehicles.

Stunt riders gather at the Trocadéro Gardens, Metro: Trocadéro; on the Champs de Mars near the Eiffel Tower, Metro: Champs de Mars; on the esplanade at La Défense, Metro: Esplanade de la Défense, and in front of Nôtre Dame Cathedral, Metro: Cité or Saint Michel.

You can join a group outing with:

Rollers et Coquillages. Groups meet every Sunday at 2:30 pm at 37, Boulevard Bourdon, 75012, Metro: Bastille. Ask about special outings for kids and families.

Roller Squad Institute organizes outings for beginners on Saturdays at 3 pm starting from Les Invalides, Metro: Invalides. For information: Tel. 01 56 61 99 61. Open Mon-Fri, 10am-1pm, 2pm-6pm.

Friday Night Fever. Every Friday night around 10 pm (weather permitting) thousands of experienced roller bladers get together at the Place d'Italie for a giant group ride. It includes police escorts, first aid workers, and emergency health crews if needed. The tour covers about 20 kilometers through the city. The line of rollers can be as long as 1-2 kilometers. If you and your teenage kids are experienced roller-bladers, this may be fun to do. Otherwise, it's better just to watch from the sidelines.

You can rent roller blades and pads from:

• **Go Sport**, in the Forum des Halles shopping center, 75001, Metro: Les Halles.

• **Bike and Roller**, 6, Rue Saint Julien le Pauvre, 75005, across the Seine from Nôtre dame, Metro: Saint Michel-Nôtre Dame or Maubert Mutualité, Tel. 01 44-07-35-89. Also located at 137, Rue Saint Dominique, 75007, Metro: Pont de l'Alma, Tel. 01 44 18 30 39.

• **Au Vieux Campeur**, 48, Rue des Ecoles, 75005, Metro: Maubert Mutualité, Saint Michel, or Cluny, Tel. 01 53 10 48 48.

• **Roller Pro Shop**, 18, Rue des Ecoles, 75005, Metro: Cluny, Tel. 01 43 25 67 61.

• **Nomades**, 37, Boulevard Bourdon, 75012, Metro: Bastille, Tel. 01 44 54 07 44.

• **Vertical Line**, 60 bis, Avenue Raymond Poincaré, 75016, Metro: Trocadéro or Victor Hugo, Tel. 01 47 27 21 21.

Skateboarding
Favorite spots for skateboarding include the:
• Champs de Mars, near the southeast side of the Eiffel Tower, Metro: Bir Hakeim or Champs de Mars-Tour Eiffel.
• Trocadéro Gardens, Metro: Trocadéro.
• Esplanade in front of the Montparnasse train station, Metro: Montparnasse.
• Esplanade at La Défense, Metro: Esplanade de la Défense.

Swimming
Paris has plenty of public swimming pools. Hours of operation vary. Most public pools are open early in the morning and in the afternoon. They tend to be open longer on weekends and during the summer holidays. Most pools are accessible to people with disabilities. Pools generally provide a basket for your clothes that you check into a cloakroom or put in a locker.
Public pools have odd dress codes. Everyone must wear a swimcap and men must wear "speedo"-style swim suits. Caps and men's/boy's suits are often available for sale at the pool's ticket office or in vending machines near the entrance.

Water Parks & Indoor Pools
Aquaboulevard. Kids love this waterpark. It has both indoor and outdoor pools, water slides, fountains, wave pools, hot tubs, a beach, palm trees, and fun for every age. There are also squash courts, food courts, and other sports facilities. 4, Rue Louis Armand, 75015. Metro: Balard or Porte de Versailles.

For indoor pools:
• **Piscine des Halles -Suzanne-Berlioux.** In Les Halles. Palm trees and cactii. Porte Sainte Eustache, 10, Place de la Rotonde, Level 3; 75001. Metro: Les Halles.
• **Piscine Saint Mérri.** Behind the Pompidou Center in the Marais. Outdoor terrace. 16, Rue Renard, 75004. Metro: Hôtel de Ville.
• **Piscine Saint-Germain.** Under the Saint Germain covered market. 12, Rue Lobineau, 75006. Metro: Mabillon or Odéon.
• **Piscine Jean Taris.** Near the Rue Mouffetard and Pantheon. 16, Rue Thouin, 75005. Metro: Place Monge.
• **Piscine Pontoise.** Art-deco style architecture. Evening swimming with lights and music. Diving boards and a lap pool with a current. 19, Rue Pontoise, 75005. Metro: Maubert-Mutualité.
• **Piscine Château Landon.** The oldest in Paris. 31, Rue Château Landon, 75010. Metro: Louis Blanc-Stalingrad.

- **Piscine de Reuilly.** Grassy areas for sunbathing in the summer. Just off the Promenade Plantée. 13, Rue Hénard, 75012. Metro: Montgallet.
- **Piscine Armand Massard.** Under the Tour Montparnasse. 66, Boulevard du Montparnasse, 75014. Metro: Montparnasse.
- **Piscine Emile-Antoine.** Windows offer a close-up view of the Eiffel Tower. 9, rue Jean-Rey, 75015. Metro: Bir Hakeim.
- **Piscine Blomet.** Art-deco style with a beautiful stairway. 17, Rue Blomet, 75015. Métro : Volontaires or Sèvres-Lecourbe.

For outdoor pools/pools with retractable roofs:
- **Piscine de la Butte aux Cailles.** Charming, old-fashioned, art-deco style. Fed by a natural underground spring. High and low diving boards. 5, Place Paul Verlaine, 75013. Metro: Place d'Italie.
- **Piscine de l'Hôtel Nikko.** A pretty hotel pool open to the public. 61, Quai de Grenelle, 75015. Métro: Javel or Bir Hakeim.
- **Piscine Keller.** Retractable roof in warm weather. 14, Rue de l'Ingénieur Robert Keller, 75015. Métro: Charles Michels.
- **Piscine d'Auteuil.** In the Bois de Boulogne, near the horse racing track of Auteuil. 1, Rue des Lacs de Passy, 75016. Metro: Ranelagh.
- **Piscine Henry de Montherland.** Large windows, outdoor terraces, and diving boards. 32, Boulevard Lannes, 75016. Metro: Rue de la Pompe.

Tennis
If you want to watch the pros, try to catch the **French Open Tournament.** It takes place in May at the red-clay courts of the Roland-Garros stadium. The stadium is located in the Bois de Boulogne, 2, Avenue Gordon Bennett, 75016, Metro: Porte d'Auteuil. The final matches are exciting, but if you get tickets for earlier rounds you'll get to see more of the players. Tickets are available by Tel. 01 47 43 48 00 or www.frenchopen.org.

The **Paris Open Tennis Championship** takes place in November at the Bercy Sports Stadium, Palais Omnisport de Bercy, 75012, Metro: Bercy. It features some of the world's top men's tennis players. For schedules and ticket information you can check the website at: www.atptour.com/en.

You can play tennis at these locations, but may need to reserve in advance:
- **Luxembourg Gardens**, on the western side of the park. The sign up sheet is in a kiosk near the courts. Tel. 01 43 25 79 18.

- **La Falguière Sports Center**, in the Bois de Vincennes, on the Route de la Pyramide, Metro: Chateau de Vincennes. Tel. 01 43 74 40 93.
- **Henry de Montherland Sports Center** in the Bois de Boulogne, at 30-32, Boulevard Lannes, 75016. Metro: Porte Dauphine. Tel. 01 45 03 03 64.
- **Fonds des Princes**, 61, Avenue de la Porte d'Auteuil, 75016. Metro: Porte D'Auteuil. Tel. 01 46 51 82 80).
- **Quai de Saint-Exupéry** has courts that are handicap accessible. 75016. Metro: Porte de Saint Cloud. Tel. 01 45 20 62 59.
- **Stade Elisabeth**, 7-15, Avenue Paul Appell, 75014. Metro: Porte d'Orleans. Tel. 01 45 40 55 88.

Bon Appetit!

In France, cooking is an art, and dining is a labor of love. Enjoying good food and companionship are a national pastime – and everyone is welcome to join! Kids, and even dogs, can enjoy a meal in the fanciest of restaurants.

One of the biggest challenges you'll face is choosing among the huge variety of food styles and traditions in Paris. Even if you just stick to French food, you'll face a vast array of regional choices and influences. Remember, this is a country that has more types of cheese than there are days in a year. Broadly speaking, French cooking can be divided into the gourmet "haute cuisine" handed down from royal recipes and practiced in fine restaurants to the everyday-style home cooking that is the joy of many a neighborhood bîstrot.

There are many regional styles. For example Normandy and northern France specialize in dishes featuring creamy sauces, richer butter, apples, and cider. Brittany is famous for fresh seafood, crêpes, and buttery cookies. In Burgundy you find hearty beef stews cooked in red wine. Around Lyon you get sausages and quenelles (a fish- or chicken-based dumpling). The eastern region of Alsace features sauerkraut with sausages, onion pies, and a form of white pizza with cream, bacon, and onions called a Flammenkeuche. The Dordogne region is famous for black truffles, foie gras, cassoulet (a white bean and meat casserole), and foods cooked in goose or duck fat. Foods from Provence and southwestern France tend to show a Mediterranean influence with lots of olive oil, garlic, tomatoes, sweet peppers, and herbs such as thyme, basil, and rosemary.

Parent Tip: To help keep children distracted between courses in a restaurant, make sure to bring along some entertainment. Drawing supplies work well, as do activity books, small decks of cards, miniature games, small toys, postcards, journals, and story books. ✤

We have included a list of restaurants in this guide that combine good food with a family-friendly atmosphere. Here are some common food terms to help you navigate the menus:

Petit Déjeuner - breakfast

Café – coffee (generally served as a small espresso cup in a café or larger cup if you are ordering breakfast in a hotel); café noir – black coffee; café au lait – coffee with milk

Grand café – big cup; café double – double shot

Thé – tea

Sucre – sugar

Chocolat chaud – hot chocolate

Lait – milk

Pain – bread

Tartine – usually a long slice of baguette bread with butter

Croissant – buttery, flaky, crescent-shaped roll

Vienneroiseries – breakfast pastries

Céréales – cereal

Confiture – jam

Beurre – butter

Miel – honey

Nutella – a spread made of hazelnuts and chocolate

Oeuf à la coque – soft boiled egg

Oeufs brouillées – scrambled eggs (rarely offered)

Oeuf au plat – fried egg

Oeuf dûr – hard boiled egg

Déjeuner - lunch

Champignon – mushroom

Cornichon – pickle

Croque Madame – toasted sandwich with melted cheese, ham, and a fried egg on top

Croque Monsieur – (*photo at right*) toasted sandwich with melted cheese and ham

Crudités – salad (usually a variety of seasonal, cold vegetables and salad)
Feuilleté – puff pastry dough generally filled with meat, fish, or vegetable stuffing
Frites – French fries
Fromage – cheese
Glaçon – ice cube
Jambon – ham
Pâtes – pasta
Potage – soup

Legumes - vegetables
Ail – garlic
Aubergine – eggplant
Carottes – carrots; *carottes rappées* – grated carrot salad
Celerie remoulade – grated celery root salad
Chou – cabbage
Choucroute – sauerkraut
Choufleur – cauliflower
Citrouille – pumpkin
Courgette – zucchini
Courge – squash
Fenouil – fennel
Haricot vert – green bean; *Haricot blanc* – white bean
Mais – corn
Oignon – onion
Petit pois – peas
Poireau – leek
Poischiche – chickpea
Pomme de terre – potato
Tomate – tomato
Cacauète – peanut

Fruits - fruits
Abricot – apricot
Banane – banana
Cassis – black currant
Cerise – cherry
Citron – lemon; *citron vert* – lime
Fraise – strawberry; *fraise des bois* – wild strawberry

Framboise – raspberry
Groseille – red currant
Melon – cantaloupe
Myrtille – blueberry
Orange – orange
Pêche – peach
Poire – pear
Pomme – apple

Poissons - fish
Anguille – eel
Bar – sea bass
Bouillabaisse – fish stew
Brochet – pike
Cabillaud – cod
Coquilles Saint Jacques – scallops
Crevettes – shrimp
Homard – lobster
Huitres – oysters
Lotte – monkfish
Maquereau – mackerel
Merlan – whiting
Moules – mussels
Raie – skate or sting ray
Rouget – red mullet
Saumon – salmon
Thon – tuna
Truite – trout

Viande - meat
Agneau – lamb
Biftek haché or *steak haché* – hamburger (generally not served with a bun)
Boeuf – beef
Caille – quail
Canard – duck
Cassoulet – meat and white bean casserole
Contrefilet or *filet* – loin steak
Côte de boeuf – T-bone steak
Côtelettes – chops

Dinde – turkey; *dindonneau* – young turkey
Foie – liver
Gigôt d'agneau – leg of lamb
Jambon – ham
Langue – tongue
Lapin – rabbit
Lièvre – hare
Oie – goose
Perdrix – partridge
Pintade – Guinea fowl
Porc – pork
Poulet – chicken
Saucisse – sausage; *Saucisse de Toulouse* – hot dog
Saucisson – salami
Steak tartare – raw ground beef, topped with raw egg
Veau – veal
Bleu – nearly raw
Saignant – very rare
À point – medium rare
Bien cuit – medium

Dessert
Crème Chantilly – whipped cream
Crème Fraiche – cream
Fromage blanc – thick creamy, yogurt-like dessert

Gâteau – cake
Glaçes – ice cream
Orange givrée or *citron givrée* – frozen orange or lemon filled with orange or lemon ice
Patisseries – pastries
Petit four – mini pastry
Petit gâteau – cookie
Tarte – pie; *Tarte Tatin* – upside-down apple pie
Yaourt – yogurt

Parent Tip: Do you have a child who functions primarily on peanut butter? It's not as common in France as in the US, but searching for it can provide an excuse for a fun treasure hunt through Parisian grocery stores. Peanut butter can be called either *Beurre de Cacaouète* or *Pâte d'Arachide*. It may come in a jar or a can. It might be located with the jams and jellies, by the peanuts and other nuts, or in the foreign food section. Occasionally you will have more luck in a small ethnic grocery shop than at the local supermarket. ✢

What's the Word?

Parlez-vous Français?

No one expects you to speak fluent French. In fact, increasingly, you'll find that Parisians want to show off their knowledge of English to you. However, you will score major points in France if you just try to learn a few key expressions:

> *Bonjour Madame* – Hello Ma'am
> *Bonjour Monsieur* – Hello Sir
> *Bonjour Mademoiselle* – Hello Miss
> *S'il Vous Plait* – Please
> *Merci* – Thank you
> *Au-Revoir* – Goodbye
> *Pardon* – Excuse me

That's it. The rest is merely icing on the cake. If you want to be adventurous, here are some more handy words and expressions:

Oui – yes
Non – no
Parlez-vous Anglais? – Do you speak English
Je ne parle pas Français – I do not speak French
Je ne comprends pas – I don't understand
Pourquoi? – Why?
Combien? – How much?
L'addition, s'il vous plait – The (restaurant) bill, please
La note, s'il vous plait – The (hotel) bill, please.
Où est? – Where is?
Où sont les toilettes? – Where are the restrooms?
Qui? – Who?
Qui est la? – Who is there?

Quand? – When?
Qu'est ce que c'est? – What is that?
Quelle heure est il? – What time is it?
Quel etage? – Which floor?
Comment? – How? or What?
Comment allez vous? – How are you?
Avez-vous? – Do you have?
Pouvez-vous? – Could you?
Lequel or Laquelle? – Which?
Donnez-moi – Give me
Je voudrai – I would like
Ca – That
Celui ci – This one
Celui là – That one

Un or *Une* – one
Deux – two
Trois – three
Quatre – four

Cinq – five
Six – six
Sept – seven
Huit – eight
Neuf – nine
Dix – ten
Onze – eleven
Douze – twelve
Treize – thirteen
Quatorze – fourteen
Quinze – fifteen
Seize – sixteen
Dix-sept – seventeen
Dix-huit – eighteen
Dix-neuf – nineteen
Vingt – twenty
Trente – thirty
Quarente – forty
Cinquante – fifty
Soixante – sixty

Soixante-dix – seventy
Quatrevingt – eighty
Quatrevingt-dix – ninety
Cent – 100
Mille – 1,000

Premier – first
Second or *Deuxième* – second
Troisième – third
Quatrième – fourth
Cinquième – fifth
Sixième – sixth
Septième – seventh
Huitième – eighth
Neuvième – ninth
Dixième – tenth

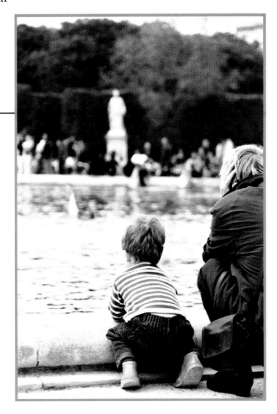

INDEX

Things Change!
Phone numbers, prices, addresses, quality of service – all change. If you come across any new information, let us know. No item is too small! Contact us at :

jopenroad@aol.com
or
www.openroadguides.com

TravelNotes

Open Road Publishing

Open Road has launched a radical new concept in travel guides that we call our *Best Of* guides: matching the time you *really* have for your vacation with the right amount of information you need for your perfect trip! No fluff, just the best things to do and see, the best places to stay and eat. Includes one-day, weekend, one-week and two-week trip ideas – in living color! Now what could be more perfect than that?

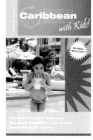

Best Of Guides

Open Road's Best of Arizona, $14.95
Open Road's Best of The Florida Keys, $14.95
Open Road's Best of Las Vegas, $14.95
Open Road's Best of New York City, $14.95
Open Road's Best of Southern California, $14.95
Open Road's Best of Belize, $14.95
Open Road's Best of Costa Rica, $14.95
Open Road's Best of Honduras, $14.95
Open Road's Best of Panama, $14.95
Open Road's Best of Ireland, $14.95
Open Road's Best of Italy, $16.95
Open Road's Best of Paris, $12.95
Open Road's Best of Provence &
    The French Riviera, $14.95
Open Road's Best of Spain, $14.95

Family Travel Guides

Open Road's Italy with Kids, $16.95
Open Road's Paris with Kids, $16.95
Open Road's Caribbean with Kids, $14.95
Open Road's London with Kids, $14.95
Open Road's New York City with Kids, $14.95
Open Road's Best National Parks With Kids, $12.95
Open Road's Washington, DC with Kids, $14.95
Open Road's Hawaii with Kids, $14.95

Order now at www.openroadguides.com